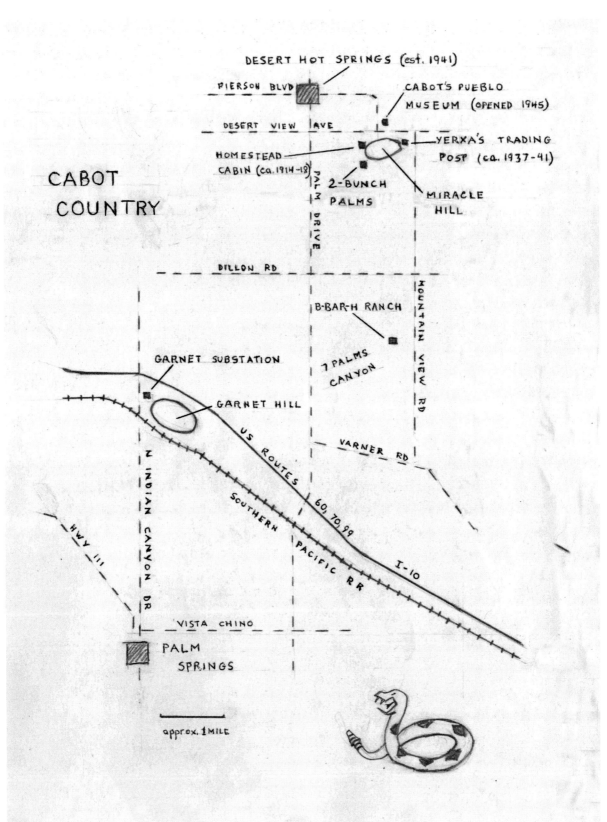

Cabot's Country map

CABOT ABRAM YERXA

ON THE DESERT SINCE 1913

Edited and Introduced by

Richard E. Brown

Second Edition, Revised by Judy Gigante and Richard E. Brown

Published by

Cabot's Museum Foundation

Desert Hot Springs, California

The Cabot's Museum Foundation Board of Directors dedicates this edition to our Friends of the Pueblo. Their gifts of time and treasure allow us to share Cabot Yerxa's unique museum and his message with thousands of visitors every year. We celebrate Cabot's legacy and our donors' vision as the Museum enters its 100th year.

Copyright © 2013 by Cabot's Museum Foundation

All rights reserved. No part of this book may be reproduced in any manner whatsoever without written permission, except in the case of brief quotations embodied in critical articles and reviews.

The photograph "Carl Eytel before his cabin, with outdoor cot where Cabot may have slept" is courtesy The Desert Magazine, The Desert Sun, where it appeared in "Bloomsbury, P.S.," by Ann Japenga (April 2004).

Printed and bound in Canada by Art Bookbindery

www.ArtBookbindery.com

ISBN 978-0-9887600-0-4

TABLE OF CONTENTS

ACKNOWLEDGEMENTS 13

FOREWORD 15

THE CHRONOLOGY OF THE LIFE OF CABOT YERXA 17

CHRONOLOGY TO 1913, by Cabot Yerxa 23

NEWSPAPER INTERVIEW: "YERXA SURVIVED LAWLESS ALASKA" 26

ON THE DESERT SINCE 1913, by Cabot Yerxa

   Introduction 33

   Article 1: 1893—The Train Stops at Garnet Station 39
   2: 1913—Homesteading
   3: 1913—Local Geography
   4: Homesteading
   5, 6: Looking for Work in Los Angeles; Back to the Desert
   7: Getting the Mail
   8: Life on the First Homesteads
   9: Carl Eytel; Indian Reveals Location of Well on Miracle Hill
   10: Digging the First Well; Indian Wells
   11: Bob Carr
   12: Walking the Desert; Shoe Repair
   13, 14, 15: Bob Carr at Mack Sennett's Studio
   16: Ford Beebe, Walter Woods, Bob Carr and Stella Carr
   17: The Carrs; Merry Xmas
   18: Struggle for Water
   19: Burros; Well-Digging
   20: Water; an Orange; Going to the Railroad Station
   21: Man Shaves with Broken Glass
   22: Buying Merry Xmas
   23, 24: Life with Merry Xmas

25: Planning a New Well
26: Digging in the Hot Earth
27: Hot Water at the Bottom
28: To the Oil Fields
29, 30: The Job near Bakersfield; 2 Mules
31: Return to Desert; Merry Xmas, the Carrs
32: Bob Carr
33: Dutch Frank, Old Man Coolidge
34: Dutch Frank, Bob Carr
35: Hilda Gray's Cabin; Rattlesnake Story
36: Orr Sang
37: Hauling a Trunk to the Station
38: Handling Rattlesnakes
39: Rattlesnake Lore
40: A Coyote
41, 42: Building a Highway
43: Rattlesnakes
44: In the Snake Pit
45: Stories of Gold Mines
46, 47: Indians and a Gold Mine
48: Types of Snakes
49, 50: Hazards of Digging Wells
51: Ford Beebe's Well Story
52: Cabot Yerxa's Cabin; Rodney in It
53: Neighbor Green's Ice
54: Homestead Housekeeping
55: Illegal to Shoot Sheep; Snake Pit
56: Chuckwallas
57: Desert Animals; Where Indians Lived
58: Indian Pottery Remains
59: Light in the Cabin Window
60, 61, 62, 63, 64: Portrait of Carl Eytel
65: Domestic Animals
66: Cat Tales
67, 68: Working in Los Angeles; Lady with Gun
69, 70: Road-building; A Peaceful Oasis
72, 73: Working in L.A., Setting Telephone Poles
74: Return to Desert--Satisfactions
75: Conditions for Homesteaders
76: Optimism of Homesteaders
78: Dreams of Future: a Healthy City
79: Dreams v. Economic Reality
80: Picnics, Amusements
81: Wild Things in Cabins
82: Reptiles, Insects in Cabins
83: Other Critters in Cabins
84: A Skunk, a Tarantula
85, 86: "The Desert Bandana"

87: Glass Bottles
88: Story about Rodney; with Bob Carr and a Lynx
89: Talking to Bob Carr, with Merry Xmas
90: Owls
92: My Mother
93: Louis Sobol's Sketch of Garnet and Cabot
94: "My Mother Was a 'Cabot'"
95: Adventures with Mother
96: Letter to Louis Sobol: Desert Situation
97: Letter to Sobol: February in the Desert
98: Letter to Sobol: View from Miracle Hill
99: Letter to Sobol: Landscape and Speculation
100: Letter to Sobol: Snakes and Chuckwallas
101, 102: Leaving the Desert; To the Train
103: Returning to the Desert after 5 Months
105: Living Alone
106: Living Alone; Beginning of Letter to Sobol
107: Letter to Sobol: Desert Description
108: Letter to Sobol: Contrast Desert Peace with City Life
109, 110: Owners of First Cars
111: Saving a Stranded Car
112: Hilda Gray Rescues Her Car
114: Hilda Gray
116, 117: Rival Carpenters: Bob Belt and Bill Anderson
118: Alaska in 1900
119: Moonlight in Alaska and on the Desert
120: Walking at Night
121: Indio Woman Makes a Track
122: Letter to Sobol: Red Racer Snake
123: Hollywood Men to the Desert
124, 125: Two Men Lose Diamonds in Cabin
126, 127: Pack Rats
128: Letter to Sobol: Building New Cabin
129, 130: Letter to Sobol: Voting
131: Greasewood or Creosote Bush
132: Journal Page on Rain, 1914
133: Walk Quietly
134: Desert Creatures
137, 138: Homes in Desert Built by Cabot Yerxa; One Burned, 1952
139: Building New House, 1925
140: Animals Watch Him Building
141: Sunday Socializing, 1925
142: Socializing, Digging a Well, 1925
143, 144, 145, 146: Big Trip to Latin America, Europe, 1925
147, 148: Letter to Sobol: Spring
149: Dutch Frank
150, 151: Old Man Coolidge; Civil War Gun
152, 153: Dutch Frank and Burros

154: Old Man Coolidge
155: Earliest Settlers
156: First Teacher, Schoolhouse
157: Building School House
158: First School
159, 160: Letter to Sobol: Desert Quiet, Lonely Rain
161, 162: Tiddles the Cat
163, 164, 165, 166, 167: Reprint from Palm Springs *Villager*: Fate of Eight Men Working on Aqueduct, 1930
169: Letter to Sobol, Continued: Snakes as Pets
170, 171, 172: Chewing Tobacco; Charlie the Mess Cook
173: Winter Rain
174: Landscape View
175: Merry Xmas
177: Watching a Snake
178: Hunting Rabbits
180, 181: Advice on Walking; Take a Crooked Stick
182, 183, 184: Reprint from Palm Springs *Villager*: Malty the Burro
185: Found Poem: "Mornin' on the Desert"
186: Store in Ventura; the Coffees Arrive
187: Return to Desert, 1937
188: Vision of Miracle Hill Development
189: Applying for Bank Loan
190, 191: The Loan Refused; B-bar-H Ranch Opens
192: Lucienne Hubbard's B-bar-H Ranch
193: Jack Krindler of 21 Club, Others Visit Trading Post
194: Lew Ayres Visits; John Barrymore
195, 196, 197, 198: Reporter from Palm Spring *News*: A Trap Door Spider
199: Snake Pit; Si Seadler to B-bar-H Ranch
200: Bugs in the Desert
201: Wildlife around the Pueblo
202, 203: Woodpeckers
204: B-bar-H Visitors, the Rich and Famous
205: Jack Krindler
206: Sol Lesser; Letter to Sobol: Sleeping Outdoors
207: Letter to Sobol, Continued: Chores, Wildlife
208: Letter to Sobol Concludes: A Mad Owl
210, 211: Early Surveys
212, 213, 214, 215, 216, 217: Hilda Gray, Her Cabin, 2 Bunch Palms Oasis
219, 220: To Los Angeles to Prove Up Homestead Claims
221, 222: Dynamite; An Idle Poem
226, 228: Letter to Sobol: Desert People Differ from City People
229, 230, 231: Smokey the Cat
232, 233, 234, 235: Letter to Sobol: Walking across Desert
236, 237, 238, 239, 240, 241: Desert Tortoise
242: Bull Snake
243: Don't Kill Snakes and Lizards
244: Animals No Longer Seen

245: Migratory Birds
246, 247: Pedro Chino Died, 1919
248: People in DHS Area, 1937
249, 250: Early Road-Building
251, 252, 253: Letter to Sobol: Views of Desert, Imagined Pains of City Life
254, 256, 257: Information on Snakes; Snakes on the Isle of Pines
258: Randall Henderson
259, 260: Randall Henderson on Harry Oliver, Cabot Yerxa, Paul Wilhelm
261, 262: Drew Oliver's Wind Contraption
263: Article from Riverside *Press Enterprise*: What Tourists Say about the Pueblo
264: Article, Continued; Cabot Yerxa a Painter of Indians
265: Article, Continued: Description of Pueblo
266: Article Interview: Cabot Yerxa's Early Memories
267: Article Sums Up Cabot's Early History
268: Article Tells Cabot's Trip to Photograph Indian Meeting, 1909; More Early History
269: Article Concludes: Cabot's Early Life, Building of Pueblo
270, 271, 272, 273, 274, 275: Desert Plants
278: C. R. Browning: Memories of Early Days
279, 280: Earliest Local History to 1937

ON THE DESERT SINCE 1913 - Explanatory Notes   211

THREE DAYS AT THE PUEBLO, 1961, by Cabot Yerxa   218

NEWSPAPER OBITUARY, 1965   227

Table of Photographs

Nome, Alaska - 1900-1901   29-32

Cabot's Family and Early Years in Minnesota   67-70

Cuba and Sierra Madre - 1902 – 1911   104-107

Homestead Years - 1913-1918   141-149

Fertilla, Moorpark, Ranch & Trading Post - 1919-1940s   184-187

Constructing the Pueblo - 1941-1950   221-226

ACKNOWLEDGEMENTS

Our admiration and gratitude extend first to Cabot Abram Yerxa, whose newspaper columns from the 1950s provide an invaluable record of early 20th century life in the northwestern Coachella Valley.

At a party in 2009, Jason Bruecks, who once served as a tour guide at Cabot's Pueblo Museum under Cabot's successor, Cole Eyraud, surprised Barbara Maron with a present. Barbara was and is a docent at the museum, a member of the foundation's board of directors, and has recently been designated the official historian for the Cabot's Museum Foundation. The gift was a scrapbook in which Cabot Yerxa once pasted some clippings of his newspaper columns, entitled "On the Desert Since 1913." As Barbara leafed through the scrapbook, the importance of these previously unknown columns quickly dawned on her. When she spoke to me about them soon afterward, she said confidently, "We're going to publish them." With my background as an English teacher and editor, naturally I couldn't wait to read them and start to work.

Over the past two years, several members of the Cabot's community have pitched in to get this book to the printer. Outgoing foundation president Michael O'Keefe gave early encouragement, and his successor, Dr. Lorraine Becker, sensed the strategic importance of the undertaking and guided us through administrative mazes.

Judy Gigante, an experienced Cabot's Museum docent and former board member, worked with Barbara and me on acquiring and selecting the photographs.

Terry Chapman, who became the museum's registrar at about the time the book project got underway, has contributed in several ways, helping us to locate photos and making suggestions at all levels of the project.

My friend Larry Hillman helped with research and drew the map, based on old maps and descriptions of the Miracle Hill area.

Barbara Maron, Judy Gigante, Larry Hillman, Terry Chapman, and Sally Rogers read the text in progress and offered useful advice.

Gabriele Mirghaffari helped in the preparation of the historic photographs for the press.

We are especially grateful to living relatives of Cabot Yerxa: his granddaughter, Laurie Segawa, and his grand-nephew, Howard Lowell, for their permission to use certain photos from the family. A visit to Mr. Lowell and his wife was a personal pleasure for Judy Gigante and me, and contributed to our understanding of the family's history.

Desert Hot Springs City Manager Rick Daniels encouraged the project. We are grateful to Mayor Yvonne Parks for her civic leadership, which has created an environment for an institution like Cabot's Pueblo Museum to mature and flourish. "A Cabot Yerxa Chronology to 1913" and "Three Days at the Pueblo, 1961" are published with permission of the City of Desert Hot Springs, as are most of the photographs.

Larry Hillman and Judy Gigante have generously lent their financial support to help me bring this project to fulfillment.

Richard E. Brown

February 2011

FOREWORD

Cabot Yerxa (1883-1965) is still remembered around California's Coachella Valley for some important reasons. He built a unique and oddly beautiful building called Cabot's Old Indian Pueblo, which is now owned by the city of Desert Hot Springs and operated as Cabot's Pueblo Museum by a non-profit foundation. Several thousand people take tours and shop in the adjacent trading post each year. The main building, originally constructed as a home and a museum dedicated to the builder's life and to Native American culture, contains a significant collection of documents and Western memorabilia.

Cabot Yerxa was one of the earliest homesteaders in the northwestern part of the valley. He arrived in late 1913, built a cabin on Miracle Hill, and took credit for discovering the hot mineral water aquifer that now supplies health spas in Desert Hot Springs. He promoted this little-known region to a land developer in the early 1930s and was instrumental in the founding of the city.

Other aspects of his life are less remembered, but equally fascinating. Cabot was an important part of the Hollywood celebrity scene located at the nearby B-bar-H dude ranch during the 1930s and 40s. He was an artist, a student and promoter of regional artists. He was an advocate of the rights of Native Americans at a time when this was an unusual position for a white man to take. He was an adventurer and a tale-spinner about his days in Alaska, Cuba, France, and elsewhere. He was a passionate desert naturalist. He was a journalist, memoirist, and publicist for causes near to his heart. He was a thoughtful spiritualist.

In the 46 years since his death, the vivid sense of the man has dimmed—obscured not only by time, but by a cloud of exaggerations and implausible stories that seem inevitable where figures of the romantic American West are concerned. Yet the real Cabot Yerxa is still knowable and still worth knowing. His story remains valuable for its illumination of early Coachella Valley history, and it remains engaging because of Cabot's appealing personality. It's no accident that members of the museum community refer to him affectionately by his first name.

The scarcity of other accounts of the California homesteading experience make Cabot's story doubly important. The only established literary classic in the field is Mary Austin's *The Land of Little Rain* (1903). Another writer of local interest, Nina Paul Shumway, chronicled her family's arrival in 1909 to start a date plantation at Coachella (*Your Desert and Mine,* 1960) and her 1930s adventure in homesteading in the mountains above Palm Desert (*Mountain of Discovery,* 1984). However, Cabot's *On the Desert Since 1913* bids fair to surpass these and all other writings about California desert homesteading in its wealth of details and insight into the early settlers' attitudes toward their chosen land.

This volume is devoted to making Cabot's story accessible to the public. The centerpiece of the book is the 280 newspaper articles he published in the *Desert Sentinel*,

Desert Hot Springs' local newspaper, during the 1950s. The series details Cabot's memories of homesteading, his later encounters with Hollywood personalities, his observations of nature, and key incidents in his eventful life. The other brief selections in this book, drawn from private papers and newspaper articles, fill out Cabot's story from earliest days to his death.

The photographs, drawn almost entirely from the museum archive and a private family collection, complement Cabot's writings but tell their own tale. From these images we get an idea of Cabot's first wife's personality and her participation in homesteading life; we meet his desert neighbors, dressed for the camera in the only decent clothes they had; we observe the Pueblo during succeeding stages of construction; we sense the comfortable intimacy between the museum-keeper and his second wife, Portia. Cabot himself had an instinct for the camera and apparently liked to pose. We catch him first as a boy in Minnesota, and, more camera-alert, at age 16 or 17 in Alaska. That familiar face gradually attains distinction and still addresses us with warmth as the decades pass.

PREFACE TO THE SECOND EDITION

The public response to the first edition has been gratifying, and the book's publication has given Cabot's Museum Foundation an opportunity to reach new audiences in a variety of ways. Meanwhile the Museum has gained additional publicity for other reasons during the 2012-2013 winter season, particularly the announcement that the building is being added to the National Register of Historic Places. Steady sales of this book have made a second edition necessary, enabling us to add some newly discovered photographs that are generously provided by Cabot Yerxa's granddaughter, Laurie Segawa, as well as a few other photos from the museum's collection that help to round out our story. Thanks to ongoing research by the Cabot's Museum Foundation's History Committee, we are able to add a few historical facts and correct a few false assumptions in the notes. We are also including an index to make the book easier to use.

It has been my pleasure to work with the Foundation's new official Historian, Judy Gigante, in making these improvements. She has brought energy and know-how to some of the less joyful tasks of book production.

–Richard Brown

CHRONOLOGY OF THE LIFE OF CABOT YERXA AND HIS PUEBLO MUSEUM

1859   Cabot's mother, Nellie Cabot Yerxa, is born in Massachusetts.

1861   Cabot's father, Fred Yerxa, is born in Fredericton, New Brunswick.

1882   Fred Yerxa, 21, and Nellie Cabot, 23, marry in Boston.

They move to Hamilton, Dakota Territory to start at trading post. The town is located in Pembina County one mile south of the Canadian boarder. Fred's brothers are living in Grand Forks and Fargo.

1883   Cabot Yerxa is born at Fort Pembina near Hamilton, North Dakota on June 11.

1885   Cabot's only sibling, Harry Chester Yerxa, is born in Hamilton, North Dakota July 13.

1886   Cabot's family leaves Dakota Territory for Minneapolis.

1889   Cabot begins working in family store in Minneapolis when not in school.

1893   Cabot and family take a three month sightseeing trip from St.Paul via New Orleans to Mexico City. The family stays at the Chapultepec castle for two days as guests of the President of Mexico, Porfirio Diaz. The family returns through Texas, Los Angeles, San Francisco, crossing the Rockies through Salt Lake. At one point the train stops at 7 Palms/Palm Springs Train Station and Cabot gets his first glimpse of the Coachella Valley.

1900   Cabot learns of the Gold Rush in Cape Nome, Alaska and decides to go for the adventure. He has saved $1,700. In April he goes to Chicago to buy supplies at Reed Murdock's grocery. He buys 50,000 cigars, some pipes and chewing tobacco for a tobacco store. He has it all put in tin cases and ships it to Seattle.

May   Cabot takes train to Seattle the first week of May. There he has his cases loaded on the S.S. Centennial. Ralph Boyer, a friend from Minneapolis, and Cabot sail to Nome. The trip takes four weeks.

June   Cabot sets up his cigar store in a 7x10 foot tent on Front Street. He rents it from a miner for $150 a month. To defray expenses, he rents part of it to a barber for $100 a month and rents a box on the outside to a newspaper man for $25 a month.

Nov	Saloon next to Cabot's store gets its own barber. Cabot's barber leaves to be a butcher and the newspaperman goes back to Seattle. Cabot has no money for next month's rent.

Elwood W. Shirk offers Cabot a job building his mercantile store, living quarters and stable in Nome. Once built, Cabot's runs the store.

Cabot and two older men build a roadhouse for El Shirk at Cape Rodney about 100 miles from Nome. Roadhouse is 12x36 with 3 sections, one for dogs, one for horses, one for men. They are still working on it when winter comes.

Cabot returns to Nome from Cape Rodney with one of the men. They build the Theobold Stage Line for El Shirk. The line makes weekly trips from Nome to Teller/Port Clarence and back. Cabot drives the stage.

1901	During the winter and spring, Cabot visits the Inupiat people, learning their culture and language. He records each word, its meaning and phonetic pronunciation. Later he sells this book to the Smithsonian.

He also sells newspapers to miners in the back country.

Cabot establishes a cigar and candy store in Nome with his friend Hood. They make their own peanut brittle. The store becomes the information center for the Inupiat people, since Cabot is friends with a number of them and knows their language.

Cabot suffers frostbite to his hands, fingers and toes while guiding a young Inupiat boy home to his family. He refuses to let the doctor cut off his fingers even after gangrene sets in. The doctor treats the fingers and eventually they heal.

At his father's request, Cabot leaves Nome in the fall for Minnesota.

1902	Cabot's family leaves for Cuba. They arrive in Havana with a steam driven car.
1903	Fred Yerxa and his sons build the first housing development outside Havana in Pina del Rio, Cuba. The Yerxas buy 33,000 acres, sell 8,000 acres @ $20 per acre, leaving 200 forty acre pieces to sell.

Cabot starts a mail order business, Cabot A. Yerxa & Company, selling Cuban cigars.

1904	Cabot's family moves back to Havana and eventually leaves Cuba for New York.

They introduce and sell guava jelly from Cuba at St. Louis World's Fair and Cabot sells his cigars. The family goes back to New York City where Cabot works in the "commission business" for a few months, then spends a few months in Boston before heading to Seattle.

1905	Cabot sells his mail order cigar business to John B. Rogers & Co. of Binghamton, New York.

In June Fred opens a wholesale grocery store, F.R. Yerxa and Sons, at the corner of Occidental and Main in Seattle. The business expands to include branch stores throughout the city. However, the stores falter and the Yerxas are out of Seattle by early December.

Cabot goes to Nome during the summer. He takes orders for goods to be shipped from the family store in Seattle and hand delivers these orders to mining camps and villages around Nome.

1906   Fred and his son Harry purchase an orange and lemon ranch in Sierra Madre, Riverside County, California. It is located on the NE corner of Baldwin & Live Oak (Orange Grove Ave.) They call it Villa Pilar Ranch.

1908   Cabot and Harry acquire the grocery store on corner where Union Service now stands in Sierra Madre. Cabot is Postmaster from January 13, 1908 to December 14, 1911.

Cabot marries Mamie K. Carstensen in San Francisco on February 8.

1909   In July Cabot attends an annual gathering of Sioux, Arapahoe, Pawnee, Shoshone and Omaha at Ghost Dance Flats, South Dakota. This year's gathering is historic because Red Cloud turns over his leadership to his son Jack.

1911   Cabot's brother, Harry Chester Yerxa, marries Edna Staples in Sierra Madre.

Cabot leaves his Postmaster position and takes over management of the family citrus ranch.

1913   On January 6 a freeze hits Riverside County and destroys the citrus crop as well as the trees. The Yerxa family loses everything.

March 13, father Fred Yerxa dies in Berkeley at age 53.

Following the freeze, Cabot has trouble finding a job in California. He travels to Idaho to run an amusement park for the Street Rail Road, operates a menagerie, becomes a deputy sheriff and works as a newspaper reporter on the largest newspaper in Idaho.

In October he arrives in the desert with Bob Carr to claim homestead land.

Cabot works as railroad agent, postmaster and store keep near Bakersfield for five months to earn money to buy supplies to take back to his homestead.

1914   Cabot returns for seven month stay at his homestead. He builds a wood frame house there.

Cabot's only son, Rodney, is born at Queen of Angels hospital in Los Angeles on October 5.

Mamie and Rodney, who is just 10 days old, join Cabot in the desert.

Cabot digs first hot water well outside his homestead cabin. It's 40' deep and water temperature is 132 degrees. The well shaft is 24 by 28 inches.

1918   February 7, Cabot proves up his homestead land.

Cabot, Mamie and Rodney travel to Seattle by ship to live with Mamie's parents.

October 23, Cabot enlists in the Army in Seattle, Washington.

Cabot is handpicked by Lt. Col. Dwight Eisenhower for the Army's small tank corps. These small tanks are called Whippets. He is Eisenhower's mess sergeant and clerk.

1919   In May, Cabot is selected to be part of a 500 man team demonstrating the Whippet Tanks all over the country to raise money for Liberty/Victory Bonds.

Cabot is honorably discharged at rank of sergeant from Camp Mead, Maryland on July 12.

Cabot works as boiler man on a ship from New York to Seattle.

Cabot opens a grocery store/post office in Fertilla near Blythe, California. He runs this store until 1925.

1920   Cabot's brother, Harry, dies in Berkeley at age 35.

Mamie and Cabot separate. She and Rodney live in Seattle with her parents.

1925   In January Cabot leaves Fertilla in a bright yellow Model T to return to Miracle Hill, where he begins to build the ranch house and lives there till May.

1925   In May, Cabot leaves via the Panama Canal and Central American for Ireland, Britain and continental Europe. He travels for almost a year.

Cabot studies art in London and Paris, where he spends 3 months at the Academie Julian in Paris.

Cabot attends the British Empire Exhibition at Wembly, England and the World Exposition of Decorative Arts in Paris, France.

1926   Cabot returns to California and operates a general store in Moorpark unil 1937. Cabot says the purpose of running the store is to save enough money to fulfill his big plans for Miracle Hill. His mother Nellie lives with him part time.

1930   1930 census shows Mamie (now called Beverly Yerxa) divorced and living with Rodney, at 16, at her parents' home in Seattle. Her occupation is bookkeeper for a wholesale florist.

1932   Cabot meets a land developer, L.W. Coffee, at his store in Moorpark. Coffee and his wife (Lillian) leave for desert with maps of Cabot's wells and letters of introduction.

1936   In July 30 friends celebrate Nellie Yerxa's 77th birthday at Cabot's Ranch on Miracle Hill. She and Cabot still live in Moorpark.

1937   Cabot sells the store in Moorpark and returns to live at the ranch on Miracle Hill. Cabot opens a trading post at the ranch.

Cabot's Trading Post is discovered by celebrities from the B bar H Ranch.

1941   Cabot starts work on the Pueblo.

1942   Cabot's mother, Nellie, dies on May 1.

1945	Cabot marries Portia Fearis Graham August 8 in San Bernardino and they live at the Ranch on Miracle Hill.
	Following Rodney Yerxa's discharge from the Air Force, he and his wife Maggie live at the Pueblo for 6 months. Rodney helps lay the telephone poles in the Adobe Room of the Pueblo.
1951	Rodney's only daughter, Laurie, is born on October 27.
1952	Cabot travels to Arizona, New Mexico, Colorado, Utah looking at ancient places of worship.
	Cabot's Altar in the Wilderness just east of the Pueblo is dedicated on November 30.
1961	Cabot's Museum is visited by 450 tourists in January and 483 in February. Cabot writes that 22,000 have visited since its opening.
1964	An article about Cabot and his Pueblo appears in the Travel Section of the New York Times on May 10.
1965	Cabot dies on March 5 at age 81.
1969	Portia dies on April 1 at age 84.
1970	Cole Eyraud reopens museum.
1978	Peter "Wolf" Toth carves Indian Monument "Waokiye." Dedication Ceremony is held.
1980	Cole registers museum in Riverside County as Point of Historical Interest.
1985	Rodney Yerxa dies in San Leandro at age 70. His wife Marguerite dies two months later.
1996	Cole Eyraud dies on October 27 at age 75.
1998	The Eyraud family donates land, building and contents of the Pueblo to the city of Desert Hot Springs.
2012	Cabot's Pueblo Museum is named to the Registry of National Historic Places.

A CABOT YERXA CHRONOLOGY TO 1913

[This undated document found in the museum collection does not include all of Cabot's jobs, his travels for adventure or profit, or his family relationships. There is no mention of his first marriage to Mamie Carstensen in 1908.

[Cabot Abram Yerxa was born on June 11, 1883, on a Lakota Sioux reservation in the Dakota Territory, 16 miles south of the Canadian border, where his father was operating a trading post near the town of Hamilton.]

Left North Dakota in 1886 and went to Minneapolis. Moved to Saint Paul in 1890; back to Minneapolis in May, 1896; back to St. Paul in '96 and to Minnetonka in 1899; back to St. Paul in 1900.

Went to Alaska in 1900 and back to St. Paul in 1901. Went to Cuba in 1902; 1903 to Isle of Pines; 1904 back to Havana, Cuba (Cigar Business in Key West in 1904); then to Boston in 1904; to Seattle in 1905; to Alaska in 1905. (Sold groceries all over Alaska. Carried groceries from town to town taking orders. No order less than $300. Biggest order was for $3,000. This was at the time my father and brother had the grocery store in Seattle.)

Went to Los Angeles in 1906; Sierra Madre in 1907 (Postmaster in Sierra Madre from about 1906 to 1913). Had four or five grocery stores in Berkeley. Newspaper reporter in Idaho and running a menagerie for Street Rail Road, Pasadena in 1908; Riverside in 1912; Berkeley in 1913; then to Boise, Idaho later in 1913. Worked from San Francisco to Bakersfield in August, 1912, for Telephone Company. Immediately following this, went to work as Construction Cashier in San Francisco.

February 14, 1910, elected to membership in Sierra Madre Lodge F. & A. M.

When in Cuba had 33,000 acres of land. Sold 8,000 acres at $20 per acre. As lots were sold, prices went up on lots. Had 200 40-acre pieces. After sold land in Cuba, came to California and bought 100 acres of orange land in Riverside. Had been offered $30,000 for orange crop on a Saturday and was to begin receiving payment the following Monday when they began to harvest the crop. This particular location had not frozen for 20 years and smudge pots were considered unnecessary. Be that as it may, the orange crop froze on the Sunday previous to the harvesting. With the value of the oranges and other properties depending upon it, we estimated our losses for that one night to be in the neighborhood of $100,000. I then started all over again with pick and shovel in Los Angeles.

COMMENTARY

Cabot's father, Frederick Robinson Yerxa (1861-1913), was a member of a large, long-established New England and New Brunswick family. Frederick was born in New Brunswick, though he married his wife, Helen Cabot, in Boston in 1880.

The family name was originally Dutch, spelled Jurkse. In the museum collection is a family tree diagram dated 1940 that indicates a Jurkse first emigrated to the New World in 1750. The Canadian and American halves of the family divided at the American Revolution.

Cabot's mother, Helen W. (Nellie) Cabot (1859-1942), bore a famous New England patronym—a source of pride for her son. In *On the Desert Since 1913* Cabot Yerxa asserts, "My mother was a 'Cabot.'" However, she was not closely related to the most famous branch of the family, which includes the Cabot Lodges. My colleague Barbara Maron is in receipt of a message from a genealogist associated with the Historical Society of Beverly, Massachusetts: ". . . three families of Cabots came to Salem and Boston from Jersey in the first three decades of the 18th C. Two, the George & John Cabots, were brothers. Anna Sophia Cabot (1821-1900), a descendant of John, married John Ellerton Lodge (1807-1862) in about 1842, and generations of Henry Cabot Lodges followed. . . . The Charles Cabots arrived about 1725, a quarter-century after John and George. They were the forebears of Helen W. Cabot, who married Yerxa. Most of the Charles Cabot branch stayed in the Boston area. Unfortunately, the male line died out in the 20th century, so that Y-DNA testing is not feasible. While they were different immigrant families, they all were related back in Jersey." In *On the Desert,* Cabot Yerxa writes that on his trip to Europe in 1925, he visited a graveyard on the island of Jersey (between England and France) which was filled with his ancestors, the Cabots or Chabots.

Despite his mother's aristocratic-sounding pedigree, Cabot describes her as he first knew her in a starkly unglamorous way: "My mother left Boston, a city-type woman, and went to live with my father in North Dakota among the Indians. They had one room, 10 x 12 foot, no water, no sink, no pipes, no neighbors, just a table and two chairs. Dad was busy in his store for Indians, etc. Mother chopped wood for fire, carried water in a pail ¼ mile; in winter no water, and she carried snow and melted it for water. The cabin leaked in rains, and snow came through cracks in winter. Wolves came to door at night and Indians ate my dogs. They had cyclones, blizzards, and more heat in summer than here [in Desert Hot Springs]. So using this for background, we start in luxury" (letter to his future second wife, Portia Graham, July 25, 1945).

*

Cabot's early movements around Minnesota were related to his father's work in the grocery business with his two brothers, Cabot's uncles. Cabot mentions in the newspaper interview that follows in this volume that he began working for his father at age six and quickly rose in responsibilities.

Minnetonka is today a suburb west of Minneapolis. In the late 19th century it was a bustling mill town, after having been a center of Dakota and Ojibway culture decades earlier.

Ever the entrepreneur, Frederick Yerxa went to Cuba in 1902, just as the Spanish-American War was ending, to sell land and build houses for Americans who would settle there, hoping Cuba might become an American possession. Then he moved to the Isle of Pines, off the southern coast of Cuba (now renamed the Island of Youth [Isla de la Juventad]), hoping to start a pineapple plantation. The Isle of Pines was mistakenly believed to belong to the United States—an error that encouraged colonization. A family story says that Frederick left because he was uncomfortable with the culture of bribery, while other settlers remained. In the newspaper interview that follows, Cabot says he left Alaska to assist in his father's projects. Much money was made in a short time, but then the adventure was over.

Within a few years Frederick and Nellie, Cabot, and Cabot's younger brother, Harry (1885-1920), had moved to southern California. Frederick and Harry bought a large orange ranch in Riverside County in about 1906. Another document indicates that Cabot's term as postmaster of Sierra Madre lasted from 1908 to 1911. The 1910 census has Cabot and his wife, Mamie, living in Pasadena. He seems to have taken over management of his father's citrus ranch in 1911.

In *On the Desert Since 1913* a journalist states that Cabot's father died in 1910, requiring that he give up the postmastership in Sierra Madre in order to manage the citrus business, though other sources indicate the father died in March after the great January, 1913 freeze. This was the calamity that left Cabot broke and led to his homesteading in the Desert Hot Springs area in September of that year.

Interestingly, Cabot's younger brother, Harry, moved to Berkeley after the freeze and, working with their uncle Ed Yerxa, started a chain of four or five stores that apparently supplied a good income within a few years. Family photos of the house Harry built for his wife and daughter in the Berkeley hills indicate prosperity and comfort. Cabot also passed through Berkeley within months after the freeze and even claims that he "had" these stores, yet it seems he rejected the possibility of working as a storekeeper for the rest of his life. As it turned out, in 1913 he was primed to become a desert rat.

YERXA SURVIVED LAWLESS ALASKA

By a [Riverside, California] Press-Enterprise Correspondent

DESERT HOT SPRINGS—A teen-ager with $1,700 in his pocket today would most likely head for the nearest used car lot, but in 1900 16-year-old Cabot Yerxa used his savings to open a cigar store in Nome, Alaska.

"Actually it was an 8 by 10 tent," the 76-year-old Yerxa, a pioneer resident of this community, recalled. "No buildings existed in Nome in 1900, only one row of tents along the waterfront.

"I had to pay $150 a month rent, so I leased the inside of the tent to a barber for $100 a month, the outside space on one side to a newspaper peddler for $25, and erected my cigar stand in what little space was left close to the door of the tent.

"I'll never forget the Fourth of July," he continued. "The miners were in such a rush to get to the saloons and gambling tents that no one was buying cigars. So the barber and I made a dummy out of newspapers, covered it with blankets and left a rubber hat and rubber boots exposed. We told a passerby that a man had been shot and no one could view the body until his partner arrived to make positive identification. We had 50 people there, smoking cigars of course, before we revealed the hoax."

"Life was cheap, law and order non-existent, every man toted a gun and killings occurred daily. When the government sent in Marines, so many of them were shot that two of them would patrol a street at a time, one marching slowly ahead, the other walking in reverse.

"They had rounded up 20 desperados to stand trial in Seattle when they got a round robin letter saying they would never be allowed to take them out. They handcuffed each thug to a heavy chain, then chained his free wrist to a Marine and marched the men down to the Revenue Cutter Bear in that fashion. For a while conditions improved."

Yerxa, a descendent of John Cabot who founded Newfoundland in 1497, was 13 when newspapers' accounts of the Klondike gold rush aroused his adventurous spirit.

"My father said no. He owned the largest chain of grocery stores in Minnesota," explained Yerxa, "and from the age of six I had worked in the store every moment I was not in school. I waited until I was 16. By that time I headed a department of 35 employees, did all my own hiring and firing, and I saved $1,700. I'll run if you don't agree, I told my father, and he relented."

Twenty days after the Sentinel set sail from Seattle, Yerxa and a 19-year-old friend waded ashore at Nome.

"We were overdue because the vessel had been stranded on the rocks at Dutch Harbor for 30 hours. In those days Nome had no docks. Ships anchored one-half mile from shore and passengers rode on lighters until they reached shallow water. Then everyone waded."

By late summer of 1900, Yerxa had mapped out plans for the approaching winter. His friend, homesick for his sweetheart, had returned to Minnesota. The cigar business was flourishing, but the price of coal was going to eat up all of Yerxa's profits.

"Food was expensive," Yerxa commented. "I did all my own cooking after I had to pay a dollar in a restaurant for three hot cakes and a cup of coffee, the first day I arrived.

"I used to make a little extra money selling my place in line at the post office. No one was allowed inside the building. All business was transacted through a window which opened to the outside. Shivering men stood in line for hours and rich gamblers offered those near the window as much as $5 for their place. Sometimes I would sell mine three and four times in one day.

"I made friends with Lolayook, the son of an Eskimo Headman who had learned a few English words from the missionaries. We exchanged vocabularies. That winter I spent three weeks out of each month with my Eskimo friends seal hunting, fishing, driving dog teams, sharing their igloos and their monotonous diet of raw meat and fish.

"I found them to be very intelligent, jovial, friendly people who were quick to appreciate a joke. They were artistic, too. Whenever they could spare time from their daily search for food, they would carve beautiful objects from walrus tusks.

"Later I profited by knowledge of the Eskimo language when the Smithsonian Institution paid me 50 cents for each word I could write."

During the summer of 1901, Yerxa and a partner opened a candy and grocery store.

"I made the candy and peddled it to the saloons. Then my father wrote that he needed my help, so I left Alaska on the last boat that fall. Months before I had frozen my fingers badly, so I was ready to leave."

In 1913 Yerxa braved the elements to pioneer again. But that time it was heat and thirst that he battled, when he homesteaded 160 acres in what is now Desert Hot Springs.

COMMENTARY

The unnamed reporter gives Cabot's age as 76, so the interview must have occurred between June 11, 1959, and June 10, 1960.

In the 1950s and 60s Cabot was a regular presence in regional newspapers. This interview is interesting for a few reasons. Cabot mentions working as a child in his father's grocery business in Minnesota and supporting himself in Alaska as a teenager under brutal weather conditions, in a very rough male society, without any family members nearby to lean on.

His attitude toward money in Alaska seems to have been: make whatever you can, spend as little as possible. His greatest earnings during a later Alaskan trip, in 1905, came from taking large grocery orders that he filled from his family's store in Seattle. Elsewhere he recorded making tens of thousands of dollars in Alaska.

The taste for physical jokes and deceptions he displays in *On the Desert Since 1913* is evident in the scheme to sell cigars by placing an effigy of a corpse in front of his cigar store in Nome. And his lifelong fascination with Native Americans is apparent in his friendship with a young Inuit man, with whom he exchanged vocabularies.

Cabot's habitual stance, well before he became a desert homesteader, was to maintain a distance from mainstream society. His delivery of merchandise to isolated mining camps required that he trek long distances through the frozen landscape alone.

Yet this punishing, isolating outdoor challenge was the type of adventure he consistently sought.

On the other hand, Cabot displays sensitivity and warmth in his description of the Inuits: "intelligent, jovial, friendly . . . quick to appreciate a joke . . . artistic, too." If he developed his Alaskan money-making schemes alone, he drew others—partners, friends—into the work whenever he required them. His eagerness to talk about his Alaskan experience in later years also indicates a strong social impulse.

The journalist's claim that Cabot Yerxa was a descendent of "John Cabot" who discovered Newfoundland in 1497 is an error that will be repeated several times in this volume. The great explorer was born in Italy around 1450, and was not related to the Cabots or Chabots of the island of Jersey where the Massachusetts Cabots originated. The modern form of the explorer's Italian name is Giovanni Caboto. He sailed under the patronage of Henry VII of England and claimed a swatch of the New World for that country; thus an Anglicized version of his name entered the English-language accounts. Centuries later the Cabots of Boston appropriated his crest to enhance their family's reputation among the Brahmins. Cabot Yerxa presumably heard this false bit of family history from his mother, who surely believed it to be true.

Cabot at far right with friends on ship to Nome, Alaska, 1900-01

Cabot in Nome, Alaska, 1900-1901

Cabot fishing with Inupiat friends, 1900-01

Cabot sitting with Inupiat children and friends, 1900-01

Three Alaskan portraits of Cabot, 1900-1901

Two views of Cabot's cigar store in Nome, 1900. Barber poles visible; tent is revealed behind advertising placards in the side view.

ON THE DESERT SINCE 1913

INTRODUCTION

The 280 articles that make up *On the Desert Since 1913* were written for an audience living in and around Desert Hot Springs, California, during the 1950s. They contain many things Cabot Yerxa thought his fellow citizens should know about earlier days in the Coachella Valley, though their focus is restricted. Those hoping for a full autobiography by the builder of the Old Indian Pueblo will find that much has been left out: the writer's two marriages and the raising of his son, Rodney; any description of his spiritual beliefs, which were unusual for a man of his place and time; an account of his life-long interest in painting, photography, and sculpture; and his role in founding the town of Desert Hot Springs. Surprisingly, even the construction of the Pueblo for which Cabot remains locally famous is not fully described.

In these articles Cabot sets himself apart from city folks and newcomers to the desert as an untamed eccentric: a hermit, he calls himself; a desert rat; a handler of rattlesnakes and chuckwallas, whose best friend was his burro, Merry Xmas. He shows himself embodying character traits that were essential for survival in homesteading days: he's incredibly hard-working, optimistic, independent. His literary character also includes other admirable qualities—curiosity, patience, empathy, civic-mindedness.

His humor is shown in his appreciation of ironies and incongruities, though his life was relentlessly physical, so it's not surprising that he also enjoyed physical jokes, like the "quail hunt" trick practiced on newcomers to the desert. In his writing, an intelligent smile can be detected on nearly every page. His description of three ways to carry a rattlesnake home with you is a classic of sly humor.

He is innocently boastful of his achievements, confident of the superiority of his old way of life. Outside these newspaper columns, he apparently had a rare gift for showing off without compromising his integrity. In the museum's collection are photographs that display him striking poses in cowboy outfits during his years as a tour guide. He burnished his creepy reputation as a snake-handler, while at the same time he could truthfully present himself as a confidant of Hollywood luminaries who hung out at his trading posts.

As for empathy, he could be moved to write stunning passages: "The goose was flying low and honking very mournfully at regular and frequent intervals. I heard him minutes before he appeared in the mist, and I heard him minutes after he was lost to vision. His heart was troubled because of separation from his flock. I might have shot him, but I did not try" (Article 132, written in 1914).

The complex impression he made on outsiders is shown in the interviews with two newspaper reporters that are included as part of this series. Both reporters begin their articles by signaling their skepticism about the desert rat they expect to encounter, but by the end of their accounts, Cabot has won them over. He comes across as good-natured, unpretentious but dignified, and authoritative about the ways of the desert.

His observations of nature were so abundant that he could spin them out for hundreds of words. He was also well trained in the performance art of the campfire tale, which unfolds like a prolonged joke, though the punch lines are not always funny. Some of the incidents he recounts he had witnessed; others he must have known only as tales repeated among his neighbors.

Many of these articles were written as Cabot was moving into his seventies. He remained physically vigorous during this period, still building on his Old Indian Pueblo grounds, traveling--often with his second wife, Portia--throughout the Southwest, engaged in various artistic projects, attending civic meetings, serving as grand marshall in parades. But "civilization" had encroached on the desert by this time, so it's not surprising to find him sounding nostalgic about the open, silent land where he'd once felt so free.

The great, unconscious irony that runs through these articles lies here. *On the Desert* often seems like a long series of love letters to the harsh land where Cabot once found unlikely sustenance. Yet all the time he lived as a virtual hermit in what was to become the Desert Hot Springs area, he was restlessly building, planting, digging, trekking, and dreaming of the possibility that someday the desert could be developed as a health spa and city (with a golf course!), exploiting the miraculous-seeming hot water aquifer that lies below the sand. Cabot may have had as much to do with the development of the first hot mineral water spa, and the building of the town around it, as anyone. He was the evangelist who first preached about the water to L. W. Coffee and encouraged Coffee and Aubrey Wardman through the late 1930s and early 40s, as they sought to buy tracts of land, and dig and build. Yet toward the end of *On the Desert Since 1913*, Cabot laments the loss of wildlife he once saw daily, and advises young men to practice target shooting at tin cans instead of harmless animals. He observes that the sound of a motor car is rudely out of place in the desert, where silence should reign—even though he was one of the early owners of a Model T, as soon as he could afford it.

The central stanza in an anonymous poem expresses this paradox:

Mornin' on the desert—I can smell the sagebrush smoke,
I hate to see it burnin'—but the land must sure be broke.
Ain't it just a pity that wherever man may live,
He tears up much that's beautiful, that the good God has to give? (Article 185)

We can find a similar irony in Cabot's funny account of a few days in his later career as a museum-keeper at the Old Indian Pueblo (included in this volume), where the groups of visitors, with their sloppy behavior, have begun to annoy him. Popularity equals success equals disillusionment?

True, but only sometimes. For the most part, the articles in *On the Desert Since 1913* are cheerful, energetic, still idealistic—though the idealism beams in two directions, backward in time as well as forward. One of the writer's most convincing lines is, "and we were happy." The long-ago episodes he describes when he returned to his homestead cabin after the regular bouts of five months away earning money to live on, then sweeping out the dust, storing groceries, investigating the new wildlife nearby, are full of satisfaction and joy.

*

This series of weekly articles appeared in the *Desert Sentinel*, with a few interruptions, from July 19, 1951 to December 27, 1957. Cabot provided the newspaper's editor with a mix of old journal entries dating back to homesteading days, newly-written articles, and pieces that had recently appeared in other periodicals. The length of the installments was determined by the amount of space available. The editor freely joined parts of unrelated pieces to fill a page, or broke a longer piece into sections and published them over a few weeks.

Determining when the various articles were written is sometimes impossible, though in other cases there are strong clues. In one case the *Sentinel*'s editor introduces a series of articles by flatly stating that they were written back in 1914; in another article Cabot refers to the way things are "here in the Pueblo," which indicates, at a minimum, that the piece was written sometime after he and his second wife moved into the Old Indian Pueblo in the later 1940s. And in one sequence there's a reference to a house Cabot built back in 1925 that has recently burned down, in January, 1952.

Just as it's hard to determine when many of the articles were written, it's also hard to date many of the events recounted here, or place them exactly on a map. The opening articles take the form of chronological story-telling, with Cabot remembering how he got his first glimpse of the Coachella Valley when, as a boy, a train he was riding from Mexico to Los Angeles stopped to take on water at the Seven Palms station. But as the articles accumulate, times and places become jumbled. In some cases the event might have happened during his earliest homesteading days (1913-1918), or on one of his visits back to the area in the 1920s or 30s while he was working elsewhere, or from the late 1930s onward, when he returned to live permanently near the spot on Miracle Hill where he had first homesteaded.

Inevitably Cabot repeats himself over the course of 280 articles, especially about his favorite subjects, such as snakes, the climate, the pleasure of solitude, his early friend, Bob Carr, and his beloved burro, Merry Xmas. *On the Desert Since 1913* might best be read today as its first readers found it, in small chunks. It's a work to dip into frequently, perhaps more than a book to read straight through.

*

This volume reprints about two-thirds of Cabot's original 280 articles. I have tried to eliminate obvious repetitions. In some passages, hasty type-setting made a hash of Cabot's meaning, and I have omitted lines that I could not confidently reconstruct. Omissions are indicated by elipses (. . .). I have normalized Cabot's punctuation throughout. Sentence repairs are indicated by brackets [].

Most of these articles first appeared with an introduction by the *Sentinel*'s editor. The first installment, printed on the newspaper's front page, is headlined: "Start This Great Story Now." The editor writes:

> We are fortunate in securing probably the finest history of this part of the desert ever written. There are few men who could tell it so well, for Cabot Yerxa is artist, writer, businessman, all in one, with wide experience, and a world traveler. Mr. Yerxa's writings have appeared in some of our best magazines. The New York World devoted a full Sunday page to one of his stories. He had the world to choose from, and made our region in the desert his paradise. The story will be run as a series in the Sentinel. It would be well to save each copy, for when the tale is told you will have an exciting, thrilling novel, proving that truth is not only stranger than fiction but much more interesting.

In the present volume the editor's introductions are omitted. In the articles that reprint letters Cabot wrote to Louis Sobol, a columnist for the New York *Journal American*, most of the fulsome introductions Sobol provided are also left out.

The explanatory notes follow article number 280.

The articles appeared under the title "On the Desert Since 1913," but most installments carried no other heading to indicate their content. The titles of the individual articles in this edition have been supplied by the editor.

ON THE DESERT SINCE 1913

ON THE DESERT SINCE 1913

[Article 1: July 19, 1951]

THE BEGINNING

The train slowly rumbled to a stop, and I stepped down into the desert sand. It was still dark, with a faint glow over the far horizon to indicate where the sun later would appear. On the wide expanse of desert there were no lights, houses, or trees to be seen. Standing in nearby brush was a single coyote, and we regarded each other curiously. The conductor later told me that the two mountains which thrust their peaks into the star-studded sky were San Jacinto and San Gorgonio.

No other passengers were up at this very early hour, and the coaches just formed a dark mass merging into a row of palm trees growing on the south side of the track. Up ahead lanterns flashed about the engine and a water tank, as the trainmen busied themselves taking on water.

This was the year of 1893, and I was just a small boy accompanying my parents on a three-months' sight-seeing trip to California. We left St. Paul, Minnesota, in a snowstorm and went by train south to New Orleans. Then leisurely down into Old Mexico with various stops and short side trips to Mexico City, where we were for two days guests of Porfirio Diaz, then president of Mexico. Diaz was a dictator, but also fair with his people.

From there north by a different route into Texas; then Los Angeles and vicinity, San Francisco, and other places, crossing the Rockies to Salt Lake City, and so on with a few detours back St. Paul.

President Diaz, his castle of Chapultepec, the floating gardens, the ancient pyramids, the train held up by two dozen bandits, a major earthquake, and other happenings are a story for another time.

Little did I realize that this desert which I thus first saw in 1893 would be my future home. But the wheels of fortune grind steadily on, change all our plans, and very often reduce us to points of beginning, sometimes putting us in the cellar below the floor of life, where fair starts are made.

[Article 2: July 26, 1951]

Between 1893 and 1913 when I came back to the desert to live, I was mostly in Minnesota, with a very adventurous two years in Alaska during the gold rush days of 1900, lived with the Eskimos awhile, then a stay with 2,500 Sioux Indians on the Dakota prairies, down to Cuba before the Spanish American war ended, over to the Isle of Pines in [the] Caribbean Sea, then lived some time in New York City, St. Louis, Boston, Seattle, back to Alaska and other places, as I have a roving disposition.

President Theodore Roosevelt appointed me postmaster of Sierra Madre—[the] next move [was] to Pasadena.

All went well and the family reassembled and joined together, pooling resources to buy large orange ranches near Riverside. In 1913 they froze. All the combined life accumulations were swept away in the few hours of undreamed-of freezing weather. We lost about $80,000, and there was nothing left. Also during that year some members of the family died. It was a tragic period.

Conditions in California were bad as a result of the general freeze. Work was scarce and wages low. However, I got a job at $10 per week. Later, thinking to better myself, I went to Idaho, ran an amusement park for the street railroad, operated a menagerie, was deputy sheriff, etc., and ended as a newspaper reporter on the largest newspaper in Idaho. There were more opportunities there than in California, but when it started to snow I became quite unhappy, because in Alaska I had experienced weather 65 below zero, together with enough snow to last a lifetime.

One day a letter came from Bob Carr in California, temporarily living at Banning. Bob was a successful writer of western fiction, with his stories appearing in magazines like *Adventure, Popular*, and other newsstand publications. He wrote under the name Robert V. Carr and had a colorful background of living with Sioux Indians, cowboy, prospector, soldier, newspaper reporter. He was an outdoor type.

Bob wrote, "We can each take up a homestead of Government land on the desert, no water, no roads, no rain, no neighbors, but we do not have to pay any rent. We can eat rabbits, write a few stories, buy a cow, the cow will have a calf, and in time we will be in the cattle business."

I wired him, "O.K., I will join you." Within a week I got off the train in Banning, had supper with Bob and his wife, Stella. That night we boarded another train for the desert. Banning, by the way, at that time was little more than [a] R.R. depot, a livery stable, and [a] half-dozen stores.

The train stopped only long enough for us to get off at 2 a.m. in the desert, then disappeared down the track towards Indio in a swirl of dust. The conductor wondered why we wanted to get off at this particular water tank, commenting, "There is nothing there." He was right. Just a water tank and a very small depot with the name Palm Springs painted on a white board. He further explained that Palm Springs was a small Indian village with a post office and a dozen white families five miles to the south.

When the fading lights of the train left us in utter darkness, I was quite surprised to recognize that this very spot was where I had stood as a boy in 1893 when first setting foot in California.

After searching the sky for the North Star, we trudged off into the unknown desert, setting our course east of north. There was no road.

We had a canteen of water, crackers, bread, cheese, sardines, bologna, and a tin pail for coffee. But no fry pan or other dishes, and no blankets. No other equipment. It was October and chilly, so [we] kept warm by walking until the sun was up and warm, then lay down and slept.

Daylight disclosed one very small wooden shack in a sandy clearing. Smoke issued from a tin pipe thrust through the roof, so we walked that way. Miss Hilda Gray, a cheerful person, greeted us at the door and praised the desert from her few months' experience as a homesteader. She said that within the 10,000 acres round about were a few other homestead shacks, but too widely scattered to be seen from here. She mentioned Jack Riley, the MacCargers, the three Green families, Coolidge, Conway, Grandma Riley,

Thieson, all of whom we later met. Then followed in closely, the names coming to mind, of Joe Bonhorn, Mike Driscol, Bill Riley, Thumb, Sweetingham, Dana, Bill Anderson, Ford Beebe, Walter Woods as pioneer settlers. Swanson, Ridings, Harding, Tex Barkay, Hicks, Edwards, Ferris, Mussen, Charlie Tipton, Robert MacDonald, and a few others followed in this early group. Then in Mission Canyon 12 miles to the west were the DeLongs; they had some gravity water, a cow, and two or three horses, which was homesteading deluxe as far as we desert people were concerned.

[ARTICLE 3: AUGUST 2, 1951]

Miss Gray showed us the corners of her land, and from them Bob and I carefully and laboriously searched out the corners of sections 30, 31 and 32, which now is the most settled portion of the desert, and other sections having possibilities as homesteads. There were then many thousand acres open, and we could choose as we wished. An interesting sidelight on these cornered stakes is this. Gold was discovered in California during the year 1849, and by 1856 the Government sent men to pick out feasible trails for overland travel to the East. Water was very necessary for men and animals, so in 1856 U.S. surveyors placed corner stakes on Section 32 and a few adjoining parcels of land, because of water seepage.

On section 32 was a large hill, and at its western end two groups of native palm trees, thus giving the name "Two Bunch" to this locality. Also there was a mud hole of evil-looking water, in which cattle waded to get a drink and small things died. Lizards, snakes, birds, and insects all slithered over with green scum. Leaves blew into the water, vegetation got tramped into the mud.

[ARTICLE 4: AUGUST 9, 1951]

It was a smelly place. The source of the water was tiny driblets of water oozing out of a five-foot clay bank. A dilapidated, rickety ladder stood there, and by going down a half-dozen rungs it was possible to fill a canteen where the slightly moving water kept the scum from forming too thickly. It was here that we obtained our water.

The only other water in 10,000 acres was at another mud hole called "Seven Palms," nearly five miles to the south. Wells were then unknown, and all homesteaders obtained water at these two places or at the railroad tank.

For a few days Bob and I tramped over the desert, searching out corners, examining land, and exploring canyons, sleeping where night overtook us, but returning to Two Bunch for water. We walked over what is now Desert Hot Springs and encountered only rabbits and a few snakes. Bob chose land adjoining Two Bunch because, as he said, he could get water there, such as it was.

I took another day alone and, returning late in the afternoon, found broken bits of pottery on the slope of the big hill. From this I reasoned Indians had lived in the vicinity. "Good enough for Indians, good enough for me"--so I picked this hill for my claim.

I later named it Miracle Hill, because at its base I discovered hot curative mineral waters, [and] on the other side cold water. Miracle Hill is not sedimentary like the others, but thrust up out of the earth's surface in ancient times. Round about it are beds of red clay and blue clay from which Indians made pottery. Also there were to be found rocks, building sand, good earth, and desert soil, all of which is ample reason for the name "Miracle Hill." But I am ahead of my story.

After paying my filing fees for the homestead location to the Government land office in Los Angeles, I had less than 10 dollars left. The law reads that homesteaders must live continuously on the land seven months of each year for three years, cultivate 20 acres of soil, build a house, dig for water, build fences, and otherwise show definite intention of making the claim into a home. And I had less than 10 dollars!

[Article 5: August 16, 1951]

I started looking for work during a period of hard times such as California has had on several occasions. My problem was not only to make a living, but I must earn enough surplus to live seven months on the homestead without any known income and somehow build a cabin in which to live.

I tramped many streets of Los Angeles, applied for work in all likely places, and visited the newspaper offices to read free copies of help-wanted sections. To save carfare I always walked.

To stretch out money I ate 10- and 15-cent meals in Jap or Chinese restaurants in the slum section of the city. I slept in "flop rooms," so called because in them 10 to 20 men just flopped on bedding. The usual charge was 15 cents. For 35 cents there was a cot and four men to a room.

Even with these unpleasant economies, my money dwindled alarmingly. What jobs did turn up, I could not take because I must earn more than a bare living.

To bolster my courage I kept the money in silver dollars and gripped them in one hand often. At last they got down to three and a few pennies. Then in the evening paper I read an advertisement for a man wanted at good salary. One who could do many things and with various qualifications, all of which I could fill. This man must be bookkeeper, grocer, butcher, experienced with horses and mules, able to run [a] Wells Fargo Express office, cook his own meals, and talk Spanish.

Next morning when that office opened, I was there, walking on air because at last I had a break. The job was as good as mine. I had eaten 25 cents for supper, spent 35 cents for sleep, and eaten 25 cents for breakfast. Never mind that only one silver dollar and small change was left, this was a break.

It was a large office with perhaps 30 clerks and typists working at different desks. A small high counter barred my further entrance. One of these fat-jowled, well-fed, lazy clerks handed me an application for the job. It was of two pages with printed questions on all four sides. Finally it was finished, and the last question [was], "Are you married?" to which I answered, "Yes."

In high spirits I handed the completed questionnaire to the lazy clerk, noting well meanwhile with satisfaction, that no other men had yet appeared in answer to the advertisement.

The clerk read slowly down one page after another, nodding his well-combed head at times as though satisfied with the answers, and I thought all was well. But he then tore the papers into bits and threw them in the waste basket, saying, "We do not hire married men."

I was stunned. Fighting mad and desperate because this was the only job in many days of search having possibilities, and my money was gone. Was this to be my final defeat?

So in explosive desperation I pounded the counter with my fist and talked to the whole office in a loud voice that all might hear. I said, "This is a big company, it hires many men. There must be a place for a man like me who wants to work. I can do many things and do them well. I want to talk to some man who knows more about this business than this counter clerk. I want to see some man in authority. I want a job."

The 30-odd clerks all stopped work to stare at me.

[Article 6: August 23, 1951]

I expected to be thrown out. But away back in the far end of the room, a small man with glasses put his head up above some filing cases and came forward. As he did so, all the clerks started working diligently, so I knew this man with glasses was important.

Quietly he inquired the cause for the disturbance. I told him, and repeated my qualifications and what I could do. He smiled and asked when I could go for work. I said, "Now." "All right," he replied, "you are on the payroll from this moment. Meet me at the railroad depot tonight at 7:30 p.m." I did not ask what the job was, or where it was, nor about the wages.

We left this train at Bakersfield, then took a branch line through the oil fields and eventually arrived at the end of the line, to a side track called Shale.

Next day I was duly installed as railroad agent, general storekeeper, Wells Fargo Express agent, bookkeeper, postmaster, ran the ice house, cooked my own meals, and took care of two tough mules and one runaway horse. With these unreliable animals, on certain days I locked up my buildings and delivered ice, meat, freight, and groceries to oil wells and railroad camps within a few miles. I was a very busy person, but made good money. After five months of this, I returned to the homestead and lived seven months without leaving a day.

The moving onto a homestead claim in the desert has many a thrill. It is a new, strange, and different life from any other.

Thornton Green met me at the railroad station with a team of lonesome mules hitched to a small wagon. We loaded in the trunk, sack of potatoes, onions, flour, canned goods, coal oil, blankets, tin stove, pipe, a few simple tools, and many other odds and ends. The wagon was full, and so we walked in the sand all the seven or eight miles to my homestead claim.

There were no roads to speak of, and so we slowly picked our way round bushes or rocks, up some washes and down others, or through drifted sand.

We arrived at sundown, threw the various things out over the ground, and he and the mules left as it was getting dark.

Here I was with one canteen of water, all my earthly possessions scattered about, and the future in my own hands. I made a little campfire of dry sticks, warmed some simple food, and spread the blankets on the sand. This was to be my home, my land, and no rent to pay!

I felt as rich as Rockefeller! There was not another building to be seen, and as darkness increased, not a light. Coyotes yapped up toward the mountains, and I went to sleep with a happy heart.

Morning sunshine and turtledoves calling wakened me to [the] desert routine. First a walk of about a mile, carrying a pail in each hand and a canteen hung on my neck to get water. Then gather dry sticks to supply an open fire on which to cook breakfast.

The various boxes contained a carefully planned assortment for seven months' needs, because homesteaders seldom got to a store during the seven months' period.

Next I dug a hole in a clay bank, put up four corner posts, then arranged a few palm leaves overhead for shade.

There was no floor, no roof, no sides, no door, no windows, no table, no chairs, no stove--I slept on the ground, cooked and ate all meals on the ground.

Later, gradually a 10'×12' rough single-board wall cabin developed, the tin stove [was] installed, and coal oil lamps gave light. Over the years three other rooms were added. They were small, six by eight feet.

[Article 7: August 30, 1951]

Living without neighbors and no phones or newspapers, it is quite impossible to keep track of the days of the week. So if it was important for me to go to the R.R. or P.O. or to work somewhere on a certain day, I would build a fire outdoors, for instance on Monday. Then each morning I built a fire in a new spot, and so on until the designated day arrived. I was sure of it because I went back to my Monday fire and counted the days--each represented by the ashes of a fire.

My son Rodney and his mother came down to take their place in the cabin. Rodney was just ten days out of the hospital and is the first white baby to be born on the Desert Hot Springs side of the railroad. So that he might have good water to drink, I walked seven miles to the R.R. station once each week, then filled canteens and walked seven miles back to the cabin.

On this weekly trip I also tended to the mail. An empty canned milk box in the corner of a freight car was the "post office." All mail for the dozen homesteading families on the desert and railroad workers was dumped into this box. Then each person who called looked through the box, picking out his own mail and neighbor's, if any. When not in a hurry, other people's postcards were read, newspapers and magazines perused.

After the cattle company put down a steel-cased well 400 feet at Seven Palms, it turned out to be a flowing well and formed a pond 30 feet across. If the day was hot, I often walked three miles out of my way to this pond. Into the pond I waded fully clothed, holding the mail above my head in one hand. [I] crouched down in the middle until water ran into my ears, then walked out of the pond dripping and continued on my way to the railroad. This was very refreshing, and in a short distance I was completely dry.

One train a day threw off a small mail sack and stopped if there were passengers. A two-horse wagon with a couple of seats called for the Palm Springs mail. The very few passengers often put wet cloth on their wrists and necks to make the journey more bearable.

The road was just a single track in loose sand, ankle deep. The horses just walked, and crossing the Whitewater Wash was often a trying experience.

[Article 8: September 7, 1951]

Freight came once a week and was stored until called for in a small building. The row of palm trees growing along the track on the south side near the small depot offered . . . "delicious shade" after a seven mile walk across the desert in loose sand and much sunshine overhead. There was a water pipe of cool mountain water by one palm tree, and the memory of this is still better than any soda fountain drink.

The R.R. water tank was fed by a pipe from Snow Creek and often overflowed, keeping some grass alive along the tiny stream which soon faded into hot desert sands. Burros relished this bite of green food.

The R.R. station was originated under the name of Palm Springs, then changed to Noria, then to Gray in honor of Hilda Gray, then finally to Garnet, because garnets can be found in the hills near the track to the east.

We homesteaders were all very poor and existed on unbelievably small sums of money. There was no work, and no money circulated. Four dollars per month per person was an average food allowance. And I have lived on less. What we went without was a longer list than what we had. No butter, no meat, no fruits, no vegetables, no bread or anything out of a store. The day-to-day menu was beans, pancakes (without butter), potatoes mostly, and wild rabbits. Of these, some were jacks and some cottontails. Every family had a different method of cooking them, but to me they were always just rabbits. And I do not like rabbits. But to preserve life we will do many things.

All of us burned brush and roots for cooking, and in cold weather for heating. A few could afford kerosene cook stoves. Lamps and lanterns furnished light. Candles could be used in winter but melted in summer time.

Walking to the post office, carrying water every day, hunting rabbits, gathering firewood, clearing land, building cabins, making bread, and doing things of lesser importance made very busy weeks. . . .

We all gradually became acquainted with the wildlife about us. The opportunity was good, because at that time the desert was alive with many things which have become very scarce or practically disappeared by this time. As civilization comes in, wildlife moves out.

I greatly miss the roving flocks of a hundred or more turtledoves which were in evidence, giving their plaintive calls at daybreak. Then too, there used to be many coveys of desert quail strutting happily about from one greasewood bush to another. Jack rabbits jumped up and dashed away wherever you might go for a walk. Coyotes were often seen, and their yapping at night was a lullaby in keeping with the mystery of the desert.

So every day we learned more about desert animals, birds, snakes, lizards, and insects. Most were retiring and kept out of our way.

Not so with the desert rat. This is the smartest little creature of them all, and it came forward at once to investigate us and our belongings. Rats went in and out of our boxes and bags. If no holes were present, then [holes] were made. Food was eaten on the spot or carried away to their storehouse in a business-like way.

A 25-pound box of prunes has 2,000 prunes, and rats left alone will carry every one away in a few nights. They will eat labels off cans, eat corks out of bottles, and cut holes through one-inch boards easily, and two-inch boards with more time. Yet they look so clean and are so smart in eluding their enemies that one is tempted to forgive their depredations.

All snakes are after them, coyotes work sly tricks, and hawks, owls and birds of prey watch for the busy rats day and night. Yet they prosper in a country where food is a problem and there is no water. Rats can climb a barrel cactus and gather seeds from its top in spite of all the thorns. . . . So until the cabin was built, with all our food and belongings scattered about the open desert, rats were quite a nuisance. Even after the cabin was finished, they dug underneath and cut holes up through the floors.

The coyotes were large and fine, with thick fur in winter, so I trapped them and sold the hides in St. Louis. The money helped in many ways. I had skinned a coyote. I got to wondering what he had eaten. So I opened its stomach, and among other things found in it was a large rat. This brought up the question, What had the rat eaten? Therefore I opened its stomach and found greasewood leaves, bark, seeds, and a small rolled paper. I unrolled the paper carefully and read, "Keep in a cool dry place." This was from one of my milk can labels.

In the homestead days there had been some good rainy seasons and the desert was green. Talmage Brothers and others brought in 2 or 300 head of white-face cattle, a few bulls among them, and they wandered at will, eating here and there, and going to Two Bunch or Seven Palms or Willow Hole when thirsty. One very dark night, I was walking home from the railroad, no moon, thick clouds obscured the stars, spits of rain fell, and a rumble of thunder proclaimed an approaching storm. In a hurry to get to the cabin and shelter, I took a short cut through the heavy, tangled brush round Two Bunch Palms. In the complete darkness I came to what I thought was a fallen palm trunk and so made a big step to get on top of it. But it turned out to be the big bull of the cattle herd lying down and asleep. He lurched to his feet, gave a thunderous bellow, threw me sky winding, and stampeded the sleeping cows off into the night.

[Article 9: September 14, 1951]

Carl Eytel was the first artist ever to live in Palm Springs and make desert paintings. We sometimes went on sketching trips together and visited back and forth. His wooden cabin was on the outskirts of the village, where the mountain rises abruptly from the level desert. As it was too small to have a stove inside, cooking was accomplished over an outdoor fire between a few blackened rocks.

One night just before dark, an old Indian with [a] wrinkled face came up to our mesquite fire, and we invited him to have supper with us. The frijoles were divided into three tin plates and [the] coffeepot filled with water. After the meal we sat round enjoying the balance of the coffee and the newly risen moon casting slowly-moving shadows over the desert floor.

The friendly conversation was mixed English, German, Indian and Spanish. However, we all understood each other very well. When I mentioned that my home was on the other side of the desert near Two Bunch Palms, the old man's face lighted up with interest, and he asked me many questions.

Therefore I took a stick and scratched a map on the ground. This showed clearly Palm Springs where we were, a trail leading to Seven Palms Oasis, and a route over to Two Bunch Palms with the location of the water hole there. Also Miracle Hill and where my cabin stood on a smaller rise.

Water is the first thought of any desert man, so he asked me what I did about water. I then told him how far I went and the time it took to carry water in pails that distance.

He listened attentively, then said in Spanish, "You go too far. Indian find water here," and with the stick he marked a spot which I recognized at once as being close to the cabin.

[Article 10: September 21, 1951]

Further questioning disclosed the fact that the place he described was the site of a very old Indian well, long since filled in and covered over by drifting sand, aided by the tramping of cattle.

He stated that as a small boy he had gone to this old well for water, [his] grandmother carrying a large red clay jar and he a small one. The Indian camp of many years ago (as evidenced by the fact that he was a boy then and now an old man and gray) was situated just below the small hill on which I had built my homestead cabin. This Indian's story explained the broken pottery I found from time to time in the vicinity.

Very early the next morning, in high spirits I walked the 14 or so miles across the desert in record time. My thoughts [were] in a whirl. Could water be so close at hand! Gee whiz! I was excited.

Early and late I dug enthusiastically. Within a week I had found and uncovered the old Indian well used many years ago! It was on the north edge of Miracle Hill just as he had described. This is the only known authentic Indian well in this part of the desert. All the others have been blown over with sand and the locations forgotten. This relic out of the primitive past is on land now owned by Tom Lipps, who also has become the owner of Two Bunch Palms.

It is necessary here to explain that Indian wells were not holes straight down in the earth as we know them. Indians had no boards or pipe, no rope, no pulleys. So therefore they dug inclined open trenches leading down into the ground until water was reached. Then women walked down to the bottom, filled jars with water, and walked out again. Some of these paths went so deep into the earth that women were afraid to walk down for the water.

We were happy to use this old Indian well for some time, because it was much closer and saved hours for other things. But the water was too hard and alkali to cook with or drink, and would not mix with soap, if you know what I mean.

[Article 11: September 28, 1951]

About this time Bob [Carr] and I learned how to witch for water, spending many hours with a witch stick walking over our claims. We started a well on a witched spot 200 feet from Bob's cabin door, finding good water at 20 feet, and this happily settled his water problem. I, too, carried much water from his new well, it being only about a mile walk for me.

Bob Carr was a delightful companion, a born story-teller and brilliant conversationalist. He had read many, many books, experienced much of life, both above and below average stratas. He had a typewriter and would work diligently until a story was in the mail and on the way to some magazine. Then to relax, he and I would go out into the desert, build a campfire and talk hours at a time, occasionally all night. If weather was bad, we retreated to the Eagle's Nest Cabin or deep into mesquite thickets.

We expanded with delight to be out of cities, and because there was no office to go to, no time clock to punch, no city editor to please, and because we were away from people. We rejoiced in being free men (we cared not how poor) in a new clean world, and we were happy.

One day we arrived at the thought that civilized life had conventionalized the hours of sleep and mealtime until man was living unnaturally. We concluded [that] people ate when not hungry and were hungry when there was no time to eat. And time to sleep was also a matter of regulation. We had both lived with rather primitive Indians who had no clocks and no regulations. So we decided to experiment to see if food would take the place of sleep. We put plentiful food, coffee and water in abundance on the strong back of Merry Xmas and started walking. Whenever hungry, tired, or sleepy, we stopped, built a fire, and had a meal. Then, refreshed, we walked on.

[ARTICLE 12: OCTOBER 5, 1951]

Our trek took us to Mission Canyon, then through Devil's Garden to San Jacinto Mountain, thence skirting Palm Springs to the general vicinity of Cathedral City, out through the sand dunes to Willow Hole, into the Mud Hills for a while, and over the Little San Bernardino mountains and home again. We paid no attention whatever to time; we talked, ate, and traveled at night the same as day, and did not sleep for 72 hours. We felt O.K. However, we decided it was cheaper to sleep each day, because the cost of [the] food we ate to take the place of sleep was alarming.

This walking episode brings up the subject of shoe repair. Every man walked most of every day, for mail, for rabbits, for water, and for firewood. The coarse desert sand wore shoes out rapidly. We could not easily afford shoe leather, and so when one man was given an old auto tire, he cut it up in pieces and distributed them among the neighbors to tack on their shoes. That auto tire was all gone when I heard about it. However, for some months I had been pounding tomato cans out flat and nailing them on my shoes for half soles. They lasted well. But Frank DeLong had a forge, and he fashioned soles and heels for his shoes out of steel shovel blades. And, man, they did wear a long time!

When the cabin was completed, we discovered there was no broom and no dustpan, and no money to send to Sears Roebuck. Some small branches and twigs bound together made a broom. But the dustpan required tin snips. DeLong had a pair, and I walked 11 miles up there to borrow them, and 11 miles home. Out of an empty square oil can the dustpan was made, tin graters were fashioned out of tomato cans, and some tin repairs made to the stove pipe. Then I returned the snips, another 22 miles. So every time that it was necessary to borrow tools, it involved a walk of 44 miles. I did this many times during the homestead period.

[ARTICLE 13: OCTOBER 12, 1951]

Bob Carr went to Los Angeles on his five months' leave from homestead. The city was all excited about the new moving-picture industry, just then organizing in California to take advantage of so much sunshine for outdoor photographing. In the East, sunny days were often far apart. Some people said it was just a novelty which would soon die out and never compete with the regular theatre. Others held that it would grow and be important to Los Angeles.

Anyway, these picture companies were paying much more than newspaper salaries to writers. Even men of no special experience hired for miscellaneous work were given wages of five dollars per day, and the application line was long.

Bob went to Mack Sennett's lot and got a job on the staff writing scenarios. Gossip of the waiting room reported that Sennett hired 10 or 12 writers during the week and fired all of them on Saturday night. Bob was ushered into a room where a dozen men, all writers, sat around one long, bare table. They were making notes, discussing plots and pictures in general. These men eyed him curiously, and from them he learned that Mack Sennett's private office was close by and at unknown times he would dash in and give the group an assignment. Then the procedure was for each man to go home and come back the next day with a story. These stories were read aloud to the group, and Sennett picked the best one. This selected story then became the clothes horse on which better parts of the other yarns were patched. Later all the men worked rounding up the story and ironing out details to make a completed, smooth-written scenario.

[Article 14: October 19, 1951]

Shortly after Bob Carr was installed, Mack Sennett came into the room, instructing the writers [that] they must use what was on hand in the studio to form their stories.

"There are now on the payroll one cross-eyed man, a jig dancer, one fat woman, an Irish comedian, one small elephant, two Negroes, and six bathing-beauty girls. Their suits are all new and we don't want them to get wet. Now you fellows go home and come back here in the morning, each with his own story. You must use these characters; they are all paid for by the month. We cannot afford to hire extra actors just for one picture. Go out on the lot and look over the sets available for backgrounds here in the studio. Search in the costume room--we have comedy police uniforms and other things of use perhaps. Your picture story can take people to the beaches and places near Hollywood. But no long trips or overnight stops, they cost too much. Income is not all we wish it was, because the public seems hard to pull away from old-fashioned theatres."

Bob stayed up nearly all night working on his story construction. The wastebasket was full of discarded copy, but he felt satisfied with his plot and action as he entered the conference room next morning.

Mack Sennett walked in early and ceremoniously laid down some typed pages and announced that he, himself, had written a story and proceeded to read it forthwith. Then he asked each man in turn what he thought of it. The assembled men all complimented the story very highly, because they hoped to stay on the payroll over Saturday night. Sennett was not above praise, and he beamed under the barrage of honeyed words. Turning to Bob, the last man, he questioned, "And you, Carr, what do you think of my story?" Bob needed to be on the payroll very badly, but shrewdly felt that just to echo praise would get him nowhere. He decided to be honest and replied quietly, "I think the story is rotten poor, and not worth building onto." There was a hushed silence in the room!

[ARTICLE 15: OCTOBER 26, 1951]

The other writers knew that Bob was a goner Saturday night, unless Sennett fired him on the spot. They waited.

But Mack Sennett was no rich man's son sitting in the easy chair of authority prepared for him by some doting father. He had come up the long hard road, lifted by his own bootstraps. Not too long ago he had been carrying a spear in a crowd of extras hired for the night on a New York stage. His present position of success and rising prominence in a new industry had been won by showing foresight, originality, and much determination. Many things far more complicated than a story lay on his desk for solution. Therefore the writing of a script was not too important. Although taken aback by the blunt criticism, he was inwardly pleased by the new man's courage of conviction. So in an even voice he asked Bob what was wrong with it, and Bob picked the story apart. Then Sennett questioned, "All right, Carr, now read your own story." Bob did.

Sennett approved, and ordered it to be used for the first draft of the new scenario.

Bob stayed on the payroll over the first Saturday night, and indeed was kept on the story-writing staff until the time came for him to return to the desert. During that time he became very friendly with two of the writers, Walter Woods and Ford Beebe, both exceptionally talented men. Walter Woods it was who wrote the great film, "The Covered Wagon," and other successes of a later period. Ford Beebe has written a long list of plots for pictures, many of them feature productions, and he still writes for the big companies. These two men caught some of our enthusiasm for the open spaces and decided to each locate a homestead claim on the desert. On one hot Sunday morning Woods and Beebe left my cabin to hunt for the corner stakes with flags on them, which Bob and I had prepared. As the desert is very confusing to strangers and all things look alike, a stake is most difficult to find without help.

They each hung a canteen of water round their necks, and in addition, one gallon of extra water was poured in a jug, which they took turns in carrying. After an hour we saw them trudging back through the greasewoods, stumbling over stones and appearing very worn and weary. "Did you find the stakes all right, and how did you like the land?" we asked. Walter answered in a whispering voice, parched by thirst, "Stakes nothing--we came back for more water."

[ARTICLE 16: NOVEMBER 2, 1951]

Ford Beebe selected the land which is now the main part of Desert Hot Springs. He moved his family out to the desert, and the cabin home which he built is now a part of the Idle Hour Café. An old Model T Ford served him instead of burros. And this machine was the first auto ever given a home in D.H.S.

Walter Woods engaged me to build him a cabin east of the new bathhouse on a small hill of red clay. This therefore was the first house to be constructed in D.H.S. (about 1914). His land joined Beebe's on the east and north of Pierson . . . .

The most picturesque and attractive cabin on the desert in homesteading days was that of Bob Carr. This was "B.A.," before autos. There is something sacrilegious about riding over the desert or up to a cabin in an automobile. The desert is so quiet and clean, and wildlife so retiring amidst the scant vegetation, that a mere man-made machine roaring about is sadly out of place.

The Carr cabin was on a sandy shelf 30 feet above the desert floor, with a clear view to the south and . . . San Jacinto Mountain. On the west was a thick, high bunch of mesquite, which gave ample shade and furnished complete protection from the west wind.

It was built of up and down boards with cracks covered by bat strips. All knot holes [were] covered carefully with tin can covers. The one living room was 10 ×14 feet. [There was a] cast iron stove at the east end, [and a] small sleeping porch at the west end. The only furniture was a plain pine unpainted table, with Bob's typewriter, the only dictionary in the desert, and a few books of synonyms. Three plain wooden chairs and a couple of boxes for extra seats and a pile of mesquite wood for fuel completed the cabin requirements.

Yet with this meager array, his quiet wife, Stella, was able by her ingenuity and feminine viewpoint to make the cabin extremely attractive. Little plants in dishes and cans, homemade curtains at the windows, spotless dishes, magazine pictures picked with care, fused with Congress [glue]. . . . Curtains and stitched covering [for] shelves made the room very cheerful.

[Article 17: November 9, 1951]

Stella was a very excellent cook and made wonderful bread. Whenever Bob was out at night, she always had a lighted lamp set right against the window glass, and we could see this for many miles as we trudged cabin-ward from the railroad post office, through desert sand in darkness. Stella Carr was a cheerful companion to Bob and pioneered all through the homesteading days, and at his death took up her home in Sierra Madre, California, where she now lives.

On that pine table Bob wrote many a magazine story, novelette, and western poetry, which has amused and interested thousands of people all over the United States. He had a flair for using characters in western settings and stories to make readers laugh. Others were war stories from his experiences in the Spanish-American War, or straight western-style [stories], cowboys, miners, and Indians.

Bob Carr was a delightful personality and a great comrade. We had wonderful days on the desert together. Just we two walking about, examining all the new things of the desert about us and enjoying endless conversations about philosophy, religion, history, poetry, books, Indians, explorers, and the strange complication that civilization has brought into human life.

And always with us was that intelligent burro, Merry Xmas. It would follow along like a dog and carry whatever was needed, the mail, water, blankets, food, books, writing materials, or paints and brushes. Merry Xmas had a wide heavy strap about its neck, to which was attached a clear toned Swiss sheep bell, and if the bell did not ring properly as it walked, the burro often seemed to shake its head to ring the bell purposely. So we three companions spent happy days rambling about, after the home cabin wood boxes were full and water carried to fill the yawning buckets and pails to supply household needs.

[ARTICLE 18: NOVEMBER 16, 1951]

One [man] homesteading, who lived alone, had an inventive turn of mind. Whenever he found bits of iron, tin cans, pieces of board, clothing, leather, canvas, etc., along the roadways or railroad track, he would carry them home and throw them near his cabin door for future use. His yard presented a strange collection of odds and ends.

During a spring season with frequent showers, he spent much time trying to graft tomato vines on potato plants. And the other way round. He argued that if tomatoes could be grown above the ground and potatoes underneath, all on the one root system and at the same time, garden space could be saved and money returns doubled.

It did not work out just right, and tiring of this experiment, the next problem taken up was that of well-digging. Going up and down a ladder to pull up a bucket of dirt and dump it was clearly a waste of time and energy. So therefore he would construct a machine to help him dig his well. When this new and complicated contraption of twisted wire and string and strips of old canvas was at last completed to his satisfaction and put to work, it operated like this:

He was down at the bottom of a hole in the ground. By turning a crank, [the machine] rotated a continuous belt reaching up to the top of the well. Fastened to the belt were many tin cans of assorted sizes. Milk cans, tomato cans, coffee cans, and some [cans] rusted by years out in the weather. As each can started upwards, it was filled with earth and then dumped as the belt turned and started down again. The enthusiastic inventor of this fantastic device had to wear seven hats on his head at the same time, one on top of the other as a protection from falling rocks, because he had not fully worked out the problem of dumping the cans properly.

The struggle for water was the first task of the day and [was] a never-ending problem with all homesteaders. In a country of no rain, the cistern idea was out. Some [who were] not physically able to carry water had it hauled to them in a barrel, and they conserved it carefully. Jack Riley in the beginning put cans in a wheelbarrow and pushed that about three miles through soft sand and returned with water. Some others went in for more frequent trips, carrying smaller amounts of water in canteens. Scott Ferris, who was young and sturdy, put a five-gallon can on each end of a pole over his shoulder like a Chinese coolie and made a walking trip of nearly five miles each way. However, he lived alone; therefore ten gallons of water would last him a long time. When there were children in the family, the usual procedure was to take all the children, all the dishes, and all the washing to the water holes, bathe everybody, clean everything, and have a campfire picnic, then return home at sunset all spotless. Miss Hilda Gray had two small burros which carried water cans from Two Bunch Palms, where she went every day on account of having chickens, a dog, and a garden. This water trip was the first of her duties each day; she cleared land in her spare time.

[ARTICLE 19: NOVEMBER 23, 1951]

Gradually every family managed to get one or two burros, and each one had an individual name, which we all knew just as well as the owners. Burros are wonderful little animals and were of tremendous help to the early pioneers. This was in the days called "B.A."--before autos. They did not require shoes or as much care as a horse, and that is why prospectors and desert men used them so freely all over the Southwest in pioneer times. Burros could carry about 150 pounds on their backs if well balanced and tied on properly. They would also work in harness and pull a wagon. Average sized men could ride them, and burros are known to be very sure-footed on dangerous trails.

However, the speeds would seem rather slow to this generation, which flits about hither and yon in autos. Burros hitched to a wagon travel one and one-half miles per hour. When saddled, the speed is increased to two miles per hour.

Here on the desert they found bunch grass at some seasons to eat, and kept in good condition feeding on sagebrush and other desert vegetation. But they had to be turned loose to range over many acres of land. Therefore when we wanted a burro, we took a canteen of water and a little food and started out walking to look for them. A burro might be found in half a day or it might take a couple of days. By staking out with a chain and moving [it] two or three times a day, a burro could be kept at home sometimes.

The old joke about the prospector and his burros has much of truth in it. The tourist, speaking to an old desert character, says, "So you have been on this desert 40 years! Have you been mining all that time?" And the Desert Rat replies, "Well, not all the time, because I have hunted burros 20 years."

I started with one burro called Merry Xmas, bought three, some had colts, so [I] ended up with seven old enough to saddle or harness, and four little ones growing up. Then I went into the army of World War I. On my return I could not find even one. They had all been stolen.

The Indian well was not on my land by a few feet. Therefore I witched a spot somewhat closer to the cabin and started to dig a new well. I did not have any lumber, and the ground was soft sand. After marking a circle 25 feet in diameter, I shoveled down three feet, throwing the earth well back. Then on the floor of that, a circle [of] 15 feet was drawn. This was shoveled down another three feet, the earth first thrown up on the first circle floor and from there over the top. At the bottom of the 15-foot circle, I then made a circle of 10 feet in diameter and shoveled down four feet this time, the earth going to the 15-foot level, then handled up to the 25-foot level and then over the top. At the bottom of the 10-foot circle there was firm ground, so I started digging straight down and kept at it until water was reached. The earth then had to be shoveled and re-shoveled all the way to the top. I worked alone and had to handle the earth four times, and so this well took many weeks of time. The water was satisfactory and about 100 degrees in temperature.

[Article 20: November 30, 1951]

When L.W. Coffee became the owner of this homestead ranch, he had a power shovel enlarge this hole which I dug so slowly, and you can see it today. A small toy lake high above the desert floor on the side of Miracle Hill, it is one of the seven wonders, not of the world, but of this desert. Water standing in a pool, on a hill, in a dry desert. . . .

A very few dollars would have purchased enough boards to case the well, but there were no dollars, and no outside employment here then. So I worked months to dig a well without using any casing, in soft sand ground. All early pioneers went through similar feats of perseverance involving much patience and some hardships.

Homesteaders were extremely saving with water. Three tomato cans full was a bath in a wash tub, and then the water went outdoors to a little tree or bush. A basin of water first washed the face in the morning, the hands followed, then into a pail to mop the floor, and finally wring the mop outside onto a tomato plant. Nearly every family had a tomato plant and one small tree to use up water driblets. Dishes were rinsed in clear water, no soap, and the rinsings stirred into chicken food or for the dog or cat. The dishes were then washed in soapy water, and this water carefully put on the tree outdoors.

Once when Merry Xmas and I arrived at the railroad, there was a train standing there waiting for orders to proceed up the track towards Los Angeles. A tourist gave me an orange to pose for a picture with the burro, to show what strange things can be seen out west. That was the first orange to be in my hands in six months. I wrapped it carefully in a bandana handkerchief and proudly took it back to the cabin for the baby and his mother. Merry Xmas relished the peeling.

Down at this railroad depot in those pioneer days came one by one, often at long intervals, all the desert residents for many miles out in the lonely sandy wastes. There was the depot itself, with a tiny counter over which trainmen received orders. Back of the counter, and in a small alcove of windows, sat the R.R agent. He had open vision of the track in both directions. In front of him a telegraph key clicked away, and so we knew there was a world outside of this desert which had become our world. Also here we could find out what day of the month it was for sure. Not that it made any difference in our lives; it was just nice to know. Watches could be set with correct time, but almost no one had a watch. Nearby was the freight car in which mail might be found. Outside was a water pipe to fill canteens, and the dozen palm trees gave welcome shade. Our homes were so scattered and so many miles apart on the desert that about the only time we ever saw our neighbors was at the R.R. depot.

Bill Keys drove six burros hitched to a wagon and hauled mining machinery supplies over this desert, through the Dry Morongo Canyon, [across] Morongo Valley, and out the 29 Palms road. He would be days on the trip and have to camp out at night. Desert homesteaders, sunburned and weary, walked in from outlying claims. Still others came some days with burros hitched to a wagon, if expecting freight. Frank DeLong always drove in with two large horses hitched to a standard-sized farm wagon. He had the only alfalfa this side of Indio, and his animals were always well fed and in good shape.

We homesteaders boasted about his alfalfa because it was cut 10 times a year. But none of us ever grew any alfalfa.

[Article 21: December 6, 1951]

On a windy, cold, miserable day a man came in the depot when I was there. His head was all wrapped in heavy cloth, with only a small aperture open for him to see out. He wanted to know what day it was and when the next train would stop. He had a raging toothache and wanted to get to a dentist. He had walked 37 miles and slept out with the small blanket which was carried over one shoulder.

Indians traveled in from Mission Canyon on tough ponies which were not shod. More Indians came from the reservation at Palm Springs. In those days there was no such thing as a stranger on the desert. We knew every man and all his animals, horses, mules, burros and dogs. To see the train come in was an event for us. If one stopped and a passenger got off for Palm Springs, it was news to tell again.

The train was a reminder of that world outside, where people had good food, meat, fruit, vegetables, perhaps even butter. And in such a world would be rain, trees, flowers and cool breezes. We would think of these things rather wistfully. But with these attractive things we remembered the disadvantages--crowded streetcars, close living conditions, and silly conventionalities, and so after all we would rather be on the desert and have our freedom.

One day a brakeman standing in the shade of a palm tree saw a desert man approaching with a scratched, cut, and bleeding face, and said in astonishment, "What happened to you, Gilroy? Fall into a cactus patch? Fight a wild cat? Or what?" and received this reply, "Oh, nothing happened special. Only I haven't got any mirror."

"Well, even so, how could the razor do all that damage?" continued the brakeman. And Gilroy replied, "But I haven't got any razor, either, and so I was shavin' with a piece of broken glass. It sort of felt as though I was nickin' myself a little."

[Article 22: December 13, 1951]

What is over the next hill is always of interest to me. So one day, taking food and water, I started climbing the mountains north of Desert Hot Springs locality. It appeared easy to reach the top and look over to see what was on the other side of them. But after a whole day of clambering over rocks and going up and up to what seemed the top, all there was to be seen on the other side was more mountains.

Then I learned about Morongo Canyon Road going through the mountains and into a valley beyond which, in turn, [the road] opened out into another, and larger, desert having Joshua trees.

Therefore again I took food and water and started walking to the Morongos. On this journey trudging slowly toward me was a young man leading a rather small black burro, on which was his camp outfit. We stopped and talked as desert travelers find it easy to do. After some dickering, he finally agreed to sell the burro for 10 dollars. That was a vast sum of money for me to part with. But the little animal had much appeal and seemed very bright and intelligent. Also it was plain to see that it would help do much of my work. It could carry water and firewood and help in many ways. So I hunted through all my pockets and managed to count out 10 dollars.

The young man could not carry his equipment to the railroad; therefore it was agreed he would tie the burro to a tree at the depot and tell the agent to look out for it until I came down.

So instead of walking to the big desert, I just stayed one day in Morongo Valley, where there were half a dozen homesteaders, and walked 40 miles home by way of the railroad, finding the burro, which I named Merry Xmas, as it was about that time of year. It had been purchased by a family in San Bernardino when very small for children to play with. But it outgrew them and the young man purchased it for his trip into the desert.

[Article 23: December 20, 1951]

THE STORY OF MERRY CHRISTMAS

Bob Carr and I wondered why the animal was so thin, as it was definitely young. We found the trouble in a tooth which was out of line and preventing proper eating. So Bob and I threw Merry Xmas down and tied it up well; then we were successful in pulling [the] troublesome tooth, and it gained weight rapidly.

This turned out to be a most unusual burro, willing and quick to learn. We were very patient with it, also making rewards of candy or lump sugar when deserved. Merry Xmas learned to follow Bob or me like a dog, to come when its name was called, to lead on a rope without being pulled like most burros, and to walk three miles per hour when the average was only two, and it was taught to have another burro or several tied to its tail, and to lead by voice command, go, stop, right, or left, etc. I sometimes had eight animals all tied to the tail of Merry Xmas, and I rode the last burro, and it would do exactly as directed. It would follow a trail and even the single footsteps of a man in loose sand if told to do so.

One thing it did, not like any other burro, was to walk side by side with me just as two men will do. On good roads we have walked four miles per hour that way and no rope or strap to keep it in place.

On exploring trips about the desert, at the end of day when camp was made, it would eat grass or vegetation nearby, but when called [it] would come to supper and eat its fair share of whatever we had, bacon, potatoes, bread, tobacco, etc. It would eat a newspaper with relish. At night when Bob and I were wrapped each in a blanket, this amazing animal would come up and lie down by the fire too. If ever a journey passed by a spot where a camp had been made at some former time, Merry Xmas would stop and look round to see if it was to be a camp again.

Out of all the 11 burros I had and the many more the neighbors had, no other burro approached this one in intelligence. Burros sold for five to 10 dollars as a rule. But on several occasions I refused 100 dollars for Merrry Xmas. I shared all my food with it on trips, and kept my pockets full of candy or peanuts to hand out for good behavior or learning new things. It followed me everywhere. Once in Palm Springs I forgot this fact and walked into the only store. Up the steps and into the store came the burro, just like some schoolboy.

Merry Xmas liked pancakes better than anything, and hot ones too. Pancakes were standard for breakfast, and when the aroma went into the desert air, it came promptly to the door and shared in breakfast. The screen door had one of those long coiled springs at the top to keep the door closed. The cook stove was right at the door as you entered. I thought up this trick. I nailed a large wooden spool on the outside of the screen door. And then by talking and small rewards, Merry Xmas was taught to grasp the spool in its teeth, jerk the door open wide with a quick twist of its head, and in the split second before the spring snapped the door shut, that big black head and neck were in the door, with mouth open for hot pancakes. This was every morning and a fair division of pancakes made always.

[ARTICLE 24: DECEMBER 27, 1951]

Merry Christmas, my burro, was always turned loose to forage and go and come at will, but on some occasions was staked out with a strong chain. It would bray if out of feed or water, and the difference in tone could often be noticed. One day it was staked out on the side of Miracle Hill and there was a distressed bray, different from normal. And so I rushed up there to find it had gotten its feet in the chain and fallen upside down into a gully. A horse would have thrashed and cut its legs badly if in such a predicament. But burros have sense. It called for help and waited for it to arrive. A horse, very thirsty coming to water, will drink too much and perhaps die. A burro, very thirsty, will take a mouthful of water, throw its head up, rinse its teeth and spit it out once or twice, then take a small drink and go lie down. After some rest it will swallow some more water. A burro never drinks too much or too fast, if overheated by work or the weather.

After the hot well was discovered and in use, tubs, pails, half-barrels, and other containers were always kept full in front of the cabin so that any animal, ours or others, could always come there and be sure of water to drink. This they did and liked it. Not so Merry Xmas! It would come and taste the water and if cold, refuse to drink. No sir! No cold water for this desert child. It knew there was hot water in the well and [was] much to be preferred. So it would start braying, paw the ground, kick the tub, overturn pails, and make such a disturbance that someone would have to go to the well and pull up some hot water for Merry Xmas to drink.

As it grew larger I could ride on some of the trips, but few strangers ever rode the animal, because as they started to climb into the saddle, it would reach round and bite them in soft places. Merry Xmas performed its part of the work everyday, hauled water and wood, made trips to the railroad, and so I saved up enough money to buy a very fine Swiss sheep bell, with a clear ringing tone that could be heard a long ways. This bell hung from a heavy strap round its neck, and every step rang the bell. This was a very cheerful help to my many hours of walking trips about the desert.

One day the burro and I were walking into Palm Springs along the one-track sandy road, the bell as usual ringing merrily. As we approached the small white schoolhouse on the north edge of town, the school teacher was at the roadside with seven children. She hailed me to stop, and the children crowded round the burro. She said, "Please talk to the children and tell them where you live. You are the only stranger to pass the school in a week, and I would like to have the children talk with a stranger."

So we passed a few friendly moments, and the next day when I returned down the road, she again heard the silver-toned bell on the burro's neck and brought the children to the roadside. The seven youngsters petted Merry Xmas and gave it grass and leaves. We waved goodbye, [and] the children went back into the small school building having talked to a stranger. Merry Xmas and I were soon out on the open desert and into a sandstorm blowing down the Whitewater wash. At such times, I walked on the lee side of the burro and let it take the brunt of the drifting sand. After some hours of walking, it was with relief that we reached Two Bunch Palms, got out of the heavy winds, and could drink at the pool. We soon reached home.

[Article 25: January 3, 1952]

I had a few tubes of artist's paint, some old brushes, and a few canvases. On a stormy day, not being able to work outside, I painted a picture of an Indian on a horse going to a water hole in a desert. A friend took this to Hollywood, and it was sold for a modest sum. With these few dollars dropping unexpectedly out of a clear sky, the big question then was: What could be the greatest good accomplished by their expenditure? Many things were needed, starting in with extra food, clothing, and so on, ending with some improvements to the cabin. But the sensible choice finally settled down to a new well. Water was of paramount importance.

The very first thing every day, water had to be carried home sufficient for the day. In the beginning, walks had been 14 miles to the railroad, then cut to less than two miles, after that one mile to Bob [Carr]'s well. The Indian well was closer, but its water too bad for full use. [The] new sand-hole well currently in use was not too far, but the water had to be carried up quite a steep hill.

Every desert man's dream of heaven on earth is "water at the door of his cabin." So I visualized water at my cabin door. . . .

The few dollars from the painting would buy a little lumber. I could dig down as far as this lumber would reach and then perhaps I could sell another painting or write something to bring in the cost of more lumber. I had written and sold small stories to the new industry of moving pictures then just starting in Hollywood.

Covering a big sheet of paper with figures and diagrams, it finally appeared that boards eight feet long would be the cheapest to buy. They would also work out for the smallest hole possible to work in, thus making the picture money reach deepest into the earth.

The eight foot boards two inches thick were cut into pieces of two feet and three feet. When put together, they left a hole for me to work in 27 inches wide by 32 inches long. In this space was a pick, shovel, well bucket, digging bar, and canteen. A ladder nailed to the wall at one end cut off five inches of the original space, leaving me net working room of 24 by 27 inches.

[Article 26: January 10, 1952]

I was pretty thin from insufficient food, but it was close working space even considering that. The well was started 10 feet from the cabin, because my dream was just that--water at the door. The few neighbors were quite concerned about my sanity or at least [my] proper judgment, because the well was started on top of a hill, where the cabin had been placed to command a wonderful view of the desert lying stretched out some hundreds of feet below. . . . There were many acres of low ground, and why not dig there? reasoned the neighbors, with sanity on their side. But water at the door was the dream, and I started.

Working alone--the procedure is simple. You go down the ladder, dig enough to fill the bucket, climb up the ladder, pull up the bucket, empty the bucket, and repeat the performance until you hit water or run out of lumber. The ground was rocky, progress slow. I was in a weakened condition, having had no meat, no eggs, no butter, fruit, or vegetables for a long period. I was doing hard work on pancakes, beans and rabbits; [there's] no strength in that food to speak of.

I seemed to play out easily on this well work and become unduly tired. Bob Carr came over to visit and saw me come up dripping with perspiration and sprawled on the ground to cool and get air. He commented, "What's the matter with you? You are getting soft like some Hollywood Boulevardere," to which I retorted, "It must be for the reason that what I have to eat has poor food value. If I just could have a piece of beef with blood in it, an apple and some butter, I could dig this well by dark."

The next day he came over again. After watching me climb wearily up the ladder and drag my feet onto solid ground, Bob questioned, "Do you suppose it could possibly get too hot down where you are?" This was a new idea to both of us.

"Great Scott," I exclaimed, "that might be so. It seems very hot down there in the bottom of the hole, and the air up here is cold by comparison. Get your thermometer and we will see what it records."

The thermometer reached a reading of 108 degrees below [in the hole], and the air above very much less. Therefore the bottom of the well was hot! We speculated as to what this might mean and the reason for it to be so. The neighbors did not believe our story and came doubtingly to investigate. Every day as I dug deeper into the earth, the temperature rose and reached 120 degrees. Then a very strange thing happened. The bottom of the well turned to stone. No more earth to dig! But this stone floor was hollow underneath!

[Article 27: January 17, 1952]

Now what would you think if you were down 28 feet in a small hole in the ground, standing on a stone floor which was hollow underneath, hot to the touch with an air temperature of 120 degrees? Well, anyway, I thought plenty. There was the Mammoth Cave in the school books, Carlsbad Caverns advertised for tourists, and here at home the boiling mud pots on the edge of Salton Sea. Then the government geological survey showing that underneath the ranch was the San Andreas Fault, with cracks presumably going down to the center of the earth, where all is a molten mass. Was I standing on the lid of a quietly boiling pot of Mother Nature's most potent brew? Would I break through into a high vaulted cavern? Or drop into a bottomless pit?

I went for Bob Carr to help in the situation. We patched up ropes and chains, tied one end under my armpits well behind my shoulders. The other end [was] made fast to a large greasewood standing near the well top. If the lifeline slipped through Bob's hands, I would at least hang in the hole on the rope tied to the bush.

When all was ready above, Bob sang out, "Everything O.K. here. Break it up and good luck to you." After several hard blows with the railroad pick, the rock floor broke. The pieces of rock and I dropped, but only a foot. There was an open space of 12 inches in the earth. Below this, moisture increased fast and so did the heat. I was only able to work a few moments at a time and then come up for air and rest. The temperature climbed rapidly to 132 degrees. That is plenty hot in a space 24 by 27 inches, with no air to breathe.

Just at this critical time the boards ran out. Every last board was nailed in place, and no more money to buy others. But I was close to water; that was sure. It was night. I had worked all day alone as usual. Every muscle ached and [my] head throbbed because of working in the heavy moist air at the bottom of the well.

But I could now squeeze water out of soil held in my hand. I could not stop here, so [I] found a lantern and went down again. Within an hour water seeped into a shovel hole and reflected the lantern light! Water at last! At the cabin door, too, and hot water at that! I knelt in the steaming light and gave thanks. The dim smoky lantern cast an eerie light and heavy shadows.

The water temperature turned out to be 132 degrees, was soft as rain water with soap, and tasted good. Bob and I sat down and built air castles. We visualized a city here with many people to make proper use of the hot water and climate for healthful purposes and outdoor enjoyment. Those who heard us rave about the future of this desert laughed at us, but today Desert Hot Springs is an actuality. The story will be related in future pages.

After a day of this fanciful dreaming, I tackled the well again. Now I dug down without casing, as the ground seemed hard enough to stand without caving. The digging was very slow! It was only possible to take out a little dirt at a time. The mud and water [were] too hot to stand in. I had no money for rubber boots. So I cut the tops out of two five-gallon coal oil cans and put one foot in each, first filling them with cold water. In this way, standing in the cans, I worked patiently down farther. As the heat of the well heated the cans of water too hot, they were refilled with cold water. When finished at 40 feet, a wooden cover was placed over the well to keep rats and snakes from falling into the water. Even then we sometimes fished lizards and mice out of the well bucket. The water was so hot that the well would steam in cool weather, if the cover was removed. We were very happy about the well both for its present use, and also as the basis for hope of future development.

[Article 28: January 24, 1952]

. . . This is the story of the discovery of hot mineral water, which has been the basis for the establishment and growth of Desert Hot Springs. This water has been found to be very beneficial for many of the human ills. Because of this healing water and salubrious climate, more and more people are coming to find health and happiness in D.H.S.

There was no money for a pump of any kind on the newly completed well. We pulled the water up with a bucket fastened to a chain. Water was now freely used with great enjoyment and appreciation. A small garden was started, and I hauled up 65 buckets of water each day to keep the sandy soil damp. Lettuce, radishes, onions, etc., did fairly well, but desert animals ate everything, so the plan was abandoned, there being no money for fencing.

When the five-month period rolled around in which the government allowed a homesteader to leave his claim, I returned to the oil fields to earn money with which to come back to the desert and live another seven months. My duties were similar to those before. I took care of outlaw mules and horses, delivered freight, groceries and meat to railroad construction camps or new oil wells being drilled, with [my] spare time used keeping books or working in the main store and warehouse of the company.

Two things are worthy of note in passing over this period. One noon I had a two-mule load of supplies at the door of an oil-well cook camp. It was in the shadow of an oil derrick where drillers were at work. My conversation with the cook was abruptly interrupted by a wild-eyed man in overalls who yelled in the open door, "Get the hell out of here, she is going to blow." The man dashed away. The cook dropped a pan full of dishes on the floor. I jumped in the wagon and lashed the frightened mules in a gallop. Just in time! Because with a deafening roar and crash, the drilling tools, weighing 2,000 pounds, flew high in the air, taking the top of the wooden derrick with them. Then followed tons of mud, rocks, water, black oil, and clouds of gas, covering everything near the well in a slimy mess. The roof of the cook house was caved in. After a half-hour the gush of material from the center of the earth subsided into a rumble and occasional belches of oil and water.

The other thing [worthy of note is:] to take the monotony out of life, [I broke] a team of large mules called Tom and Mandy. Tom was the worse of the two. Several men had tried to take care of them, failed, and quit. The boss said to me, ". . . you have to take care of those mules or quit." So I started in to use all my animal experience to make friends of those two outlaws.

[Article 29: January 31, 1952]

To harness Tom, I first must put a heavy chain round his neck from the next room, reaching in over the manger, then pull his head down by dragging the chain through a hole in the wall. By holding one ear very tightly, it was now possible to maneuver a bridle and bit into place. To get alongside the animal in the stall without being kicked into the next world and throw a harness on his back was a daily battle. Finally, when both mules were harnessed to the wagon, we were off for a joy ride with all the freight and supplies. They unharnessed fairly easy if tired.

Two other, smaller mules . . . would run to the corner of the corral and stand with heads close together and kick anything that moved behind them. Going over the fence in front of their heads only caused them to run to another corner. Maggie was a white horse that ran away at any opportunity, out of the barn door, over the corral fence, with or without a wagon. It took much time to harness all these critters every morning. . . .

But the big fun was when Tom and Mandy had to have shoes. As soon as I drove to the little town of Fellows, out of Bakersfield, and stopped at the blacksmith shop, word went down the one street from saloon to saloon, barber shop, and general store. "Tom and Mandy are going to be shod"-- and all unoccupied men gathered at the blacksmith shop to see the fun.

[Article 30: February 7, 1952]

One blacksmith came out and held Mandy, while I took Tom in and chained him to the wall. Then Mandy was chained farther down on the wall. Now the two blacksmiths and I went to work to truss Tom up in such a way that he would be a good mule for the time being. Two four-by-six inch timbers were swung out from the wall, where they were securely hinged and ironed. One timber fitted closely on each side of the mule and extended four feet beyond his heels. Then the three of us working carefully put a leather-bound canvas sling under his belly. Ropes and chains were passed under this, round the side timbers, and over his back and well secured. Then by turning a crank slowly, Tom was lifted off the floor. There was a struggle here, but when tired of kicking, his four legs hung down but could not reach the floor. On the heavy side [of the] timbers were iron arms, two in front and two behind. Now came the ticklish part of the performance. We had to clamp each of the four feet into one of the iron arms. They held the hoof in a proper position to be shod. His head was chained to the floor. So thus fastened, all an animal could do was squeal and groan. The blacksmiths now proceeded with the shoeing operation. When [the] shoes were nailed in place, there was a minor battle to get them hitched to the wagon again so I could drive away.

These two mules had been abused and mistreated to the point where they were resentful, suspicious, and outlaws. However, by kindness and fair treatment, in a few weeks I could walk in the stall without danger and harness with little trouble.

[Article 31: February 14, 1952]

It was very wonderful to return again to the desert after the five months' interval to bail out the well, to freshen the water, and stop up holes where rats had cut through the cabin wall. The opening of fresh grocery boxes was better than a storybook Xmas. When the cabin was somewhat orderly, I took a canteen of water to search for the burros. They are gregarious in character, and usually all the loose animals in the valley would be found ranging within a mile of each other. Knowing that they must go to a water hole when thirsty, I first went to Two Bunch, then Willow Hole and Seven Palms. By examining the tracks in the sand, it could be determined if they were ranging in the locality. If so, the freshest hoof marks leaving the muddy bank of the pool would indicate in which direction they left. After finding the last trail in the desert, it was just a case of following it until the animals were found.

They knew that capture meant work, and often the smart ones would lie down to escape observation. But if a man approached on their trail, they would pursue one of two tactics. Either walk 20 steps out of reach all day, or kick up their heels and run for a mile, thus prolonging capture. This is where the payoff came in for the time spent giving Merry Xmas an education for proper behavior. It would come like a well-trained dog when I called. But not for strangers.

This day Merry Xmas was with a band of animals near Willow Hole, but came up readily to eat peanuts and jelly beans from my pockets. Its coat was jet black and glossy, shining in the sunshine like some expensive fur in an exclusive shop window. It was entirely black except for a creamy white muzzle, truly [a] beautiful animal. For a burro it was in excellent condition, fat and full of spirit, kicking up its heels now and then. It seemed happy to again take up duties as beast of burden at the ranch. We called our place a "ranch" now, because we had a cabin, a well, and one burro.

Bob and Stella Carr arrived on the desert from their Los Angeles vacation a few days later and rehabilitated the two-room board cabin nestled out of the wind next to thick mesquite trees. Life again took up where we all [had] left off to go away for the five months. We were just like two families on a desert island. Only here we had a surrounding ocean of sand instead of water. Consequently, we lived very much alone and completely isolated from everything that city people have in their daily lives. We had no neighbors, no street cars, no phones, no newspapers, no mail, no grocery store with fresh foods, no moving pictures or other amusements.

[Article 32: February 21, 1952]

Bob Carr was a most unusual person. Bob had been reared in the Black Hills of South Dakota, going to a country school for a meager education out of a few school books. But his real education had come from contact with life itself and very extensive reading of good literature. His father, a frontier doctor, was called from many miles round to attend white pioneer settlers for all their physical ills, both natural and accidental. Sioux Indians, too, were given medical care, and often domestic animals were treated.

In a country like that, there were no nurses; therefore Bob started under 10 years of age to accompany his father on medical calls and helped in every emergency from childbirth to murder victims. Bob was a prime favorite as a small boy with cattlemen, prospectors, miners, and Indians, too. So from early boyhood, he lived an outdoor life and experienced real adventure with grown men in a wild new country. Also with Sioux Indians, those denizens of the plains, still living in their traditional tepees.

His first practical job was on a country newspaper. He learned to set type and developed a flair and marked ability to write. Setting type taught him spelling and grammar. By the time he was 20, he had a small country newspaper of his own. The Spanish-American war came up and Bob volunteered, serving throughout in the Philippine Islands, seeing much actual fighting. He was top sergeant.

On return, he again entered newspaper work, always in the writing field. Going east to Chicago, he spent time with some of the big dailies. He tried St. Paul papers for a while, Kansas City, and other places. However, there was an interval when he was publicity man for big meat packers, contacting cattle ranchers of the west in order to have them ship cattle to certain meat packer plants. Eventually Bob got out to Los Angeles and did a special column under his own name, and general reporting for the Los Angeles *Evening Herald-Express*.

Having had so much actual adventures and an interesting style of writing, it was easy for him to write stories appealing to men which sold readily, giving him opportunity to move and live where he pleased. Besides newspaper articles, stories, and novelettes, Bob wrote two published books of poetry dealing with the Western life of pioneer people and Indians.

[Article 33: February 28, 1952]

About the turn of the century, Dutch Frank and Old Man Coolidge were two of the very few men to be found in this corner of the Southwestern desert. They were prospectors and partners. Traveling with burros and replenishing [their] water supply from widely separated water holes, they prospected up one canyon and down another, climbed mountain ranges, struggled through deserts searching for gold or mineralized rocks. They met with some small successes, but never found a mine of big importance. After many years of this hard-roving program, Old Man Coolidge became too old for the rigors of camp life and took up a homestead claim on the flat in front of Two Bunch Palms. On one of his widely separated trips to Banning for supplies, Bob [Carr] contacted him. He listened to the old man tell stories of the desert, found out that government land was open, notified me, and we took up adjoining pieces of land.

Dutch Frank continued life as a prospector alone. He was still ranging these mountains and nearby deserts when we came, and presented a very picturesque appearance. He spoke broken German with much profanity if directed to misbehaving burros, of which he had three. The best dash, dang, blank, ding burros in the desert, if you asked his opinion. Frank was a small man with noticeably short legs. Two burros carried his camp outfit and supplies, with pick and shovel on top. He always rode the third animal. Frank could walk, I have even seen him walk, but only on rare occasions. Because no matter what he did, he always rode a burro. If only a few hundred feet to a waterhole, Frank rode a burro, and if firewood was needed for the camp, he rode a burro to look for it. When he visited me, he arrived on a burro and left on one, even though the distance was no more than a city block. While making the visit and carrying on our conversation, he sat on a burro. He smoked a pipe, and never the hand-rolled cigarette of cattlemen.

Dutch Frank carried his German thoroughness into all that he did. The burro harness, straps, saddles, and equipment [were] always in the very best of repair. His animals were well-shod, and extra shoes in the packs. I have been to DeLong's T-cross-K ranch often when he was there shoeing his burros, riveting straps that were broken or showing wear. His camps were carefully picked. Near Two Bunch he had searched out a wonderfully protected, depressed sand pocket in thick mesquite. The entrance was narrow and thorny, leading downhill from small dunes. But once in this retreat, there was no wind whatever, plenty of firewood, and not too far to get water from the palm trees. In here he set up camp in an orderly manner, with a place for everything. His bedroll, extra firewood, and water canteens always had a fixed spot. Saddle blankets were hung up to dry, harness equipment kept on mesquite limbs out of the sand.

[Article 34: March 6, 1952]

There he sat and smoked his pipe in peace and quiet. Frank did not crave company, but rather resented intrusion. I never saw him read a book. He would glance over a newspaper. However, he valued it as an easy way to start a fire. He could have homesteaded any piece of land in the desert from Banning to the Mexican line, but nothing in this world could get him to live in a house settled down in one spot. He liked to roam, and he liked his three burros. He was a thoroughly contented and happy man. So who can say that it is better to live in a city and chase the elusive dollar, in the hope that at some future date, enough dollars will have been captured with which to buy happiness. Dutch Frank was already happy without the dollars.

He paid no attention whatever to desert animals. He in a good-natured way took them for granted, and was amused rather than angry at what they did, never resentful. He protected his outfit and belongings as best he could, but if they outwitted him and cut a hole in the flour sack, he only laughed. Snakes meant no more to him than flies; they were a nuisance, but nothing to be afraid of. He slept on the ground in a rattlesnake country without the slightest thought of them or any nervousness.

Bob Carr always viewed any situation from the dramatic angle, because he was a born story-teller. One day after the wood boxes were heaped high and all the water pails full to the top in both cabins, he and I got to discussing what two men could do with their bare hands if lost in the desert without food or equipment. Or [if they were] two Indians running away from marauding tribes. So we approached the problem this way. We hunted round for clay, carried some to Two Bunch water hole, formed a shallow wide dish, and hastily burned it. Although badly cracked, it served our purpose to bring more clay to our pottery work spot.

We had used matches to start our fire, as twirling a stick to get a flame we considered unnecessary time loss.

Having now abundant clay and water, we fashioned a crude olla to hold a gallon of water, and a rather deep dish with thick walls to cook with. Also we formed two small bowls to eat out of, and made two clumsy spoons. We placed these articles to dry slowly, and later in the day fired them in hot ashes. They held water. With carefully selected stones of the proper size, we set out on the prowl for food. We succeeded in obtaining three small birds, and after a time one small cottontail rabbit fell to our barrage of stones. We could not in fairness use a knife, so we used sharp pointed sticks to aide in skinning and cleaning our game.

After searching, we found a rock with an edge sharp enough to sever the heads and feet, and to cut up the birds and rabbit into small pieces. We filled the deep dish with water, threw in the pieces of meat, and started them to cook over a fire. Some mesquite beans were gathered, cut up, and added to the stew. Several sage leaves were added to give flavor. After considerable time the food was ready and served in the individual bowls, and we had our clay spoons to use. Thus refreshed, we gathered branches and palm leaves to build an Indian-style wickiup and were well launched in the business of house-keeping.

[Article 35: March 13, 1952]

A SUSPENSE STORY OF UNUSUAL BRILLIANCE COMPLETE IN THIS ISSUE

When Hilda Gray completed her homestead requirements and proved up, there was nothing here for her to do, so she returned to Los Angeles and resumed her vocation as expert stenographer. She sold all her buildings and a fence to me, and I started to dismantle them. I had a nail-puller, and as time was not of value, I pulled every single nail and straightened them for future use.

Every day or two I came down with two or more burros hitched to a wagon and hauled the boards home at a speed of one mile per hour, as the route was uphill.

Miss Gray had kept chickens. They scattered food. Mice came in to eat the food and for the shelter of buildings. Sidewinder rattlesnakes came in to eat the mice and make a home. It was a happy family. Chickens, mice and snakes. Hilda often killed one of the little gray-horned sidewinders. In cleaning up the barn and yard, I found one or two snakes every day or so.

Finally everything was wrecked and moved home except the floor of her main cabin. In this was a trap door which gave access to a half- cellar underneath with sandy sloping sides. No floor, no walls, no steps, no light--you just opened the trap door and reached down for wanted things, or dropped down into a crouching position and then could move about somewhat in almost hands-and-knees fashion. It had seldom been used, and here I expected to find rattlesnakes having a happy home-time. I did. One day by dropping into the sandy cellar below the floor where all was semi-darkness, I killed five horned rattlesnakes and thought that was all of them. However, there was just one more. This is the story of that "one."

In the middle of the so-called cellar was a neat pile of single glass window sashes 20 inches square, six of them. As my eyes became accustomed to the darkness, I looked down through the six panes of glass and saw fully coiled in the sand under the last one, the largest rattler of them all. So I straddled the windows with one foot on each side and carefully picked up one window at a time and slid it as noiselessly as possible up onto the floor above my head. The snake was fully awake now and kept watch of my movements. The rattles buzzed nervously as each window was removed. When [I got] down to the last glass over him, the sidewinder moved round a bit, the better to watch me, and buzzed without ceasing. When in this mood, they will strike at anything and quickly, too. At this point I could have, of course, broken the glass window and killed the snake. But a window on the desert is a valuable thing, and I was getting some kick out of matching my defense against the belligerent rattler. The danger was apparent, because if bitten, the nearest doctor was 14 miles away and no way to get there. I was alone. So [I] proceeded with utmost caution. I kept my eyes focused into the dark, so as to retain the full use of them. The snake kept up an angry, never-stopping buzz which had to be ignored; otherwise it tended to be disconcerting.

Then very cautiously and with measured slowness I put the fingertips of each hand on the outside edges of the one remaining window. With a slow-slow motion I reached it above my head and up onto the sunlit floor above. Meanwhile I never let my eyes wander from the snake's eyes, so as to anticipate any further action on its part. My feet had not been moved at all and were still in the same relative position. My trusty snake stick had been laid for some time in the sand by my side, and as my hand came down from moving the last window upstairs, I grasped the stick and dispatched the rattlesnake, now twisting about my feet. But the window was saved and is in use to this day.

Cabot's father and mother Frederick (Fred) Yerxa and Helen (Nellie) Cabot Yerxa, ca. 1880s

Young Cabot in Minnesota

Fred Yerxa in middle age

Nellie Yerxa in middle age

Nellie, Fred and Cabot Yerxa

Cabot as a young man

Yerxa Brothers' store in Minneapolis on Nicollet and Fifth street. It took 22 delivery wagons to handle the Yerxa Brothers' grocery trade in 1896.

One of the 22 delivery wagons for the Yerxa Brothers' grocery trade.

Yerxa Brothers' Minnesota bakery plant where Cabot briefly worked to learn the grocery operation.

Inside Yerxa Brothers' Minnesota store.

[Article 36: March 20, 1952]

Orr Sang lived alone and homesteaded north of the now B-bar-H Ranch. He was handy with tools, and his cabin had two stone walls, a fireplace, and [a] cement floor. Another novelty was a crude, shallow cement bathtub which would hold five gallons of water. It was the first and only tub for many years on the desert.

Near his cabin was a good corral, with [a] small barn for feed and shade for his two burros. Molly was white, strong and willing; Fanny of Maltese color and always sulky and slow. They were generally in the corral with hay and grain to eat.

Orr Sang was a retired policeman from Los Angeles and had a pension, so he was sort of an aristocrat amongst us homesteaders. He did not have to turn his burros loose on the desert to eat. His was the only burro carriage in the whole desert. It was a small four-wheeled affair with a canopy shade overhead and fringe all around the edge. This had one cushioned seat and a padded backrest. When Sang went for mail to the railroad or to Seven Palms for water, he sat on a cushion in the shade and smoked his pipe in full comfort. We other men tramped in deep sand with the sun burning down all the way. Also having money to spend, he could go to Banning at times and return with fresh meat, green things, and better canned goods than we could even dream about.

He was an excellent shot and [a] good trapper, too. He did not go in for hard work, so used his time to secure skins of coyotes, badger, and fox. These he tanned nicely himself and sold, thus further augmenting his money supply. After Sang had completed his homestead, he spent much time in Banning and the mountains. Not wishing to have the continued care of his burros, he sold them to me. The price was 50 dollars [for] two good burros, [a] fancy wagon, [an] excellent harness that fitted well, a riding saddle, and [a] few odds and ends. Paying for it was difficult, but I set more traps, caught more coyotes, cleared land for others, and dug wells by hand. Finally the 50 bucks was paid in full. Some small income was derived from . . . hauling things about the desert in [the] wagon.

[Article 37: March 27, 1952]

One commission that came my way was hauling a very heavy lady and her trunk to the railroad--a trip of several miles. Far be it from me to be disrespectful or curious about a lady's age or weight, but I am explaining a problem of the transportation. So in all honesty the estimated weight for the lady was over 200 pounds, and her trunk was near that figure, too. With this task ahead of me, I patched up enough harness, with short straps, wire, and ropes, to have three burros out in front of the two [burros] in good harness attached to the wagon. This gave pulling power of five animals, which seemed sufficient for the project.

Very early on the appointed day, I arrived at the cabin door where she was visiting, loaded in the trunk and the lady herself. We then proceeded to cross the desert bound for the railroad at the time- clocked speed of one and one-half miles per hour. The lady was on the cushioned seat under the canopy, and of course I walked all the time to encourage the burros and keep them in movement. Left without proper driving ability, they would stop and eat dry brush or lie down and rest. I had allowed ample time, which was fortunate, because that day a strange thing happened.

When [we were] still a long way out from the railroad, there galloped up to us a group of loose burros. The leader was a large male animal, and I could see they were bent on mischief. Twice I scattered them when they approached too close to my team. Then they drew off a hundred yards and seemed to be planning trouble. All at once they wheeled and dashed closely packed together straight towards us. The big male burro was in the lead, and he guided the band at full speed just in front of the tails of those in front. The impact broke the improvised harness [and] threw the three lead burros to the ground. Then all the animals, my lead three and all [the] loose burros, galloped out of sight, leaving bits of harness here and there. Now there were only two burros left. This called for [a] readjustment of plans. So I told the lady, "From here on, two burros can haul the trunk and you must walk. Or we can leave the trunk here on the desert, and you can ride to the railroad." She chose to ride. So the trunk was left in the sand for me to get later. But it was two weeks before I found the runaway burros and recovered parts of the harness.

[Article 38: April 3, 1952]

Rattlesnakes were very common in the old days. They multiply very slowly and so have been greatly reduced in number over the intervening years by boys, dogs, and autos when in the roadways. But in homestead times a trip to the post office always meant killing three to seven of them. Sidewinders in the lowlands and diamondback rattlers along the foothills. They will not attack, but the danger lies in not seeing them nor hearing the warning buzz. Snakes would fall into open wells as they were being dug, crawl into doors of cabins if left open, [or] into empty boxes and among firewood. The peeping of little chickens attracted them to come and eat them one by one. Rattlers like to coil up under boards, old sacks, and in the roots of bushes, so keep that in mind. One schoolgirl stepped on a sidewinder in such a way that its head was between her big toe and the others. She ran and screamed with the snake dangling from her foot and finally dislodged it without being bitten.

They will crawl into blankets for warmth if sleeping on the ground, so have a look at your blankets now and then. I have found them on the doorstep, in with the chickens, mixed in the hay, under boards, on a shelf in the house, under the kitchen table, along paths, in rocks, by moonlight, under my cot, and other places. They can be anywhere at any time, but are supposed to hibernate from November until March and usually do. Fortunately of late years they have become very scarce. If you hear one buzz, stand perfectly still and look to see where it is. You ought to know. There may be more than one, so do not jump from the first one or you may tangle with the second. The rattlesnake, no matter what the variety, [is] distinguished by a triangular head and small neck. Harmless snakes have small heads pointed in appearance, and the neck is streamlined. Rattlesnakes are the only dangerous ones, all others are harmless and friends of man. Some of them destroy rattlers, so never kill any harmless snakes.

If you want to capture a rattler alive, there are three methods. First, lift the snake and put it into a gunnysack that someone holds open for you. Second, take a stick and get it to coil without too much excitement. Then take a water pail and place it slowly over the coiled snake. Now if you slide a wide shingle or piece of tin under the bucket, it can be tipped upright and you have a convenient handle to carry anywhere.

The third method is done in this way. If you have no sack and no pail with shingles handy, use a cane-like stick about forty inches long to get the rattler in a good tight coil, then thrust the stick through the middle of the coils without hurting it. Now you lift and carry towards home. The snake will always make its way along the stick towards your hand. When too close, drop it gently to the ground, encourage recoiling, again insert the stick and, lifting it up, resume your journey towards home. Repeat if necessary.

[Article 39: April 10, 1952]

If you only want the skin of a snake for a memento or hatband, cut off the head and it will coil tightly about your arm like a large bracelet and is easy to carry this way. In skinning, some cut down through the middle of the belly. Others cut along the side, leaving all the large scales on one side and those of the back on the other. Stretch the skin in a shady place, rub with salt until dry, then with glycerin, which will make it pliable. Snakes can be eaten, but be sure it has not bitten itself or the meat will be poisoned. They will die if held in hot sun a few moments; consequently in hot weather they stay in the shade during the day and are moving round at night. In cold seasons they are out in sunshine in [the] daytime and lie quiet at night, cold and unhappy. Snakes can be noticed in moonlight, as they cast a slight shadow, so if walking in moonlight, look for shadows.

Cowboy Bill one day caught a large diamondback, took out the fangs, tied it in a gunny sack, and threw the angrily buzzing snake, sack-bound, inside a small tent during the night where a tenderfoot was sleeping. The man was in such haste to leave the tent alive that it collapsed about him, and the snake, gunnysack, tent, and frantically struggling man were just one grand mess.

Snakes will come to water. One day a large diamondback was coiled round a standing water pipe and enjoying the drip of water from the faucet. Walking into a new building, it was necessary to tread a plank where in one place a hose was running underneath to a tree. There was a strong hissing noise, and I thought the hose broke, but on taking up the plank, it was a rattler resting there doing the buzzing.

Sidewinders are so named because of a peculiar side-like method of going forward. This is to aid them in soft sand and is of prime importance when climbing sand hills, which is their natural and preferred home. They move rather slowly [and] cannot overtake their prey, so they have this habit to obtain food. They get in soft sand and turn and turn many times like a dog sometimes does to lie down. The result is that the snake is coiled closely in a plate-like pattern with its head exposed on top. The rest of the body [is] nearly submerged in sand, and here it waits for hours to watch for some unsuspecting bird or small animal to come its way. We used to find many snakes coiled like this in the desert sand, even though they are difficult to detect. Sidewinders are also called horned rattlesnakes because of one distinct horn over each eye.

[Article 40: April 17, 1952]

If walking on the desert and becoming tired or sleepy, an old trick of desert men is to take a large bandana handkerchief, look at the sun to see its position, and place it spread out on a small greasewood bush in such a way that it casts a shadow on the ground. Then clear out the small sticks and stones from the base of the bush. Now put your head on the edge of the shadow so that as the sun moves, there will be more shade instead of less. By placing your hat over the eyes, you can have a wonderful rest and sleep, even in the middle of a desert under blazing sunshine. Indians did this if on extensive journeys. It seems not to matter that [your] feet and legs are in the sun, if the head is kept cool in shade. I have done this many times on long walks through the desert where there was no natural shade.

However, one day I awakened with that uncomfortable feeling that I was being stared at, as you have also experienced in streetcars or other places to find some person staring at you. On the desert you should never do anything too quickly. If sleeping outdoors, do not jump up or wave your arms about when awakening. There may be a rattler resting on your blankets. This time, I knew something had caused me to waken, so I slowly turned my head right and left, lying still otherwise. 25 feet away was a very large coyote sitting down, looking intently at me. His mouth was open and water dripped from its protruding tongue, as it was noon and a hot day. I did not have firearms or even a walking stick, which is always a good thing to carry on trips.

I was not much concerned about the coyote as such, because they almost never attack a human unless mad with rabies. And so I was glad to observe that it looked normal. Slowly getting to my knees, I could reach a few rocks. The animal stood up as I moved, but did not retreat. It took several rocks thrown at him before he left. The coyote had found me asleep and was investigating if I were dead, which would [have] furnished good meals.

[Article 41: April 24, 1952]

. . . Autos were just then getting in-going through the Coachella Valley, getting stuck in the sand and losing many hours of time, [so] that [the drivers] complained bitterly about the general use. There was an auto road race from Los Angeles to Phoenix, Arizona. The race drivers found it [a] difficult and hard fact that there were no roads autos could use in the desert here. The newspapers took it up in headlines and in editorials. Sacramento took notice and arranged that an engineer would be sent down to pick out a roadway from Banning to the Arizona line.

Jack [Thelson] and Frank [Green] learned of this, wrote to the engineer, and guaranteed he would be met at [the] Whitewater River crossing by a group of road scouts to take him through this desert safely and deliver him to Thousand Palms, where another group would pilot him to Indio. Palm Springs was quoted to have said, "A road is impossible on the north of railroad tracks, consequently the only route must go through Palm Springs."

On the appointed day Frank Green, Jack Thelson, [and] Thornton Green, with two mules, a couple of other men whose names I do not now recall, and myself met the engineer at Whitewater River. There was no bridge there at that time. Travelers had to ford the stream, bumping over boulders, and if too much water was running, they sometimes camped out for hours until the water decreased.

[Article 42: May 1, 1952]

The engineer was driving a very small single-seat auto of that year's vintage when we started out on our expedition. Frank and I went ahead, picking out the routes. One had a shovel and the other a grub hoe. We merely indicated the path to follow, whether to the right or left of bushes, rocks, or deep-cut wash banks, and making minor improvements in the terrain, however always keeping a fairly straight line towards an objective. Jack Thelson and the other men kept close to the engineer, who drove the auto. At times they pushed the auto, or filled in holes and cut down brush. But when the auto could no longer proceed with its own power, Thornton Green came up and attached the mules, who hauled the car to better ground.

It was fairly easy as far as Garnet. The real work started when the group left there bound for Thousand Palms. Water, food, and blankets were carried along for the men and forage for the animals. We ate and slept as circumstances required. The other bunch of men from Indio, intent upon the road being established north of the railroad tracks, were waiting for us at Thousand Palms.

Of course there was no pay of any kind for us, but we pioneer men were glad to give a few days' time and much hard work to see an improved road come into the desert. And that road now has become Highway Number 60-70-99. Because of our efforts it is on the north side of the railroad tracks. The names of Frank Green and Jack Thelson should be written in the record, because it was these two who learned of the new road survey and called upon the rest of us to volunteer services. Just think how important that highway has been and still is to the growth and happiness of this community and the desert region, in fact, the entire state, as a gateway to California carrying trucks and vehicular traffic all over the country--one of the most active highways in the world.

[Article 43: May 8, 1952]

I have had many close calls with rattlesnakes. Then one night came a new one. It was quite dark, I was walking gingerly through a patch of cholla cactus, slowly making my way so as not to contact the vicious spiny stalks which I could barely distinguish in the gloom. Twice the noise of my feet crunching on rocks had disturbed snakes and I heard the buzzing, so I knew this was snake country.

Perhaps I was giving most of my attention to the cactus. Anyway, all of a sudden, without warning, I stepped right in the middle of a large coiled diamondback rattlesnake! He was asleep or would have rattled. Or perhaps his mama did not teach him to rattle. But this rude awakening made him mad, and he buzzed angrily. I can feel the strong coils twist and squirm under my feet, even now, and its head thrashing about my legs. You can be assured that I made two or three big steps. Fortunately my boots were heavy, because I still had five miles to walk in the dark.

On one occasion Bob Carr and I were walking from the railroad to the mountains on this side of the desert in snake season and after dark. We both had on just ordinary city shoes of rather thin leather, with no protection for our legs. First one man would lead and the other follow until it was embarrassing, then he would take the lead for a while and the other very thankfully follow along. We several times heard buzzing near us, but reached home safely. In those times it was really rather silly to be out at night without some protection.

On moonlight nights, rattlesnakes cast a narrow shadow, and if watching closely it is quite easy to see them. In fact I have on occasion gone out on moonlight nights to find rattlers for my snake pit. At the old ranch house I kept 15 to 20 snakes and chuckwallas for pets. They were in a pit five feet deep and 13 feet square. Many people came to look at these, which brought in some revenue.

[Article 44: May 15, 1952]

One morning I was down in the pit with the snakes, giving a lecture to some visitors who were leaning on the fence top watching me with curiosity. In counting the rattlers, I told them one was missing and might be in the old coat thrown into one corner to give them shade at noontime. As I started to examine the coat and its pockets looking for the missing snake, a well-dressed fellow from Chicago exclaimed hurriedly, "No, don't do that, you may get bitten. Send the coat to the cleaners!"

On another occasion I was in the same pit alone and cleaning it. All the rattlers were moved to one corner--the other snakes need not be worried about. Counting was difficult, but I made the number as 17, which was the correct number. Then I proceeded to clean their den, which was a box partly underground with only one rather small opening. My snake count was wrong, because when I thrust my arm through the hole and into the box, there was one rattlesnake in there! I felt its scaly coils! But it did not strike! It only licked my hand with its black forked tongue! During the past several months I had handled them so much that it is my belief that they recognized me as a friend. . . .

[Article 45: May 22, 1952]

. . . In homestead days there persisted a story, told in different ways, to the effect that in the '80s two Chinamen carried water in cans on burros from the Whitewater River to some spot on the big red hill in the west end of this desert. The ground was worked with a hand rocker and yielded small nuggets of gold far above wages. The hill is there, you can go look it over. We homesteaders did, but never found the old workings, nor any gold either.

The other story pieced together by Old Man Coolidge, with some unidentified rumors current at the time, was this. Two prospectors who had been in this country before 1900 spent several years prospecting the desert mountains east and north of Desert Hot Springs; [they] were at last successful and found a rich gold pocket in one of their diggings. They were elated to have at last been fortunate enough to find a mine and extract gold therefrom. Three deerskin sacks were filled with gold dust and pieces the size of wheat. These precious sacks were wrapped in their blankets and packed on burros with other camp equipment. They started the long journey towards San Bernardino. One day, as the story went, they reached Two Bunch Palms to replenish the water supply and camp for a day's rest. They thought this a good time to make the division of the gold into two lots instead of three sacks. Here the story is confused, and it is surmised the men quarreled about the division. The argument became so heated that one man was killed, and the other took all the gold and disappeared. Coolidge repeated this story . . . and believed it, because he was still hunting this lost gold mine when we arrived on the desert.

[Article 46: May 29, 1952]

This much I know about lost mines. About 1914 when I was working all alone clearing brush on a 20-acre piece of my claim and had seen no stranger for many days, imagine my surprise to see approaching me slowly from the west, a horse-drawn wagon and figures of two rather small men. There was no road, and it took some time for this group to reach the clearing, as they had to go around bushes and piles of rock. As they came closer, I could see that there was an old Indian man with long gray hair streaming about his shoulders, seated on some blankets in the wagon. His feet were stretched out in front of him, and with each withered hand he grasped the sides of the wagon, the better to keep his balance, as the wagon bounced and swayed in its slow journey. One young Indian walked some distance ahead, picking a route for the wagon to follow. A smaller boy was driving the two scrubby ponies as he walked beside the wagon. Only the old man could ride under such circumstances. At my well the horses were given water and a short rest. The Indians also drank and filled all the canteens they had in the wagon. After a little relaxation and some questions as to the best route to Long Canyon, they again got underway.

[Article 47: June 5, 1952]

We spoke mostly in Spanish, but they maintained the traditional Indian attitude of non-communication. But they did drop a few things, so by inquiry from other Indians and some cowboys, the story pieces together like this.

The old man, when young and vigorous, had seen for himself the value of gold when taken to a trader for flour, bacon, blankets, and other desirable things. So he, having remembered a legend among his people [about] the existence of a hole in the ground out of which gold could be taken with little effort, set out to find it again. This spot was in a side canyon entering into Long Canyon, which leads from this desert into the Morongos . . . . With persevering tenacity and much lonely traveling in and out of many canyons, he at last found the old Indian mine of legend. It was not as rich as he had hoped, but by energetic work he could extract small amounts of gold. This he did at intervals throughout his life, telling no one of its location.

But now suddenly and without warning, he had been stricken with nearly complete blindness. So he decided he would take his two grandsons out on the desert and into the canyon, with hope and prayer that he could find the spot where the Indian gold lay close to the surface, before it was too late for his old eyes to recognize landmarks.

I shall never forget the pathetic figure of the nearly blind old Indian clinging to the sides of the wagon, one lad walking by his side and driving the small ponies, the other boy, straight and erect, bronzed and hatless, walking resolutely ahead and picking a road where none existed. The little cavalcade disappeared as they had come, silently into a panorama of sand and cactus, ringed about with pale blue mountains.

Their expedition was fruitless, because nothing was ever heard of their venture again. A few men and some other Indians have searched the canyon, but it is 20 miles long and no gold has ever been found.

[Article 48: June 12, 1952]

Among the harmless snakes are many that are beautifully marked and differ widely in size and description. Quite often we see the red racer, usually three or four feet long, but [which] has been known to reach five feet. It is reddish in color, moves very swiftly, has teeth, and is a good rodent catcher. Photos have been taken of this type of snake eating rattlesnakes. Once I saw a red racer swimming in an open well in which it had fallen.

Various attempts failed to catch it, so finally I went down a short ladder with gloves on and purposely had it bite my finger, and so was able to capture it and get it out of the well and above the ground. One night at the home ranch a large racer was in the hen nest just swallowing a hen's egg, so I grabbed it, took out the egg from its mouth for my supper and placed the snake in the pit with the other pets.

Then there is the California pink boa, a very friendly and harmless snake. It will form a ball in your hands, twine round your wrist, and feels like smooth rubber. It is small but crushes its prey by constriction. King snakes are very clean looking and are strikingly marked always. They, too, kill rattlesnakes, so never injure a king snake, as they are good friends of man, as are, indeed, all snakes except the rattlers.

Rattlers are camouflaged to match their location, so come in reddish brown color, quite white, nearly black, and almost green. A rare kind, quite lazy but very large, is the true desert rattler. It can swallow a full-grown cottontail rabbit. Very hard to find, its home range is the mesquite thickets that reach from here down into old Mexico. The candy snake is a little fellow with a coat of bright colors. Small as it is, like a lead pencil and less than eleven inches long, it will, if cornered, coil and present a brave appearance. It is so small and so harmless that this is funny. I imagine it has seen big snakes do this to frighten enemies, and so it tries to [imitate] the same tactics. Another big snake is the heavy, slow-moving gopher snake, often five feet. Harmless and friendly, it can be handled like a kitten. I saw a coil of rope one night in the headlights of the auto and stopped to pick it up, but found the rope to have a head and a tail; it was a large gopher snake! Again-- never kill any snake but a rattler.

[Article 49: June 19, 1952]

In pioneer life the first necessity every day was that of water. So water was our number one problem. Homesteaders carried it to their cabin in many different ways, which to them seemed easiest. But all had hopes of digging a well on their own land. Wherever men gathered, wells and water were always the main topics of news and conversation.

Digging a well by hand is hard work by any method. Almost never could a well be dug in an open hole. All must be cased with boards to prevent cave-ins and to protect the diggers from falling rocks.

Jack Riley cased his walls from underneath. I cased mine from the top. We both dug wells for a living, in part. Frank DeLong in Mission Canyon had a forge and some tools. He invented a collapsible metal form which could be placed in the well at night, filled with concrete, and removed next day. The resulting well-hole was a continuous cement tube going straight into the earth.

Jack Riley and I, working together, dug the first attempt after water in [the present city limits of] Desert Hot Springs for Walter Woods, on his claim just east of the present bathhouse. We very laboriously, taking turns at top and bottom, dug a hole 120 feet deep, but found no water at that depth. It was found in a deeper stratum more recently.

When we were working on Thornton Green's well in the west Dillon Highway area, his four goats kept jumping over the open hole at the top and showering us with sand rocks. The goats had to be tied up.

Van Dusen had a deep well on his homestead claim north of B-bar-H Ranch. Van had a series of trap doors at different levels, arranged to prevent injury from falling rocks as he worked in the bottom. A strong steel cable went through these doors to the bucket on the bottom. At a signal, a man in a Model T Ford drove away with the top end of the cable, and the heavy bucket of earth and rocks bumped its way upwards, forcibly opening all the trap doors in its journey to the top.

One day at nearly noon Van gave the signal to the Ford man that he, and not the bucket, was riding to the top. This fact called for a slow trip and stops for trap doors. But the man with the Model T Ford misunderstood the signal, and with great enthusiasm and determination to get the last bucket up before dinner, he drove gaily, dragging the steel cable at full speed. The unfortunate Van was standing in the well bucket hanging to the steel cable. He was dragged up the hundred and some feet, in the dark and through all the trap doors, very unceremoniously. He was nearly killed. He was bald-headed and wore no hat. When Van stepped out of the bucket at the top, all scratched and bloody, his profanity and opinions about Ford cars and one Ford driver just burned the sagebrush and bushes for a hundred feet around the well-top.

[ARTICLE 50: JUNE 26, 1952]

The nicest well I ever dug was one for Bob Carr near his cabin, now on the land near Two Bunch Palms owned by Tom Lipps. This well was down through soft, pleasant-smelling blue clay all the way. It was not deep, and the sides stood up straight and needed no boards. The location was in thick brush, and lizards and snakes took much interest in what I was doing, some of them falling into the hole during the night. Birds came and sang as I worked. I was out of any wind and in sunshine. And best of all, I was alone. To be absolutely alone and out of sight and hearing of people and civilized things is a very enjoyable experience.

Ford Beebe dug the first successful well in the now village of Desert Hot Springs, at a point near the Idle Hour Corner. Very slowly and patiently he dug down deeper into the earth, mostly by himself. Neighbors were few and busy, his children too small to take part. Many days went by, but gradually he dug down deep enough to begin to hope for signs of water.

But one day all further progress was obstructed by a very large rock squarely in the middle of the well-hole, too hard to break with any tools he had, too large to get into the bucket. It indeed was discouraging and looked like the end of this well effort. Ford was never a man to get mad, and neither one to be beaten easily. He smoked a few cigarettes and analyzed the situation. Should he give up his many weeks of work in this hole and start a new one close by? No, that would be foolish, he argued with himself. He must get the rock out. So with much determination and ingenuity, he gathered all his wire, chains, rope, and barbed wire together. For one whole day he was down in the bottom of the new well, struggling alone with that big rock. Finally he was successful in tying and wrapping it into . . . a crazy sling affair, with a large, strong, wire-twisted loop on the top. Into this he securely fastened the well rope, which fortunately was a tough, small steel cable, but quite strong. No more could he do this day.

[ARTICLE 51: JULY 3, 1952]

Early the next morning, even before the dishes were washed or the cabin tidied up, Ford Beebe assembled his wife and all the children at the well. This would be the day that the rock might come out! The children were promised homemade candy. He told his wife that after the rock was out, for two whole days he would do all the cooking and wash every dish himself. Everyone was happy. It was like a real picnic, but with no lake and no band.

Cheerfully everyone helped turn the iron windlass handles. And slowly, oh so slowly, the rock came, twisting and bumping upwards. All were tired now, out of breath, and the mounting warmth of the day made visible perspiration. At last the rock appeared at the top of the well casing. There it hung. The sling still held it well balanced. But what to do now? How to get it on the bank? It was like the man who caught a bear and then could not get loose from the bear.

Ford thought over the situation quickly, and he instructed his wife and the largest boy to push on the rock and get it to swinging freely and widely. He would watch and at the split second moment [he] could release the windlass, and the rock would then drop safely on the bank to be dealt with later. With much effort and persistence, the rock finally swung fully over one side of the well, and Ford with skill dropped the rock on the bank. Everyone was exhausted. They just dropped where they were and rested on the ground. Ford lit a cigarette and lay on his back, blowing rings into a clear blue sky. His thoughts drifted to the satisfaction of having a well and plenty of water!

He stretched his tired muscles and closed his eyes. Just then the silence was broken by the smallest boy, who in a thin piping voice exclaimed, "Daddy, Daddy, the rock is slipping." And so it was. The great weight of the rock had caused it to slip and slide in the soft earth bank, and down it dropped with a heavy thud into the bottom of the well.

[*Desert Sentinel* editor's note: "Cabot brought out last week that Beebe's was the first successful well in DHS. He must have finally conquered the rock."]

[Article 52: July 10, 1952]

Early homesteaders' pioneer cabins were all very much alike. The YERXA cabin was typical to type, built of 1 x 12 boards placed on end, with wooden bat strips nailed over the cracks. All knotholes were covered with tin can tops to keep out blowing sand, rats, and mice. For furniture, there was one small unpainted drop-leaf table. One second hand Morris-type chair. All other seats were made of empty grocery boxes. Coal oil lamps and one lantern furnished meager light. The one stove was sheet metal with a cast-iron top. It consumed much wood gathered on the desert in an ever widening circle about the cabin. A three-gallon pail of water was perched on another grocery box near the stove, and seemed always empty or nearly so. Carrying water for household requirements is a never-ending task.

The cabin floor was of wood, and desert rats were always under the house trying to gnaw a new way in. The roof was of paper. Portions of this often blew away and necessitated many patches. It usually leaked during rains. The one door was on the east end, and one small window on each of the other three sides gave light and ventilation.

My son Rodney was the first white child north of the railroad and was brought to this cabin a few days after birth. In four years he grew to run around actively and to talk freely. He took a great interest in food. As soon as any dish was put on the table, he grabbed a spoon and dragged his small box seat from a corner and exclaimed, "Here's me." At a very early age he rode in a wooden box on the strong back of Merry Xmas, the ever-faithful burro. A similar box [on the opposite side of the burro's back], with a stone inside of equal weight, kept both boxes in safe balance. In this pioneer, desert-style baby buggy he was carried everywhere and in all weather. To the railroad for mail or small packages seven miles each way, up into mountain canyons where there was not even a trail, out into the sand dunes, or to call on neighbors miles away. He crouched in this box through sandstorms and in the darkness of night. Occasionally trips were made to T-cross-K Ranch 22 miles [round trip], but he never cried, and Merry Christmas never stumbled or fell.

[Article 53: July 17, 1952]

Only once in the four years of homesteading did we ever have a piece of ice. It happened this way. Neighbor Green had to drive his mule team one day to Palm Springs to get a bottle of liniment or something. When he started back he purchased a piece of ice from Mrs. Coffman's Desert Inn, just then in the beginning. At that time [the inn] was not much more than an idea. But anyway, she had a large icebox with different things in it. Also at that time a Chinese cook was in charge of the icebox. He charged 25 cents to each and all who wanted the icebox "opened." And then you paid extra for what you selected out of the icebox. It might be a bottle of pop, a cucumber, or whatever it was, you paid its value, plus 25 cents for having had the ice box "opened."

Green wrapped the piece of ice in many blankets and at last reached this side of the desert. The day was hot. He drove three miles out of his way to break off a very small piece of his dwindling cake. This he wrapped in many gunny sacks and left at the Yerxa cabin door, as no one was home, unfortunately, on this historic occasion.

We had five hens loose in the yard and one of them, investigating the cool wet sacks, decided that this was the very first cool place she had ever seen in the desert. Therefore she sat down on this very comfortable place and laid an egg. So when we came home at dark, at the cabin door were some wet gunny sacks with one white egg on top, but the ice had entirely melted and disappeared under a temperature of 110 degrees. . . .

The baby had no toys except homemade ones, but [he] enjoyed them much more than today's youngsters do with expensive playthings. He had a rocking chair of uncertain action, constructed out of a grocery box. Another smaller box was mounted on a wooden wheel, far from round. This had two wooden handles and served as his wheelbarrow, and in it he gathered many small sticks for the stove. But his most valued possession was a crude wooden horse which had four straight wooden legs. It had a wild cat's ear and a coyote's tail. Patches of rabbit's fur were attached here and there over the horse. But this was a very wonderful animal in his estimation.

[Article 54: July 24, 1952]

After the well at the door was completed, I fenced in a very small lot of ground and planted a garden. There was no money for a pump, and so I pulled 65 buckets of water each day out of the well and carried them to the garden. The sand was only damp, and the effort too great for the result, so the plan was abandoned. A valuable dollar was expended for one small peach tree, but it perished for lack of water.

One hen hatched out 13 little chicks which scratched round energetically, and we envisioned a chicken to eat later on. But after a couple of weeks, a baby chick disappeared nearly every day without a trace, until only two were left. Then, hearing a commotion outside, I discovered a rattlesnake eating another baby chick. The very next day I killed another rattler just swallowing the last chick. They were both red diamondbacks and three feet long.

Homesteaders' cabins had always a small screen cage nailed to the north side of the building. They reached through a window from the inside and stored perishable food in the cage. No one had ice. But a surprising coolness can be created by wrapping any dish with a wet cloth. Desert air evaporated the water so fast that most food kept very well by this plan.

Another novel and practical idea of cabin life was to cut a hole through one wall, so that firewood could be taken from a box nailed to the building on the outside of it. This box was covered to prevent snakes and rats from nesting among the firewood.

Homesteaders never had enough dishes, so many of the plates in use were of tin. Extra cups were always cleaned tin cans; Eagle Milk cans made the best ones. Tables were frequently just homemade affairs of ordinary boards. Almost no one on the desert ever had a real tablecloth. But quite often the table was covered with a piece of oilcloth, which brings up a story. One family, building their own cabin slowly, had up the four walls but no roof. Late in the afternoon of a hot day, heavy black clouds formed in the west near San Gorgonio. They lowered and came steadily nearer; rain was sure to fall. So all the small children were crowded under the rough table, which had an oilcloth cover, until the rain was over. And the father and mother sat crouched together on a box under one umbrella, which was a relic of city life.

[ARTICLE 55: JULY 31, 1952]

30-odd years ago, pieces of meat would occasionally be handed round with the explanation that the animal fell off a cliff and broke its neck. No questions were asked as to where it happened or who found it, or what kind of an animal it was. However, the meat often tasted like mutton.

But on one occasion a group of men organized a party to hunt for a mountain sheep in the Little San Bernardino Mountains. The day was very hot, and mountain climbing is very laborious even in good weather. The terrain and natural obstacles separated the men, until finally just two men were climbing a high ridge. And these two as it happened were enemies. Suddenly a big buck sheep appeared as a silhouette on some rocks not too far away. It stood there and looked at them with quiet curiosity. Both men raised their rifles with unruffled care and precision, and each took careful aim. But before pressing the trigger for the sure shot, each looked sideways at the other man, waiting for him to shoot. But not a shot was fired! There was a 500-dollar fine for killing a sheep, and neither man trusted the other. The sheep walked slowly away and out of sight. The two men came down the mountain in complete silence. . . .

[ARTICLE 56: AUGUST 7, 1952]

The friendliest [reptiles] of all were the chuckwallas, the largest lizard we have here. Often from 12 to as much as 18 inches in length, they are found only in the mountains and among rocks. Wide and flat, they have a strong heavy tail with which they fight each other. The scaled, pebbled skin is very tough and loose on the body. They have the strange ability to inhale air and inflate this skin to nearly double their size. This is nature's protection for them, because when chased, they run for rocks and wiggle into a small space and then inflate their skin, filling all the rocks' unevenness, and so their enemies cannot drag them forth. Snakes, birds, coyotes, foxes, and Indians hunted them for food. In color, they often resemble the rocks where found, and so the colors run from tans and red to black, sometimes mottled with several colors. A large male chuckwalla usually has a white tail.

I spent much time with these intelligent lizards, training them to play dead for some moments, to sit up in a corner and say their prayers. They also learned to climb a toy ladder and jump down into a net like circus performers. Also they would jump into my hand, climb to my shoulders, nibble my ears in play, then climb on top of my hat and blink in the sun. They would come when called and eat from my fingers without fear. They eat at 10 in the morning and enjoy lazing in strong sunshine. Desert tortoises will also learn to come when called and eat out of hand. They are vegetarian and enjoy lettuce, bananas, peaches, tomatoes, etc. They cannot swim. Never place them near deep water. In November they withdraw inside their shell and do not eat or drink or move until March. The eggs they lay have a soft shell, and ants have always destroyed the ones mine laid, so no small ones ever hatched here.

Skunks are reported to be very interesting house pets. However, I have never tried them. But you can.

[Article 57: August 14]

For some months I kept three desert chipmunks. These are the active little fellows with two white stripes down their backs, and with tails that they snap like flags in a wind.

Their favorite nesting place was a two-pound coffee can closed with the cover, which had a small door for them to enter. Inside were placed some small squares of flannel cloth to serve as nesting material. They looked like miniature blankets. During that winter these bright little animals would every now and then bring all the cloth pieces out of the can, dry them in the sun, and carry every one back into the can before dark.

Chipmunks, with their sharp teeth, can cut into sacks and boxes. They can make a standing jump from the floor up onto a table if food is expected there. They can climb cactus plants and gather the seeds at the top. Two of them were observed one day rolling a small gourd full of seeds towards their nest.

Horned toads will relax and stay quiet in the warmth of one's hand. They will eat flies as fast as you can catch them. They are certain to catch them. They are entirely harmless and helpless and should be protected in every way by us humans. They have a film which can be dropped over their eyes to keep sand out. In this way nature has provided so that they can dive into sand and have some idea how close to the surface they are for protection.

As late as the last century, Cahuilla Indians lived in a small village at Two Bunch Palms [on land] now owned by Tom Lipps. Another group of Indians, more numerous in numbers, made their homes in the sand hills both east and west of the Seven Palms Oasis in this part of the desert.

For the most part they lived in small wickiups of brush and palm leaves, always near some source of water. Springs were popular locations, of course. But in a few places they dug wells. An Indian well is not dug straight down like ours, because they had no tools and no lumber. Therefore their method was to dig a long trench in the earth sloping downward, so that the women could walk down this incline, fill a jar with water at the bottom, and walk out again. Old Indian women relate that some of these paths had walls so high that many were afraid to go down for the water.

[Article 58: August 21, 1952]

It is evident that all cooking utensils and jars used by Indians for any purpose were made of local clays, red in color, but sometimes blackened by too much fire. Rather small arrowheads are found in the sand of different materials, often obsidian or quartz and flint. The game hunted was mostly birds and rabbits. Coyotes and foxes were valued for their fur. Occasional expeditions were made into the nearby mountains to obtain a deer or mountain sheep, because of the food value of the animals, and also many uses were found for the hides. On these trips to the mountains, many acorns and other seeds were gathered and carefully stored for later use. These desert Indians were very peaceable by nature and were never warlike. They had no horses in early times and so never went anywhere except on foot.

Among the pottery shards found on the desert are some tan-colored pieces, often with simple attempts at decoration. These are supposed to be much older than those of red clay.

Always on the lookout for Indians relics, over the years I have found arrowheads of many designs and materials, arrow strengtheners, broken jars used for cooking or water storage, metates, mano stones, beads, and many pieces of broken pottery. Jack Riley once found a water jar, but placed it on some hay in his burro wagon, and the burros broke it while trying to get the hay. The only perfect water jar ever found in this section of the desert was discovered buried completely in the sand just east of Miracle Hill by two small girls 30-some years ago. It was full of seeds and too heavy to carry, so the children threw the seeds away and traded the jar for candy and things in Miss Gray's pocket-size store, then on the desert in front of Two Bunch Palms. It would have been interesting to know just what kind of seeds they were. . . .

On another occasion I uncovered in red clay the remains of an extinct sea turtle. It had evidently been trapped in soft mud, because there it lay complete. The shell was high-domed, 28 inches long and 15 wide. But the head and feet turned to dust when I attempted to move them. The shell, later sent to the University of California, was pronounced to be that of a sea turtle when this desert was under salt water, having an opening into the Gulf of California, and no one knows how many centuries ago that was.

[Article 59: August 28, 1952]

Poems ought to be written about "the light in the cabin window," because to it can be associated much of real sentiment, and because of it many a homeward-bound man in the night has trudged on with renewed courage.

In pioneer days when all travel was on foot or occasionally by burro, it was customary to place a lighted lamp or lantern right against the glass window pane of the cabin, so that the missing member could be guided and cheered homeward through the darkness. This tiny spot of light could be seen many miles out on the desert, and it became a source of inspiration to spur the traveler onwards and to give renewed energy to tired muscles.

Stella Carr was very thoughtful about the window lamp. The Carr cabin was on a sand hill shelf above the desert floor, and so when Bob and I returned from our 14-mile walk to the post office, we were always glad to see this tiny pinpoint of light glimmering in the darkness. The desert at night is very confusing unless one has a very clear sense of direction. Some amusing stories are remembered of men who became lost in the darkness and ended up miles from their homes when daylight disclosed their error.

The first school in the desert was started about 1916, in a building built by the county on one acre of ground on the now Dillon highway, near the B-bar-H road. Three McCarger children needed schooling, Hicks had one, a new family moved in with one, and two more children were borrowed from friends or relatives in the city--all this trouble to get eight children together, which was the minimum to open a school. The teacher boarded at McCargers'. The school building soon became the center of community activities, picnics, meetings, and some dances or box picnics, which were always popular. This building, which was a link with the past, burned down a few years ago, and only a few blackened boards mark the site of the first school.

[Article 60: September 4, 1952]

CARL EYTEL AND DUTCH FRANK

[Articles 60 through 64 originally appeared as a single article in the Palm Springs *Villager* in 1952.]

Carl Eytel was the first artist to ever live and paint in Palm Springs, and that was nearly 40 years ago.

One day in 1914 I was hunting my burro Merry Xmas in the vicinity of Seven Palms. Carl Eytel was camped there, making interesting sketches of sand dunes with San Jacinto Mountain in the background. And so we became acquainted.

His camp was by a small pool of water near the base of a large native palm tree. It was a very simple affair, just a faded blanket and piece of dusty canvas showing wear. By the grayed ashes of greasewood roots was the inevitable well-blackened coffee pot. Carl was German and liked plenty of coffee at every meal. Upright in the sand, handy to the fire, rested a covered tin pail in which to boil cereals. One tin cup, tin plate, camp-style knife, fork, and spoon completed his outfit. Palm fronds cast shade over a canteen leaning against his saddle, which had been thrown carelessly on the ground. A bright-pattern woolen Navajo saddle blanket hung to dry in a mesquite tree. There was no gun, as Carl had an aversion to killing any desert creature.

All of this equipment was tied back of the saddle when moving camp, as he never liked to bother with a pack burro. His horse was an old cow pony raised on the desert, bay in color, with stiff knees, but it had been his trusty companion on many miles of rough country travel, and he was very much attached to it.

[Article 61: September 11, 1952]

Carl Eytel and I were good friends and often went sketching together. Sometimes he would come to my cabin near Two Bunch Palms and stay several days. At other times I would go over to Palm Springs and visit him. His cabin was of redwood shakes and very small, scarcely 6 x 8 feet, in which was a single cot, small wooden unpainted table, homemade, and his painting paraphernalia. Of necessity I slept out of doors on the ground. There was not space enough for a stove in the toy-size room; therefore cooking was accomplished over an open outdoor fire, ringed round with a few small blackened rocks.

One day when I was visiting him, two ladies who were strangers in Palm Springs came to buy a picture. He seated them outside on campstools in front of the cabin. Carl then went into the tiny building and would bring small pictures to the open doorway for them to see. One lady purchased a sketch for 12 dollars and he was elated, because finances were low and paint and food items needed, one of which was canned milk. Carl was a very indifferent and haphazard cook. He relied upon canned milk as the mainstay of his every meal. It took no fire, no time to prepare, and was always ready and satisfying.

J. Smeaton Chase, who was then writing a book about the desert, lived nearby and occasionally joined us by the campfire. Palm Springs Indians were friendly to Carl and often sat around without saying much. Edmund C. Jaeger always called at Carl Eytel's cabin when down that way.

[Article 62: September 18, 1952]

One night a desert character named Dutch Frank, whom we both knew, came over for supper. We divided the beans three ways and put more water in the coffee pot. Coffee was served black, because Carl's milk supply was again non-existent.

Dutch Frank always traveled with three burros, one of which he rode, and the other two carried his camp outfit. This included a pick and shovel tied on top, because he was a prospector who investigated all the desert regions round about.

That night he had just returned from a trip as far as Thousand Palms Canyon. Dutch Frank extolled its beauty and the wonder of so much visible water in an otherwise very dry desert country. He traced a map on the ground with a stick and explained to Carl with many gestures the location of this marvelous canyon oasis, and where the water could be found. This much I gathered, but could not understand the details. Frank's English was very broken, and when both men reverted to German, I lost interest, not being able to understand what was said. So I spread out blankets and went to sleep, leaving them still talking about landmarks and directions.

Before I left in the morning, we had set a day for Carl to come over to my place, from which we would start our journey to see the wonders of Thousand Palms Canyon and make a few sketches.

He arrived as planned. The following day we put the pack saddle on Merry Xmas, a black burro and the best one I had for a camping trip. Roped onto the saddle were our blankets, together with food for several days. We each carried only a one-quart canteen of water, which we thought enough, for were we not going to a place where the water was in abundance and ran away in a stream!

It was June and the day turned out hot, made sultry by low-lying white clouds. There was no road. We often had to make detours for thick patches of cholla and steep sides of arroyos, which delayed our progress.

The water in our canteens became less and less, even though we merely wet our lips, knowing well that we could not take a drink.

[Article 63: September 25, 1952]

Eating cold pancakes spread with lard at lunchtime further depleted the canteen of water. In the mid-afternoon there was no breeze, and it became so hot that we rested awhile in the partial shade of a steep bank in a wash.

The sun went down, darkness gathered about us, and still Carl had not located the landmarks as described by Dutch Frank. Each mile now was an effort, and we were walking more slowly. After dark we tried one entrance into the hills, but it was a dry one. We drained the last drops out of our canteens in retracing our steps to that canyon entrance.

Surely the next opening to the east, we thought, must be the right one, and into it we stumbled over boulders and through thickets. Because it was now too dark to recognize any landmark, one canyon was as good as another to us and we plodded on with tired muscles. Deeper and deeper into the Indio Mud Hills we struggled, but still no palm trees and no water. We kept going, our throats parched and dry, our feet dragging with fatigue. Finally emerging through the hills, we found ourselves out onto [the] soft sand which drifts along the southern side of them.

It was about midnight, very quiet and hot, with oppressive humidity. We were desperately in need of water. We had eaten nothing since the cold pancakes, because in our food supply was only beans, lard, rice, corn meal, coffee, flour, potatoes, and some sugar. No wet canned goods of any kind. So without water we were stymied.

[Article 64: October 2, 1952]

Carl was for staying where we were until morning. But when I thought of the agonizing thirst to be endured for the rest of the night, I doubted if we could walk at all in the blazing sun of another day on the desert--still without water! So I argued with him that we must somehow struggle on tonight while it was yet dark and get somewhere where water might be found, before the sun of another day burned up over the horizon. We knew that Indio was southeast, and if we kept on we must eventually find water of some kind.

So stumbling through deep, soft sand and desert brush, sometimes tripping over roots or stepping into animal holes, we often lost our balance and fell sprawling on the ground. By the first faint light of day we dimly discerned through the heat haze the outline of a few trees and something of a fence, and made our weary way to them. We found there a wet ditch where irrigation water had run during the day. Walking along the ditch, we found a depression where a little water had settled into a small muddy pool. We moistened our parched mouths, drank sparingly, bathed our faces and arms in the warm water. We gave heartfelt thanks and stretched on the bank in exhausted sleep. Never has any liquid tasted quite as good as that muddy water.

Next day after resting in the welcome shade of trees, we walked into Indio and continued our exploration trip to [the] Salton Sea and back by easy stages to Indian Wells, where we stayed a day and then on to Palm Springs, where Carl found his cabin in perfect order. Next day I walked across the desert to Two Bunch Palms. All of the country we walked over now has paved roads, comfortable homes in most places, and the future of this desert land is marvelous.

Carl Eytel was so beloved by the Indians that he was buried in the Palm Springs Indian Cemetery.

He had [a] true and deep appreciation for all these colorful western lands. His pen and ink sketches and paintings show careful, sincere effort to reproduce the beauty and mystery of the desert.

[Article 65: October 9, 1952]

Many people brought to the desert as pets, domestic house cats. [Unless] they became desert-wise, they disappeared, because once out of the cabin, wild animals hunted them for food. In the heavy brush near Two Bunch Palms and at Seven Palms, and also near Willow Hole, lived wild cats and linx, which hunted the desert round about and would pick up and make short work of eating dogs or house cats. However, the tame cats that survived became partly wild themselves and often hunted out in the desert for rats and mice. Coyotes are fast and smart about capturing domestic animals. A coyote trick is for a single coyote to approach a cabin at night and start yapping. The cabin dog will bark back and go forward bravely. The coyote retreats and yaps again, the dog advances. The coyote's effort is to entice the dog well away from the cabin; then his coyote pals dash in to finish the dog.

Many domestic animals disappeared in those days. R.H. McDonald had a famous cat that hunted the desert for food and eluded wild animals for years. But in one race to the cabin, a coyote followed it so closely that it bit off half the cat's tail. One day Mac was digging post holes with a post digger, which makes a hole six inches in diameter. During the night a large trade rat fell into one of them. It could be seen at the bottom of the hole, but no way to get out. So Mac called the cat [and] showed him the rat. Then Mac took the cat by the end of its stub tail and lowered it head-first into the deep hole. The cat accepted the indignity of being held by its tail, grabbed the rat in its strong claws, and still held it fast as Mac pulled him out of the hole by the stubby tail.

[Article 66: October 16, 1952]

All cats have an aversion to water, as we all know. But the desert and hot weather changed that, in this story anyway. Mike Driscoll lives alone and is fond animals. So he always has cats and a dog or two around the cabin. On one very hot day he came in from the desert to find his two kittens, much distressed by the excessive heat, lying in some damp ground near a tub of water. Their tongues were out and dripping. So he grasped one cat in each hand and firmly held them in the tub of water. They struggled and scratched and fought the water as you might think they would. But next day, when Mike again returned, they stood at the tub and took a second bath with less objection. This performance was repeated until the cats learned to like the water and enjoy its coolness. And finally, Mike would take both cats and put them into the deep tub of water. The kittens then would, of their own accord, sink down into the water until only their noses were out. But each had two paws grasping the tub's edge. When well cooled, they would clamber out by themselves. And until the coyotes eventually caught them, they were always at the tub on very hot days.

Even now there is a big yellow tom cat here at the ranch which comes in, days apart, for a pan of milk, always waiting at a distance from the house. This cat hunts out in the desert, never meows, and it is impossible to approach it closer than a dozen feet. Every now and then cats have gone completely wild, going to live in the desert, taking their chances eluding wild animals. They grow in size, the fur is coarsened, and they revert to the type of their ancestors, becoming fierce and suspicious. One or two police dogs have gone wild and mated with coyotes. The offspring have been seen at times, very large for a coyote, but having the same looks and characteristics. Such a mixed breed was seen here on this desert a number of times. It would follow men on horseback, as though wanting to . . . be friends and become a pet dog like one of its progenitors. But the men never could capture it, and the strange animal eventually would disappear in the brush, only to reappear and act the same some weeks later. Captured coyote puppies make smart, cunning pets, but as they grow older they will steal chickens and revert to the wild ancestry.

[Article 67: October 23, 1952]

On one of my money-raising junkets to Los Angeles, I reached the city flat broke and had to take the very first place that could be found. This turned out to be an office clerk to the agent of the Pacific Electric Building, at Sixth and Main Streets, wages $65 per month. Two of us collected all the rents in the building, kept the books, hired and fired all elevator operators, all cleaners and mechanics needed to keep the building in operation.

The building agent and I had an office all to ourselves. Next to us was the office of George S. Patton, a business associate of Henry E. Huntington, and it was his son who later became the famous General George Patton of history. George Patton, jr., often came to the office when home from school in the East. Through Patton's office I walked into the private office of Henry Huntington. He used our office to go and to come, thus escaping observation of visitors in the front office, where [there] were secretaries and general office help. Henry Huntington was many times a millionaire. He owned the Pacific Electric R.R., the red cars, and the Los Angeles Street R.R., the yellow cars of the time, and also owned a very great part of the Southern Pacific R.R. Most of his personal friends and important business visitors came through our office to escape the formalities of the front office. Therefore we knew very well who were privileged to enter through our office.

One day a woman of average size came to our office. I was alone at the time. She was dressed in black, heavily veiled, wore black gloves, and carried a good-sized bag, which she kept in her lap. She said, "I am here to see Mr. Huntington personally, and I must see him alone." She did not offer a card. Knowing well that Mr. Huntington did not have any "woman in his life," I excused myself to her and said I would go see if Mr. Huntington was in . . . . I closed the door tightly as I entered Patton's office and related the situation to him. He became agitated and exclaimed, "It is 'the woman in black' again. I will summon help. Tell Mr. Huntington I am leaving now." And he did.

[Article 68: October 30, 1952]

When I carried out instructions to inform Henry Huntington, he said hurriedly, "It's the woman in black. Stay and watch her. I am going to the Jonathan Club." And he disappeared into the outer office. I returned just in time to see the strange woman wipe a large revolver with a black handkerchief and replace it in her bag. She wanted to know how soon she could see Mr. Huntington, rather brusquely.

I said, "He was not in his private office, but I will look in others for you."

I went through the door on my left into the office of a big official sitting at a large heavy desk. Briefly I told him the circumstances. He too, showed much alarm and exclaimed in an authoritative voice, "You go back and stay with that 'woman in black.' Watch her, don't let her leave. I will get help. I am leaving here now," and he disappeared.

I went back into my office and engaged the woman in casual conversation. But she mistrusted me and fingered her revolver in an affectionate manner, meanwhile asking where Huntington was and why I could not find him. Just when things got into a nervous tension, the door was opened by a policeman accompanied by plainclothesmen who subdued the "woman in black" after a short struggle and took her away. In explanation, it seems that the woman was demented because one of her family had been killed by the railroad, and she held Mr. Huntington to be personally responsible. She had given trouble on previous occasions, it seems, and was known to officials as "that woman in black." But the humorous part of the story to me was the fact that I was the cheapest man involved, just a 65-dollar clerk, and yet they left me to cope with the situation.

Well, the city interval passed and with the October sun casting golden light over the Angel on San Jacinto, I was again in the desert hunting up all my strayed burros.

[Article 69: November 6, 1952]

Desert men can take a pint of water and walk a long distance because they are used to hot weather and intense sunshine. But this story has to do with the reverse of the usual conditions. Once came a very hot day on the desert in summer season. Riverside County had authorized a few dollars to be spent breaking a rough road through the sand and brush, from the old schoolhouse towards Two Bunch Palms. Wilbur McCarger and I were allotted the task. . . .

We started at the old schoolhouse very early one sultry morning. We were reluctant to leave the welcome shade of this unpainted wooden building. But shouldering picks, shovels, heavy mattocks and some canteens of water, we dragged our steps out into the soft sand of the open desert.

We set up small flags to guide our direction and to keep the broken trail as straight as possible. The sun climbed higher in a pale blue sky and shone down on the desert without benefit of any breeze. Big rolling clouds appeared over the Little San Bernardino Mountains, and humidity increased rapidly. We drank from our canteens often, and our few clothes were wet with perspiration; white patches of salt appeared on our shirts where this evaporated. When near Orr Sang's cabin, I walked a half-mile to it with empty canteens, trusting to find water. None was there. With labored exertion I made my way back to where we were working, and the last canteen of water. We chopped down a few more greasewoods, drank all the remaining water from the canteens, and then quit for the day. We had each brought water and had drunk seven gallons, but the sun was yet high in the sky. We learned later that the temperature in Palm Springs on that day was over 128 degrees.

[ARTICLE 70: NOVEMBER 13, 1952]

We separated. McCarger returned to his family cabin, and I trudged off towards Two Bunch Palms through heavy sand. My canteen was entirely empty. At last, very weary and mouth parched with thirst, I neared Miracle Hill, which, ashen-colored, rises abruptly from the level floor of the desert. The palm trees [at Two Bunch] grow on a sandy shelf well above the flat land. This shelf is quite high and consists of soft, wind-blown sand. To scale the shelf from its desert side is very laborious, because as you take a step forward, you slide partly backward. Finally I gained the top and could see the heavy green palm leaves glistening in the sunshine. They cast a very welcome bit of shade at their base, and to this spot I waded through the muddy pool of water which gathered from the runoff of the very small spring that made this an oasis in a sun-drenched desert.

As I rested and drank slowly from my refilled canteen, the wildlife about the pool again resumed its natural expression, which I had interrupted. A red racer snake slithered down the bank and partly into the water. A few mourning doves flew into a tree and then dropped down to drink. A male quail strutted cautiously into the sunshine at the water's edge, and when satisfied [that] all was well, he called to the rest of the covey and a dozen more small birds joined him to drink and twitter, then all flew off in a whir of wings. A small cottontail rabbit hopped out of the brush and into the sunlight. Lizards of two or three different varieties appeared, each intent upon their own affairs. Besides the need for water, some were intent upon catching ants; others relished only flies as food. The vegetarians looked about for small leaves of grass and tender leaves. A few winged bugs hovered about the pool, only to be snatched up by small birds, darting out from shady spots in the mesquite thickets. A single tarantula hawk with orange-colored wings skimmed about in the sunshine. There is much to see in the desert if you will be still and observe with patience the interesting life around you. . . . .

[ARTICLE 72: NOVEMBER 27, 1952]

I always hit the city [Los Angeles] without a cent and so had no chance to look around, but must get any kind of work and start at once. One year this turned out to be a pick-and-shovel job for a utility company. Our gang dug ditches and manholes all over downtown Los Angeles. The pay was very small, 25 cents per hour. I sat on the curbstone and ate my lunch out of a paper bag along with Mexicans and Negroes. For water, the company had a water boy who carried a pail of water into which was thrust a tin dipper with a long handle. This lad walked about where the men were and gave each a drink out of the same dipper. Sanitation was not thought of in those days, and when the wind blew, the pail caught lots of street dust.

The work was hard and indignities many, but I always kept up my courage by thinking of the desert and the joy of freedom.

On another summer period, I got a job digging holes for telephone poles between Los Angeles and San Fernando. We had to dig so many per day per man, and men not used to hard work had to quit. Sometimes we were assigned to digging anchor holes for steel guy wires to brace the telephone poles. This work was often risky. The holes had to be approximately three feet wide, six or eight [feet] long and about eight feet deep. One day I was down in an anchor hole near the railroad tracks when a very heavy freight train roared by at high speed. The loose ground in which I was digging shook, pebbles and little streams of sand started to drop out of my wall, and then part of it gave way and buried me up above my knees. I yelled for help because the rest of the wall was insecure.

[Article 73: December 4, 1952]

The water boy, fortunately nearby with his pail and dipper, heard me and summoned others. The predicament was not pleasant.

When the holes were all dug, I was put into the pole gang, raising telephone poles by hand. This was difficult work and dangerous, doing it all by hand as we did in those days. This pole-raising is now done by machinery. On one occasion when the wind blew a telephone pole towards me, which I was holding upright with a pike pole, part of the skin on my left palm slipped off before other men could come to my assistance.

The gang's boss then made me time-keeper. The superintendent in the main office liked my work and promoted me to be time-keeper for all men working in the city outside of the central buildings. I learned to ride a motorcycle, which was then quite new as transportation. I rode more than 100 miles per day around Los Angeles, keeping records of all men and materials for the telephone company, [which was] then expanding service. My duties took me in and out of all the moving picture lots, and I planned to work in them after my homestead period was over. But . . . World War I came up and then I joined the army, which changed the course of events. My commanding officer was Dwight Eisenhower, then a colonel of the Tank Corps. I was his mess sergeant for a period, supervising his and other officers' meals, together with 100 to 400 soldiers.

It was always with great relief that we left the city and once again headed back to the desert. City clothes were hung up in a closet, city shoes shined and put away in a box. Then we happily donned overalls, heavy shoes, a cotton shirt with open neck, and some favorite old comfortable hat. A comfortable hat never looks well, and a hat that looks well never feels comfortable. Think that one over, and any man will agree it is a true statement. Once again in desert clothes, we set about cleaning out wells, removing rats or snakes, or anything that fell in during our absence. Then followed an hour of bailing out water and throwing it away, to freshen up the water. If any tree had survived the summer heat, it was drenched and given new life.

[Article 74: December 11, 1952]

The cabin was swept and dusted, beds made up fresh, dishes put through a bath of soap and water. Then holes in the roof were repaired and firewood gathered. Boxes of groceries were opened, and it gave us a great sense of security to see packages of food on the shelf. We, very few of us, would see a store again for seven months, but we cared not. There was flour and yeast to make bread, sugar, salt, dry beans, cornmeal, canned milk, molasses, and a few other items to make many meals. But the greatest overall joy, with a thankful feeling of independence and satisfaction, was the fact that the land under our feet was ours! To no man must we pay rent or tribute for water, gas, electricity, phone, newspapers, or streetcar rides. We were free men in a new, clean, fascinating world.

I know that it was this desire for freedom and for the ownership of land under one's feet that brought all early settlers to this desert. These two things motivated all that they did and carried them through the many hardships and privations with a cheerful heart. . . .

[ARTICLE 75: DECEMBER 18, 1952]

No man ever refused to work, because we were glad to get anything that would turn into a dollar. The wage scale was not important. I have often walked as much as seven miles, carried a pick or shovel or other tools, worked all day and walked seven miles home again to earn $1.60 or $2 for the whole day. And . . . I carried a canteen full of water hung on my neck to last all day. Other men did the same. In the beginning there was a very large pile of big rocks between Rolly's corner and the R.R.depot. The County paid Jack Riley and me to break up these boulders and make a passable road. We each walked back and forth each day to work. My pay was $2 per day and his was $3 a day, because Jack placed the dynamite to blow up some of the largest ones. . . .

[ARTICLE 76: DECEMBER 25, 1952]

No person in this world will ever get enough money, or gain enough distinction over his fellows, to equal the thrill and quiet joy of the ownership of land, which was mine when I stood on my desert claim for the first time. All papers signed and filed, there round me were some boxes of groceries [and] a canteen of water with a blanket spread on the ground. This was my land. This feeling was, I am sure, the same with all pioneer homesteaders.

The future of the desert and the future reward to each man differed greatly according to his slant on life's picture. To some it was a field of alfalfa standing strong and green in winter sunshine. To some this alfalfa would turn into money as baled hay, or be fed to cows for milk, or to pigs to get fat and go to market. Some men talked chickens of different types, and turkeys too. A few expanded the idea of winter vegetables, or early fruits going to market. We heard stories of fantastic prices sometimes paid for the first grapes, figs, tomatoes, etc., which were then growing in very small quantities at widely separated spots on the desert between here and the Mexican line. Every man had a dream of the future in which he would be the man who had a large bank account and could write checks freely. It mattered not that no man in the desert could change a five-dollar bill at that time.

Another fact to be noted besides the general optimistical outlook, was that each settler was sure that he had the very finest claim in the whole desert. Each man would listen politely while another was explaining the good qualities of his homestead, but at the first break in the conversation, the listener would then expound at great length with convincing detail why his very own claim was by far and above any denial the best ding-busted piece of desert land between here and Mexico. . . .

[ARTICLE 78: JANUARY 8, 1953]

. . . My own dream in the distant past day was not of alfalfa, chickens, or pigs, little or big, but based on beef cattle. The beef cattle would provide money for an art gallery, museum, and time to paint desert pictures. But World War I came up, and I volunteered into the Army. . . .

My entrance into the ownership of cattle was to have had a very meager start. I planned to buy one beef cow, which was all the money I could then hope to get. The cow would have a calf, and in the years following I would be in the beef cattle business.

But when I discovered the hot mineral waters and we found that it would help ailing people, all plans were changed. Bob Carr and I reshaped our dreams of the future to take recognition of this very surprising circumstance. He and I sat often on hilltops, gazing at many thousands of uninhabited acres of hot, dry desert land. If the weather was bad, we crouched by small fires in deep arroyos or in thick brush. But always, much of the long talks was the same. Bob and I visualized a health city, growing up out of the greasewood here on the desert!

[Article 79: January 15, 1953]

In this city would be established sanitariums, hospitals, rest homes, many swimming pools and bathing facilities for those seeking better health. Following naturally would come paved streets, electric power, stores, churches, schools, and homes for many contented people. To this city would travel thousands of people from throughout the whole United States, people seeking winter sunshine, and those who needed the desert and the hot mineral water to greatly improve their health. Many would be cured of their various ailments.

We talked about it so much and visualized it so well and in such detail, that we were impatient with people who could not see the future and the importance of the healing hot water. Bob said that our land was worth over $1,000 an acre. This talk sounded very foolish to all who listened to us, because we had on ragged overalls and could muster no more nickels or dimes than anyone else. And also, true to relate, we could not sell an acre of land at any price. People simply were not interested in such fantastic dreams. . . .

[Article 80: January 22, 1953]

There were a few picnics to someplace that offered any shade. People walked and carried canteens of water or, if possible, traveled on burros. Sometimes there were sandwiches, but homemade bread was not suitable. Therefore, generally, the meal centered around one main dish over a campfire. Rabbit stew, boiled beans, or chowder made of canned fish were popular, and also many different dishes using rice. The dessert would be some kind of cooked dried fruit, prunes generally or raisins; peaches and pears, etc., [were] too expensive.

Once in a while there was a quail hunt, so-called. In this game the victim is placed at night with a sack at the end of a small runway built of sticks. He is told to hold the sack well open until the quail have all run in, then he must close the sack quickly else they escape. The other men in on the fun then go out into the brush to drive in the quail, as they explain to the man with the sack. But there are no quail, and all the men go home, except the man left alone in the dark. And this is one version of the expression you have heard, "Holding the sack."

There never was a big gathering, nor any gay parties; no one on the desert had any money. And city people or those in the [motion] picture world never came out, because they could not get into the desert at the time without walking. And they cared not to walk.

It was better, so. The quietness and natural peace of the clean, open desert without many people is very wonderful indeed. We loved it. . .

[Article 81: January 29, 1953]

. . . My chickens have been robbed by wildcats, desert foxes, coyotes, and linx with tufted ears. From time to time, but not all the same month, representatives of all things living in the desert have come into some cabin where I was living. Centipedes, scorpions in three models--the smallest being the most poisonous, the other two being a greenish one and the large clumsy type, which is not as bad as it looks. Bats that sleep all day fastened to roof boards or in dark corners, [which] then fly all night, catching millers and bugs of the darkened hours. Horned rattlesnakes have appeared among the firewood, and so have black widow spiders, the large wood spiders, and others. Ants have been troublesome at times; the very small ones have been the worst offenders. They go after meat and fats first, but will swarm over other food items as well, just to keep in practice.

Large red ants enjoy out-of-door life most and seldom enter buildings. They will bite sometimes and raise a big lump on many people. The large black ants never come in the house and never bite; they tend strictly to their own business and are very efficient in gathering their food. They march like soldiers, seeming to work under supervision. Wild bees come from the mountains for water and do not sting while on this mission, [but] are quite harmless. Vinegarones and tarantulas look formidable, . . . have a bad reputation and are feared by Mexicans, but are not very poisonous. They move fast, hence are difficult to kill. Small field mice of two or three different kinds are a nuisance. Kangaroo mice and two kinds [of mice] large enough to be called rats have tufts on their tails and are so clean and cute that one can well forgive their small thefts. The desert rat is a pest and a problem wherever found. . . .

[Article 82: February 5, 1953]

. . . The lizards that play round the dooryard are all harmless; some eat only ants, others choose flies, a few larger varieties are vegetarians and eat only grass or tender leaves. One variety is carnivorous and has teeth, and then there are the racing lizards which at high speeds progress mostly on their hind feet. Sand lizards of different kinds are equipped with webbed feet. Strikingly marked "collared lizards" often came near where I labored and sat on loose boards, observing my work with a seemingly critical eye. They became very tame. A few dark, strong lizards with scales have visited me on occasion; their choice is a tree of any kind, but they enjoy palm trees mostly. The so-called horned toads are really horned lizards, and we should always give them special protection, as they are so helpless that they are becoming extinct in this area. Chuckwallas, large and clumsy, are seldom encountered, because they are usually in the mountains. But two of them lived in some rocks near one of the cabins and were my neighbors for years. Chacos, or child-of-the-earth, you will never see unless you dig in the ground. They look very ugly and are feared because of their strange appearance, but are quite harmless. Another curious fellow is the banded gecko. They are seen only at night and move very slowly. There are no gila monsters here.

In the insect world, many live on the desert, but only a few are worthy of notice. The tarantula hawk is one, two inches long, body of metallic blue, with two large, orange-colored wings. It presents a striking appearance and will sting hard if handled. Leave it alone and it will not harm you. Then there are the small fuzzy fellows always alone, always in a hurry; they come in white, bright yellow, and bright red. They also will sting hard if picked up. The Walapi tiger or kissing bug is after blood, but fortunately its hunting season is short. They fly at night and try to get a few drops of blood when people or animals are asleep.

[ARTICLE 83: FEBRUARY 12, 1953]

Of the birds, most all of them stayed out of my cabin. But often fly-catchers came in and built nests and were not afraid. Once a roadrunner came in the barn, built a nest and raised some small youngsters. Roadrunners kill rattlesnakes! Protect them! The other birds stayed in the yard or nearby bushes. Shrikes, sparrows, wrens, ground owls, and humming birds. Coyotes came up to my cot some nights, but went away when I threw stones. Rattlesnakes have twisted through the door, before I had a screen up. They have been on kitchen shelves, under my bed, and other places. They use no judgment in where they ought to stay. So be glad that they rattle.

[ARTICLE 84: FEBRUARY 19, 1953]

Rabbits range well out of doors [and] eat any plantings. Desert chipmunks are great thieves and will watch all you do and take advantage of any mistake you make in protecting food. There are badgers and gophers occasionally, but you will likely never see one of them. Hawks, eagles, and large white owls have been killed off here.

My greatest surprise of life alone on the desert came in this fashion. One morning in summer I got up at 3:45 to have an early breakfast, and into the dimly lighted kitchen walked slowly a large black-and-white skunk. It looked at me curiously, examined my shoe laces, investigated under every table and chair. Finding nothing important, it went out the same door as it had entered. The next morning at the same time, just at daylight, it came again to the kitchen, followed this time by five small baby skunks! Now you know I am very friendly to animals, and so I did not kick those skunks around. I just let them take their own time to examine everything they wished to do. After a few days they left the house alone, but I saw them about the yard at night for some months, and they perhaps moved away or coyotes got them, because they disappeared.

One afternoon a large tarantula walked into the room, and in a few moments a tarantula hawk flew in looking for it. Then ensued a battle between the two of them, but the tarantula lost the fight. The lady with the orange-colored wings was too much for him.

We must not forget the nighthawks, that interesting small bird that nests on the ground and sails about the cabin at night catching millers and mosquitoes. I am sorry that the mourning doves have nearly disappeared from the desert since people have come here to live. Their mournful note is part of the real desert. The almost complete absence of the valley quail is also very regrettable, because they added so much to the cheerfulness of our surroundings when we first came to live among desert creatures.

[Article 85: February 26, 1953]

THE DESERT BANDANA

[Originally published in the Palm Springs *Villager*; concludes in Article 86]

A red handkerchief round his neck is not something just to make a desert man or cowboy look picturesque. We are talking about the man who walks or rides a horse in desert country, with no room for extras or non-essentials. A big bandana is part of his equipment for the life he leads. With a good handkerchief, he can tie it tight around his neck in bad weather and receive much protection from cold and wind. It creates quite a noticeable degree of warmth. Paradoxically, in hot seasons, if tied loosely with the large part kept high on the back of the neck, close to his hat, the heat of the desert sun is modified and the blood stream kept cool as possible. . . .

A red handkerchief is the towel of a man traveling light, performing its use as such, and washed when opportunity offers. It is a napkin if one is needed. And for handling hot dishes or coffee pots at campfires, it is indispensable. If mosquitoes are a nuisance, the face can be protected in sleep. When the weather is too windy for a hat, the same handkerchief knotted up makes a practical head covering. In case of cuts, burns, or bruises, the handkerchief is available for bandages and can make a sling if one is needed. Should rest be necessary in the daytime, the handkerchief folded over the eyes induces sleep. As a tourniquet in cases of snake bites it might save a life or retard the effects of poison until a doctor arrives.

[Article 86: March 5, 1953]

A bandana is very practical as a marker for a camp in heavy brush [and] makes an excellent flag in running survey lines. On camping trips, money or watches tied in a handkerchief are kept free of sand and are easy to find. If robbing wild bees of their honey, a handkerchief on the hat gives some protection. Placed over open dishes of camp food, it keeps flies and bugs out until meal time.

I do not know of any greater joy than bathing the face with a wet bandana after a grueling day's walk through deep sand on the desert. If there is enough water and soap, it can be used as a satisfactory wash rag. It dries razors and dishes with equal efficiency. A large bandana spread over a small bush in the desert makes enough shade for one's head to lie down and rest. When wet and used on wrists or back of neck, it will prevent injury from too much sun. While wet over bottles and canteens, the evaporation will keep the contents cool. . . .

Hunters can use the handkerchief to tie the feet and legs of small game together, thus making them easier to carry. Bandanas spread flat on the ground answer as a table on which to play cards or place lunch. Tied over the head, [a bandana] keeps sand out of the hair when sleeping on the ground. Should there be an alarm clock, wrap it up in the bandana, and it will ring on time without getting dust in its insides.

When placed on a counter in a store with the four corners tied together, it will hold a surprising number of small articles and will not break like a paper bag. I used to have a one-armed man come to my desert store. He scorned paper bags or any help in tying up his purchases, preferring the handkerchief he used to carry his varied articles to a waiting pack burro.

So the next time you see a sunburned man with a big bandana around his neck, do not think, as the sweet young thing says, "He just does that to look cute."

[Article 87: March 12, 1953]

. . . Today let us consider glass bottles--not liquor bottles, but just water bottles.

On this desert, any empty bottle left in the sun gets so hot that when water is poured into it, a temporary pressure is created that will often break it. I know one man who attempted to fill a bottle which had stood in the sun, and the bottle burst and destroyed one of his eyes instantly and left the other eye with only 50 percent of vision. Another man on the desert, trying to fill a five-gallon bottle under similar conditions, was cut so badly by flying glass that he died.

Bottles left in the sun can cause a fire in this climate. Three or four houses have been set on fire in Desert Hot Springs by bottles being left carelessly about the premises.

It is quite a general custom to carry a bottle of water in the back of automobiles. In one case here in the village, the hood was left standing open, the sun shone through the bottle and set fire to the car, but fortunately the people were at home, smelled the smoke and extinguished the fire before the car was entirely destroyed. . . .

[Article 88: March 19, 1953]

All parents recount amusing things said by their children. This one amuses me. When I left the desert in 1918 to volunteer into the army of World War I, Rodney, then nearing five years of age, was taken on a slow boat from San Pedro to Seattle. He was the first white child born on this side of the desert and had spent his whole life up to that point here in the sand. During this time he had only seen water twice that did not come out of a canteen. There was a very small muddy pond at Two Bunch Palms and what was explained to him [as] a reservoir at T-cross-K Ranch in Mission Canyon, about 20 feet square.

Rodney never talked much. For several days out on the ocean he never said a word nor asked a question. Then about the third day, when we had been out of sight of land for a very long period, he exclaimed, gazing at the immensity of water in view, "Gee, Daddy, this is a big reservoir!"

Bob Carr and his wife homesteaded on land joining mine in 1913. They kept a dozen chickens, which were well locked up at night. But at one period a chicken was missing every few days during daylight hours. Large animal tracks were noted, a few feathers scattered about, and some drops of blood in the sand. That was all.

Bob cleaned his rifle and kept it near the door. On one bright sunny morning, he and I were sitting in the shade of his cabin speculating as to whether it was a coyote or lynx responsible for [the] missing chickens. Just then we heard a chicken squawk near the edge of [some] mesquite brush and looked in time to see a big spotted lynx retreating with a full-grown chicken in its mouth. Bob grabbed the rifle, and we took up the trail. In a few moments we saw the lynx with its prey, and it saw us, too. Whereupon the lynx promptly dropped the chicken and advanced slowly towards us, menacingly. Stopping now and then with teeth bared and snarling, its glinting eyes [looking] steadily in our direction.

We three were very close together now, and just for an instant the lynx crouched low and steadied itself for a spring upon us. But Bob was cool and had been holding a line on the animal with his rifle. His shot went true to the mark, and the lynx never completed the spring, but fell within a half dozen feet of us, screeching and clawing the small brush and sand. Had we been unarmed, we would have been in for a very serious encounter, indeed. Such a large animal could kill a man, or at least make extremely serious injuries.

[ARTICLE 89: MARCH 26, 1953]

Lynx, coyotes, and wild cats used to live in the heavy brush round Two Bunch Palms, and I have seen many in the days gone by, but not for quite some years lately. The last lynx came to the Pueblo early one morning eight years ago, but coyotes are still with us outside of the village.

The Bob Carr single-pine-board cabin, with a one-slope roof, was on a sandy shelf above the flat desert and half hidden in thick undergrowth of mesquite and greasewood. Bob and I had cleared several pockets out of the sandy depression amid the sand hills near his cabin. These pockets were circular open spaces in which a campfire was safe and out of any adverse wind condition which might be affecting the open desert.

To these secluded spots we often went for talks and long discussions of outside news which had trickled in to us by mail, sometimes to wonder at the way nature had provided plants, birds, and animals, and other desert things with qualities which made their survival possible in such a land as this. For variation we talked about books, famous people, historical events, and pages out of history which have changed the course of the world. Sometimes Bob would recount again parts of his past life which had been very eventful, and on some days we went over the trials and experiences which had befallen me, which were many and varied. Anyway, we spent very interesting hours crouched by small campfires buried out in the desert without benefit of radio or television, which people find so necessary today.

We did not even have a newspaper. There we were, just two men by a fire, in the middle of many thousands [of] acres of land, with no roads and no strangers prowling about. After I found the black burro called Merry Xmas, it would follow us and lie down by the fire, and I am not at all sure that Merry Xmas didn't understand much that was said, because its intelligence was so much greater than any ordinary burro.

[ARTICLE 90: APRIL 2, 1953]

In a large mesquite tree of venerable age lived a family of seven great spotted white owls standing fully 20 inches high, and the wing-spread of these beautiful birds of the night was astonishing. During the darkened hours they would often fly slowly and close overhead with a ghostly swish of wings. Sometimes they would come quietly to rest on a convenient limb and call a very mournful "Who, who." This was all very eerie in these primitive surroundings.

To our campfire hideouts Bob and I took the occasional city visitors who chanced to come to see the desert and us. We would start out at night in the dark from Carr's cabin, walking single-file, with the city man in line. We walked in circles and loops, through thick brush, sometimes on hands and knees under low-lying mesquite branches. Then over sand hills, through rocky washes and patches of cactus, until the weary visitor was nearly exhausted, and at last drop into one of our secluded camp spots. Here a small fire was built and stories told of wild cats, mountain lions, lynx, rattlesnakes, etc. The visitor thought he was miles away from the Carr cabin, and with the background of night and location of the campfire spot, all the stories seemed very real. But in fact we were never more than a quarter-mile from the cabin. Often coyotes would yap, desert rats scampered about in the brush, and sometimes the firelight glinted back from animal eyes peering out at us from the darkness. So therefore, when the large white owls sailed overhead slowly with a very audible swish of wings and called "Who, who" in the blackness of the night, all visitors were ready to return to the cheerful lamp-lit cabin.

We walked them the same long way on the return journey, uphill and down and round about, so they never suspected that it was all a game which Bob and I enjoyed very much. The stories these men told in Hollywood about visits to Carr's desert cabin were very amusing. . . .

[ARTICLE 92: APRIL 16, 1953]

. . . After my father and only brother died, my mother spent some winter months in different years with me at the old ranch house, up until the time that she also passed from this life. No words of mine can give adequate praise for her unfailing courage and cheerfulness under many trying conditions.

[ARTICLE 93: APRIL 23, 1953]

Louis Sobol is one of the nation's foremost columnists and is one of Hearst's highest-paid special writers. When the B-bar-H Ranch was first started years ago, he was a guest there along with other New York celebrities, and one day with the help of a guide, he called at our ranch home at Miracle Hill, the house that later burned down. An acquaintance was formed which has lasted to this day. He, a typical New Yorker in the literary field and of the ultra, ultra city type, and me, just a desert rat in the rough, with sand in my shoes.

Louis Sobol's column, "New York Cavalcade," in the New York *Journal American* has a combined reader public of 10 million to 14 million people. First his special space is allotted in the New York papers, and then it is . . . reprinted in about 85 other newspapers throughout the country.

Louis Sobol in his column wrote, many years ago, "Garnet is a flag stop some seven miles from Palm Springs, and this is being written from our temporary headquarters, the B-bar-H Ranch. I have already been initiated into the Order of Pamperers, founded here a season ago. The code of the Pamperer is never to do today what can be done tomorrow. There is laziness in the air. The desert abounds in colorful characters. Today I drove over a winding, sandy ribbon of a road to Cabot Yerxa's place. Cabot, a mild-mannered fellow, lives here with his white-haired mother in serene aloofness from the outer world. Single-handed, he has built himself a house with a cellar, upstairs rooms, and an ingenious kitchen. Mother Yerxa proudly escorted me into her kitchen and started pumping water. I tasted it, and then I knew the reason for her pride. It was boiling hot--for that is how it comes out of the ground--and they drink it when it cools and swear by its mysterious medicinal properties. Cabot, who studied both in Paris and London, has many of his paintings hung round the walls. But his chief decorations are newspaper matrices, dating back 25 or more years when he first came to the desert after having hermited for a spell in Alaska. He is not averse to selling his art--nor selling anything, for he has a little store outside in which a few sundries are on display, but unfortunately few people drift up his way, except a casual guest from a ranch, wandering by accidentally on [a] horse's back. Yes, this desert recluse has visions of a day when all the world will come flocking to these magnificent outdoors, regain health from these still unpublicized magic waters, and drink in the hot sun."

[Article 94: April 30, 1953]

My mother was a "Cabot," from that aristocratic family well-known in the New England states and educated in Boston amid the civilized and ease and many conveniences of the times.

And yet she went with my father as a bride out to the frontier West in North Dakota only 16 miles south of the Canadian line. They lived in a one-room board cabin in which my brother and I were born in the early '80s. We two lads were the first white children born in the entire county of Pembina. Many groups of painted Sioux Indians came on ponies and set up tepees outside my father's store to do some trading. They always ate my dog, so after every powwow I had to have a new dog. Some few cowboys in the area also came for supplies. In those early days we ate buffalo meat and burned buffalo chips to keep warm.

Years of normal city life passed, and then before the Spanish-American war was over, we all moved down to Cuba while the shooting was still going on in many places. There we were one of the first pioneer white families to settle in the jungle portion of the islands. Spanish-speaking, quite primitive natives each carrying at least two sharp knives were in the yard, and boa-constrictors in the trees. Very large centipedes, scorpions, hairy tarantulas, and other poisonous things crawled round the floors and were often found under the pillows or in your shoes. Through all these varied conditions my mother kept a smiling cabin, even when a wild man from the mountains crowded past the cook and forced his way into the room where we were then eating breakfast, and explosively exclaimed in Spanish, while wielding a large sharp knife, that he would cut all our throats unless we bought the eggs that he carried down with him on his horse in a dirty cloth. We bought the eggs.

[Article 95: May 7, 1953]

Then in later years my mother spent many winter months here with me on this desert before Desert Hot Springs had gotten underway. In the beginning of those past winters, the few neighbors were miles away. And yet during her whole life and under all circumstances she was always cheerful, happy, and optimistic in every way. Truly a wonderful personality.

Oh, we experienced many prosperous years, too, when we all traveled much, stayed in the best hotels, lived in private railroad cars attached to fast trains going here, there, and yonder. At times we had private yachts on lakes or rivers, owned big houses, and in the days of horses, we each had one or two horses for personal use. There were at times cooks, waiters, butlers, stable boys, yard men, and other servants.

We associated with governors of states, senators, and the rich and prominent of the times. Once in Mexico City we were the guests of Porfirio Diaz, the then- president and dictator of Old Mexico, at the Castle of Chapultepec. The National Band was sent to the train to play in our honor when we arrived in the city and again when we left. We owned the very first automobile ever used in the state of Minnesota, and we took the first automobile ever seen on the island of Cuba to Havana. Police and soldiers had to clear the streets of curious natives every time we appeared.

In contrast to all this luxury, I have lived with the Eskimos up near the Arctic Circle, eaten chunks of meat raw, cut from long and smelly whales, and lunched on unclean frozen fish dipped in rancid seal oil, head, eyes, and sides just as they came out of the water. But Alaska is another story. . . .

[Article 96: May 14, 1953]

[A letter from Cabot Yerxa to Louis Sobol, originally printed in his column "New York Cavalcade":]

We had an unusual rain—so rare, and the desert was drenched and every plant got green; flowers came out and the bunch grass made seed as it does in April and May. I think we will be able to hold flowers in bloom all winter.

[The] B-bar-H Ranch is open, and Charlie Bender has oiled the road from the old schoolhouse into the ranch, so you can take the corner in high and no dust. Here on my ranch I will have a new rough cabin to show you, a wishing well building 13 x 20 [feet], and we have dug down to water.

This water temperature is 95 [degrees], and nearby is my other well, temperature 132, and another 140, and at odd times I dig on still another, to be hotter. Mother was 80 in October and is back here with me again. Oh yes, Gary Cooper bought another 160 acres close by, and Norma Shearer also purchased 160. And I think up in the skies I have located two new and larger stars, bright and close. I wonder if they will stay on. Yours out West, Cabot Yerxa

[Article 97: May 21, 1953]

[A letter to Louis Sobol, originally printed in his column "New York Cavalcade":]

Letters are my only amusement. I do not have radio or visitors. I live entirely alone. I have not seen even a moving picture in seven years, nor have I been in a restaurant or . . . anywhere classed as amusement in seven years.

It is February. In much of the United States that is still a winter month. But here on this desert, all the delightful feeling of spring is in the air. Everywhere green things are pushing up from the sand.

We walk, I and the goats, who follow along like well-trained dogs, except that they will playfully butt each other. We walk leisurely from the corral and up the side of Miracle Hill to the stone cabin named Eagle's Nest, built 30 years ago. This is the cabin built at the top of the hill dug into the clay bank, the cabin for which the burro I called Merry Xmas and I carried 100-pound sacks of cement on our backs for seven miles. The faithful animal lived out its life-span and rests beneath the sand nearby. So today I carried green things there and also placed some on three old Indian graves of tribesmen long since departed.

[Article 98: May 28, 1953]

[A letter to Louis Sobol, originally printed in his column "New York Cavalcade":]

I wish you might have taken this morning walk and stood with me for a while on top of Miracle Hill and filled your lungs with clean, pure desert air, having the fragrance of greasewood, of sage, and other wild pungent plants. The slight breeze was from due east, and so perhaps no other human being was breathing this air for the next 100 miles. Neither was there a single factory or any automobile casting out fumes in all that distance. . . .

Villa Pilar, Yerxa's plantation house in Cuba, ca. 1903

Cabot with his Cuban "guard" harvesting timber for building homes, ca. 1903

Nellie & Fred on porch of Villa Pilar Home, Cuba, ca.1902-1904.

Cabot in Cuba, ca. 1903; his mother's caption: "Still going"

Cabot's brother Harry, probably taken after the family moved to Southern California, ca. 1908

Cabot on horseback in front of Sierra Madre home, occupied from 1907-1911

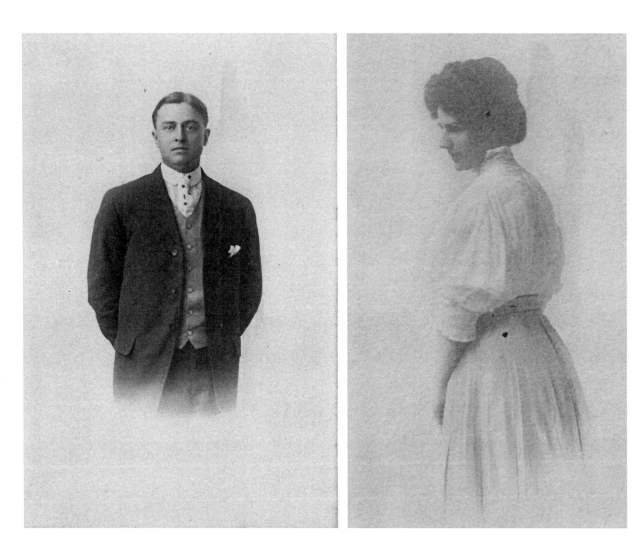

Cabot and Mamie Carstensen Yerxa. Married in San Francisco in 1908.

Interior and exterior of the couple's Sierra Madre home. Cabot published an article extolling the house's conveniences for California living, signing himself "architect."

[Article 99: June 4, 1953]

[A letter to Louis Sobol, originally printed in his column "New York Cavalcade":]

Snow still lies heavily on towering San Gorgonio and the other grand old mountain, San Jacinto. Mountains have personalities, and so we feel better acquainted with San Jacinto, because it is possible to walk easily to its very base and enter the various canyons with little effort.

The goats and I seemed to be in a small world, rimmed about by vague barriers of dull purples and distances of Maxfield Parrish blues. The dry sand between plants presented the appearance of having been swept. The many small stones of different colors lying about were a temptation. Soon my pockets were full. Among them were two broken arrowheads and some fragments of primitive pottery, evidence that ancient people had preceded me in living on the mesa.

Perhaps in eons of time, . . .when man has taken entirely to the air for his traveling, someone will find on this land a broken piece of iron which archeologists will determine to be parts of some Model T Ford. From this they will speculate as to the owner and his life, just as I did with the broken arrowheads and artifacts.

[Article 100: June 11, 1953]

[A letter to Louis Sobol, originally printed in his column "New York Cavalcade":]

It is too early for snakes to be out yet, as they are still hibernating. There were a few of the fly-catching lizards sunning themselves, hungrily watching for stray flies. Several small birds hunted diligently for scattered seeds under greasewood bushes. Two large black crows flapped their wings clumsily not far over our heads. They were steering a course toward more civilized parts, as the desert is not a place in which a crow can make a living.

One small desert fox dashed among the undergrowth with all the speed and fixed ideas of a motorcycle policeman, but without the noise. These foxes are the dandies among the denizens of this region. They have the finest fur and are the most dainty and cleanly in their habits.

I replenished water for my pets in the snake pit, and of all the different reptiles there, only two chuckwallas were in evidence. Not a single rattlesnake. That's because the 4th of March is usually the time they select for their convention. I picked up one of the chuckwallas and placed it on my shoulder, where it examined my ear, then turned its head and eyed me quizzically. The other I held in one hand and stroked [it] with the other. The warmth was pleasing to its cold body, and so we re-established trust to each other. They have intelligence, these chuckwallas; they will eat out of my hand, and I have taught some to play dead, say prayers, and to climb a five-foot ladder and then jump into nets like circus performers.

[Article 101: June 18, 1953]

We homesteaders back in 1913 were required by the government to live seven months out of each year on the claims. A five-month leave of absence was granted to earn money with which to buy supplies to live another seven months on the desert.

The going and returning was a matter of much planning. If on the desert, the prospective traveler must take a canteen of water and walk several miles in soft sand to talk with Wilbur McCarger or Jack Riley, who each owned two burros and small wagons. If neither was home, then journey on to find Thornton Green, who had two very sad-faced and slow tan-colored mules.

With the day of departure agreed upon, the animal owner then took his canteen of water, some food with perhaps a blanket, and walked out into this 100,000-acre desert to find his animals. When found, they were staked out near his cabin to eat desert vegetation until needed.

On the appointed day, he left his home very early in the morning with two animals hitched to a very light four-wheeled wagon. He thus proceeded to the cabin of the family wishing to leave the desert. Mileage, train schedule, and hour of departure had to be very accurately determined with a safe margin of lost time, because the rate of speed accomplished by the desert animals while hitched to a wagon was a little over one mile, but never more than two miles per hour.

On the eventful day we would begin at daylight to scan the lonesome desert with field glasses in the proper direction. Finally we would be able to dimly discern among the many greasewood bushes moving objects ambling very slowly towards our location.

After seeing their approach, we usually had over an hour to finish tacking cloth or paper over the windows on the inside of the cabin, to keep out the strong rays of summer sunshine while we were gone.

[Article 102: June 25, 1953]

All the last residue of water was put carefully on any small tree, with the hope and a prayer for its survival until our return.

At last the creaking of the wagon and the voice of the driver could be heard encouraging his sweating animal to keep moving. If not watched, they would stop to eat bushes, to bite at flies, or even lie down with complete unconcern about train time.

The trunk and bags were hastily loaded on. Any woman or child could ride, but the driver and all men must of necessity walk, because the tired animals could only struggle through the sand, pulling the unpainted, rickety wagon with its burden.

So in this fashion the small cavalcade would start on its laborious journey to the R.R. station at Garnet. Sometime there were wheel tracks to follow, but in most cases the faint trail was round greasewood bushes or up and down banks of sand in dry washes, where some shoveling was necessary. At the tiny Garnet depot, goodbyes were exchanged, tickets bought, and the welcome shade of a few palm trees enjoyed. The palms have since been cut down.

At last the slow train, puffing black smoke, arrived to take us to civilized parts. We were always burned to a dull brown by the desert sun, feeling very uncomfortable and ill at ease dressed in city clothes and tight shoes. Ice water on the train was a forgotten novelty. We drank slowly, with enjoyment. It seemed very strange to be sitting down comfortably and to see, out the windows, trees and green things after many months on the desert.

The other passengers looked very pale and white to us, and because of our sunburned appearance, we were very noticeable to them.

Once in the city, the noise and confusion was very disturbing to us, and a year's absence always had made some changes in clothing and style. Women's hats were of course always different. . . . .

[Article 105: July 16, 1953]

. . . The very early desert had no roads. Each homesteader made sort of a road, sometimes only a trail, to his cabin. Straight lines were forgotten, because it was easier and more practical to go around greasewood bushes than to make the effort to cut them down.

Seldom did any stranger ever venture into this land of no roads and almost no houses. Therefore we early people were very curious if we saw strange footprints in the sand while out hunting rabbits for food. We would follow those footprints until satisfied as to whose cabin they originated from. Then when next we met the man living in that part of the desert, we would ask about the footprints going that way. Always some explanation was forthcoming to explain them.

I often thought of Robinson Crusoe and his excitement at finding footprints on the sand in his realm. Our situation was similar, but not so important.

Every cabin-dweller had field glasses and surveyed the desert carefully several times a day. We had no other excitement in our lives. We looked curiously for any sign of life, human or animal. Many days passed when nothing could be noticed.

[Article 106: July 23, 1953]

Then perhaps two or three burros or a small group of cattle would show in the glass circle [of the binoculars]. If burros, we looked long enough to determine to whom they belonged and their names. Every burro had a name, and each person here then knew the name of every burro on the desert, no matter to whom it belonged. The cattle we counted, and remembered in what direction they were moving, so that when a cowboy showed up looking for lost animals, we could then tell him what we saw. Besides occasionally discovering men or large animals at a distance, the field glasses afforded us much entertainment. We watched coyotes, birds, lizards, snakes, or other small denizens of the desert busy about their small affairs and daily search for food.

Very occasionally a man could be seen far out in the desert, and we would follow this figure in the glass until his identity was disclosed or his destination determined.

Frank DeLong, who originated the T-cross-K Ranch in Mission Canyon, and I signaled each other by means of large colored cloths on a 50-foot line, or with lights at night. The distance was 11 miles, but strong field glasses made this practical. I often helped him with his work, making hay, handling cattle, or at other times when he needed the help of an extra man. . . .

[Article 107: July 30, 1953]

[Articles 107, 108, and 109 continue a letter to Louis Sobol, originally published in his "New York Cavalcade" column:]

"Here in these primitive surroundings it is hard to realize there is a war. We desert rats do not go in for radios much, and only occasionally the newspapers. There is something incongruous about filling a small cabin with sales talks about pills and whatnots, the armchair conclusions of news commentators, or the shrill voice of some barbwire soprano whom you know to be painted and marcelled out of all resemblance to a really beautiful woman as nature intended woman to be.

"The desert and nearby mountains without my cabin door are the same as they were a thousand years ago, and wildlife goes on in all its fascinating and efficient ways. Required foods are gathered for the day and proper amounts stored for the winter season. Small habitations are repaired for the coming of the annual rains. Chipmunks, very smart-looking in their striped winter fur coats, are making a last hurried search for extra seeds. The snakes will stay close to their dens, and the first rains soon to come will cause them to go into hibernation.

"My pet wren which flies north in the spring is back here now for the winter and bows to me in solemn manner when I open the cabin door and see it hunting bugs under the greasewood bushes. The fly-catcher is also back again and whistles very cheerfully each morning just before sunrise—and the shrike, a very early nester, is clearing out last year's collections of twigs. My desert tortoises have dug themselves a hole in the bank for winter.

"I have turned most of my snakes loose in the yard to find their own feed. One day I found a five-foot snake in the hen's nest swallowing a chicken egg, so I grabbed him and took the egg away for my supper and dropped the snake into the pit with other reptiles."

[Article 108: August 6, 1953]

"For some months I have searched for a rare type of desert rattlesnake, and one night in the dark I found a beauty coiled up on my doorstep and picked it up and added [it] to my pet collection. It has been a very good-natured snake with a good appetite. Some do not eat well in captivity.

"Another night my lights picked out a coil of rope in the road, and when I examined it, I found it had a head and tail and was the largest bull snake ever found in this desert, measuring over six feet. I was sad for days when this snake escaped from the pit by climbing over walls more than five feet high. . . .

"New York people seem to enjoy their city and the crowds of other pale cliff-dwellers who battle each other for seats in subway cars or an entrance to Brooklyn Bridge, and they rush from one place to another, live in an electric-lighted world, and sink exhausted at unreasonable hours into restless sleep within four very confining walls. . . .

"The next time you come out here, I will take you to my hideout, where I go when wanting a really quiet day. You see, there are neighbors now only three miles away from my cabin, and that makes me feel hemmed in. So I made a road with pick and shovel into a mountain canyon as far as a car can go. At this point we leave the car, and we walk as far as it is possible to go without climbing the steep side walls of the canyon. To this secluded spot I laboriously carried on my back over a period of many days, some lumber and palm fronds to build a palm cabin. There is a fireplace to make coffee, a table, and rough seats. All very primitive and wild--but it is peaceful."

[Article 109: August 13, 1953]

"Blue sky is overhead, the sun gives warmth and vitality, desert plants fill the air with fragrance, one or two birds will call cheerfully, clean dry sand is underfoot, and you will feel a regeneration of all life forces and realize that man is of divine origin and destiny and has a soul--if only he will, for a time, withdraw from the world and listen to its precepts. Adios Amigo, Cabot Yerxa."

. . . One of the first autos brought in was owned by old man Dana, who lived south of Long Canyon. He was rather advanced in years and not too strong. The roads were almost hopeless for autos, and his car got stuck in the sand very often. He would then walk to the nearest cabin for help, and we all have taken part in digging that first car out of heavy sand.

Ford Beebe had a Model T and kept taking off or losing parts of it until its identity was nearly lost. But Ford kept it running nevertheless. . . .

Mrs. Lucy Woods and [her] small daughter, Tinka, then lived on the small hill just east of the new bathhouse, and they chugged round the desert in another Ford car which someone kept going, to haul water and go to the post office at Garnet.

[Article 110: August 20, 1953]

EARLY CARS IN EARLY DESERT

Jack Riley lived near the now-B-bar-H Ranch and had the first Model T car. This he drove very successfully almost anywhere he wanted to go, throughout the desert country. Jack never paid much attention to roads. He was used to burros, and burros could go anywhere, and he expected the auto to do likewise. It usually did. He had surprisingly little trouble. His car was trimmed down to a skeleton basis, and he carried extra water, gas, and a shovel always. Jack had a keen and understanding eye for all desert conditions, and the driving to right or left of any obstruction often made a lot of difference, but he always made a quick choice of the lesser of two evils.

Frank DeLong from Mission Canyon had a forge and many tools and was mechanically-minded, even though he was a typical cowboy. One day Frank bought a Ford in Banning and was instructed how to start it and to stop. He managed to reach the ranch without incident. But the very next day he took the thing all apart, filling boxes, cans, and pails with its many wheels, nuts, and bolts. Then he put it all together again, because he said, "He wanted to know what made it run." He never had mechanical trouble with his car.

Bill Anderson had one of the early autos with a flat bed so that he could carry lumber and building supplies, as he was a carpenter when any work appeared in this area. Bill was a steady pipe-smoker, and unfortunately, one day on Dillon Highway near Indian Avenue corner, he forgot that he was driving an auto and not horses, and took both hands off the steering wheel to pack his pipe with fresh tobacco. The car swerved out of the wheel tracks, overturned, and Bill was killed instantly.

Also in those early days Mike Driscoll acquired a car, as did Joe Bonhorn, Rube Halstead, Cabot Yerxa, R.H. McDonald, and others followed, until cars became somewhat numerous and burros gradually disappeared.

[Article 111: August 27, 1953]

This story of Mrs. Lucy Woods, who lived in one of the first two houses ever built in Desert Hot Springs (Ford Beebe lived in the other one), is a desert classic. One day in August, nearly 40 years ago, she was en route to Banning, which was really a venturesome journey at that time. The desert just shimmered with sun-glazed heat, bushes were dried up and looked without hope of survival. The sand roads were powder dry and the air stifling hot with no movement. Big white thunderhead clouds stood suspended motionless in the pale blue sky. And yet on that day she must go to Banning.

There was but one pair of wheel tracks in the deep sand from Garnet to the Whitewater Crossing, and no bridge either. Travelers for Indio and beyond crossed the wash from Garnet to Palm Springs and proceeded down that side.

As Mrs. Woods drove her car slowly round the Whitewater point, she came to an auto badly stalled in the one-track road headed into the desert. She stopped her car and got out to talk with the two men who were resting in the scant shade of their auto. In those days of only one-track sand roads, it was the custom to always stop and talk the situation over, because in such cases one car had to be taken out of the road tracks to let the other go by, then everyone had to help get the sidetracked car back into the road again. This task might take from a half-hour to as much as two hours, depending on [the] size of [the] cars involved and other factors.

The two men were from the city and exhausted by their efforts to get their car out of the sand hole they had dug by spinning rear wheels, and were at a loss to know what to do. They said they had been there over three hours and no one had come by, and that everything they did just made the car sink deeper down, and that "this was a gosh-awful country anyway."

Mrs. Woods had been surveying the situation and figuring out a solution. Now it just happened that the auto [from the city] was buried in the sand quite near the crossing, and there was a small stream of water running in the channel, so she said to the men, "You two lads can carry water from the stream and put it in these sandy road ruts, and enough water will make traveling possible again." So the men happily carried water for quite some time, and finally both cars left the bad spot and Mrs. Woods reached Banning, and not too late. These men had been working and cussing the desert for over three hours and never thought about using the nearby supply of water!

[Article 112: September 3, 1953]

This brings up another stalled auto story. Miss Hilda Gray, who was one of the very first homesteaders here, came down on a visit some years ago. She was alone and driving a coupe. It was after dark, and she attempted the short-cut road round the east end of

Miracle Hill, which is exceedingly soft. Her car stalled and settled down in the sand like a setting hen on a nest.

Now Miss Gray is not a young woman, neither is she strong or husky, but alone in darkness she got that car out, because she knows the desert and has courage. There was no shovel, but she had a frying pan and tin pie plate. With these two implements, she got down on her knees and shoveled the sand away from in front of the wheels, then pulled small brush, filling the holes and some of the sand ruts ahead of the car to give the wheels some traction. Thus by careful driving she was able to move her auto to safer ground. And then she went back and repaired the roadway so that no one else would get bogged down in the same place. This would even have been quite a feat for a man.

Miss Hilda Gray was one of the limited few women who homesteaded all alone on this desert in the very early days. Even for a man the experience was quite rugged, but for a woman the many problems were multiplied.

Of necessity one of the first things every day was the procuring of water. Miss Gray surmounted this task by having a small burro and going each morning to the waterhole at Two Bunch Palms. There she filled cans or canteens, which were hung on the burro's pack saddle and securely tied. Then they both trudged back through soft sand to the small wooden cabin out in the desert on her claim. On such a trip she often killed sidewinder rattlesnakes, not as large as diamondbacks, but just as poisonous. . . .

[Article 114: September 17, 1953]

Hilda Gray was well-known and loved by many people in the village, because she was one of the very few pioneers who came in here to take up government land in 1912 and 1913. Her homestead claim was about a half-mile out on the desert, just south of Two Bunch Palms. . . .

Hilda Gray was reared on a cattle ranch in West Texas, and her father early taught her to ride cow ponies and to be an expert shot with a revolver and other guns as well. She grew up being familiar with horses, rattlesnakes, camping, and campfire cooking. As time went on she received a very good education, some college years, and also musical instruction. Before she was 20, it came to pass that Hilda was a schoolteacher in a one-room school, instructing the mixed-aged children, from little tots to nearly grown cowboys.

When she came to California, her work was that of stenographer for a prominent lawyer. She was very efficient and liked the work, but chafed under city living conditions. She loved the out-of-doors. So when opportunity offered, she took off four years from her city life and homesteaded 160 acres of land on this desert.

The desert that far back was a lonesome and rough sort of place for a woman to be living alone. Hilda's dry sense of humor and intelligent handling of her problem of self-protection is illustrated by the following incident.

In a casual way one day, down at the railroad station at Garnet, when a mixed troupe of men were waiting for the train, she suggested a shooting contest. Small five-cent tin milk cans were placed on a pile of railroad ties, and then everyone took turns to see who was the best shot. Dutch Frank, Old Man Coolidge, Jack Riley, a few more from this desert and some more living over the mountains in the Morongos all tried at the tiny cans. To carry a revolver in those days was not uncommon, so there were several guns in the group. But Miss Gray beat them all. The word soon got around this country that she was an expert shot, so she never was troubled by unwanted romance-seekers in her lone home on the desert. . . .

[Article 116: October 1, 1953]

Bob Belt was one of the first carpenters to take up a home in this desert and built cabins for several early homesteaders. His claim was at Seven Palms. The artesian well there was the first drilled well of that type completed in pioneer days. This was known as "Belt's Well." He was a cattleman as well as a part-time carpenter. To the pond made by run-off water from the flowing well came, at intervals, all the many head of cattle then roaming over the desert. Loose burros could be found near the water often. Many rabbits and other specimens of desert life made tracks in the wet sand. Clouds of wild doves and other birds winged their way to this very welcome water home, and in season came ducks during their migration flights.

Bob Belt was young, attractive-looking, and good-natured. He could expertly roll Bull Durham cigarettes and light them with one match, even in a wind. Tall and slim, he was a typical cowboy type, always wore a clean blue shirt, western hat, high-heeled boots, spurs, brown leather chaps, had a good saddle, and rode well on young, showy horses. He was also deputy sheriff for this district. One time a long while ago, he was called upon to lead a posse of men to capture a desperado who had fled into the rocky country out on the Mojave Desert. In this chase Bob Belt unfortunately was shot and killed by the hunted man from ambush.

Soon after this, two other carpenters came in and took up widely separated homesteads. Bill Anderson had the land above the Coffee Foundation Bathhouse, which was one of the most northerly ones, and Mussen took as his claim one of the most southerly pieces down below Seven Palms.

There was a rivalry between the two men. On the Mussen place the sand was very soft and would blow into clouds of dust in windstorms. The view of the mountains was not so good, Bill said. But the water there was very shallow and easy to get. Mussen boasted his 160 acres had more water than any other claim, and rightly so.

[Article 117: October 8, 1953]

Anderson's land was rocky and hard, so Bill proclaimed to the world that he never had any dust storms and called attention to his superior view of the mountains. He made no bones about being able to look down upon the Mussen location far to the south. However, Bill Anderson had no water at that time and of necessity had to haul every drop he used several miles, which openly pleased Mussen. Bill balanced this handicap by stating to all who would listen that he had 320 acres, owing to peculiar quirks in the law which the rest of us could not fulfill, so we only had 160 acres each.

Then in addition to these points of irritation, both men were carpenters, and the only ones here at the time. All the rest of us pounded nails and put up cabins, but when either of these two men appeared, we retreated to the sidelines and let them plan the work at hand. But sometimes their rivalry as carpenters appeared on the surface as well as in land matters. Also, it just happened that each man had a small tractor, the first ones ever to be brought into this desert. So you will understand the background for this conversation.

One day Anderson and Mussen, together with a few other local men, were working on a job together. After an interval of silence, Mussen growled at Anderson, "Bill, that tractor of yours is no darn good. You need more than 160 acres to turn it on," and there were laughs in the gang, because Bill's tractor had something wrong with its steering apparatus, and it was very difficult to turn it any direction.

Bill snapped back, "Perhaps that is true, but I have got full 320 acres to use when necessary." Then to get a dig in at his rival, he added, "Mussen, that tractor of yours is worthless. Just see how deep it digs in the soil. Throw it away and get a couple of burros." The men all laughed at this sally. Mussen thought that one over, then exploded with this retort: "Well, what if it does dig too deep, I own that land all the way down to China, don't I?"

[Article 118: October 15, 1953]

The moon has many aspects, some good and some bad. It affects tides, plants, animals, and many people in different ways. The word "lunatic" is derived from the old word "luna," meaning moon.

Its most unpleasant effect to me is the blackness of shadows cast by the moon. Sun shadows have warmth and subdued color, as all artists know, but moon shadows are black.

In the year 1900, that is 53 years ago, I was very far north in Alaska, nearly to the Arctic Circle. To sell newspapers, and for various reasons, I often walked 10, 20, even 30 miles from one place where there was a fire and men, to another place of warmth. This was so far north that daylight was only a matter of two hours, then night closed in again. So it was the custom to travel during the moonlight periods.

All that winter I stayed in the fringe gold camps of the region or lived with Eskimos at times. The whole ocean was frozen solid from Alaska to Siberia. The ice and all land surfaces were covered with a thick blanket of gleaming white snow. No trees existed to break this terrific expanse of unbroken white.

Into this seemingly never-ending silent space I walked many, many miles in the semi-darkness of starlight. Temperatures were 40 to 60 below zero. If the moon was in the sky, visibility was good, but the moon caused my body to cast a deep black shadow on the scintillating snow. Sometimes this shadow appeared on the right and sometimes on the left. It walked when I did, stopped when I paused to rest. It gave me a very eerie feeling to always have this shadow close to me and imitating all that I did. Sometimes, of course, it followed. . . . Sometimes it preceded me on my endless lonely walks.

[Article 119: October 22, 1953]

There were no birds, no lights, not a sound except crunching snow. Nothing to see except that black shadow, always there in silence. Just me and the shadow! I often wished that I could whistle, but had never learned. The situation was very spooky at best.

Then as I approached some small Eskimo habitations, there would be the dogs! The Eskimo dog is not the tail-wagging, friendly dog you are familiar with. The Eskimo dog has wolf ancestry and is suspicious, snarling, and vicious by nature. Being partly wolf, it is never entirely subdued and distrusts all strangers. I carried a stout staff to protect myself. Even then I had some close calls to serious injury from these wolf dogs. They would hear my approach and run out in packs of five to 20 animals to contest my further advance to Eskimo camps. Each dog cast a shadow, which made them look twice as many.

In 1913 I was on this desert, 40 years ago. The scene changed, but not the shadows cast by the moon. My moonlight walks here were never over 16 to 20 miles at night. However, the moon and its shadows were even more of a disturbing factor on the desert.

To glance behind and see this black shadow following closely or traveling along one side or the other was disconcerting enough. But with the moon behind, thus throwing the deep black shadow in front, it was often the cause of real complications. Owing to the heavy, obscuring shadow preceding one, it was impossible to see any animal holes, . . . stepping into . . . which caused loss of balance and sometimes a sprawl upon the ground amid thorny brush. Cactus was blacked out until too late to escape painful jabs. And sometimes that shadow covered up rattlesnakes until the last moment to observe them properly.

[Article 120: October 29, 1953]

It seemed to me that more than half my effort in walking through the deep sand was caused by pushing that black counterpart of myself over the desert! When a boy, I was impressed by some realistic sermons in which the devil was described in detail as being a real person who followed people about in the world only to cause them trouble. And so this shadow on the desert in moonlight seemed to be a real devil who came to plague me, because I was walking all alone in 100,000 acres of sand and cactus.

No birds, no lights, no trees, no trail. The two or three cabin lights in this desert always went out after nine p.m. The then less than 15 houses in Palm Springs showed not a single light. [The town was] too far away, and no electricity [was] there then. Only once or twice of a night would a train come down the hill from Banning with its engine headlight shining a few moments on one stretch of track, and once more complete darkness.

If a diamondback or a sidewinder rattled, I would stop and maneuver my shadow to see where the snake might be, to kill it. Then all would be silent once more, but the shadow took up the march with me whenever I started out again on my journey.

If you want a new thrill, go to some desert where there are no houses, no lights, no road, and take off alone into the brush. Walk all night with your shadow in the moonlight, through cactus, thorny vegetation, and where rattlesnakes wait patiently to greet strangers! And I will bet that you get a chill up your back before dawn.

[Article 121: November 5, 1953]

We all use and value the aid to safe driving afforded by that white line down the center of the pavement. But few have been told of its origin, which happened in this fashion under desert conditions. Many years ago there was a widowed mother living two miles out in the open desert north of Indio. Her only transportation was one of the old, time-honored Model T Fords. This was equipped with small three-inch tires, which were not too good in sand.

At that time and on the route she traveled, there was one wheel track leaving Indio on the right of the road, and one wheel track on the left entering town. Both were very sandy and soft, [with] chuckholes close together. Autos were supposed to keep in the wheel tracks on their proper side, but in hope of finding better tracks, they criss-crossed from side to side until the road was a labyrinth of chuckholes. Sometimes they drove out into the desert searching for harder ground. At night, and with the old inadequate Ford lights that dimmed when the speed of the car slackened, this road became very difficult indeed. Many an unfortunate driver had his car stalled until daylight, and then could go in search of a man with a team of horses to drag the car out.

Therefore to lessen the hazards of the trip somewhat, this lady prepared a bundle of sticks, and to the top of each one she tied a piece of white rag. These stakes, with white rags fluttering, she drove into the center of the road at proper intervals from her homestead to Indio. This line of rag-topped sticks made it easier to drive in the dark and was even some help in daytime. Her idea was very practical. The plan spread as others found it helpful to desert driving. And it was eventually developed further into the white line in the center of paved highways now so familiar to us all.

[Article 122: November 12, 1953]

[Letter to Louis Sobol, originally printed in his "New York Cavalcade" column:]

Silent Sam is a five-foot red racer who is not poisonous, but will bite if handled. He moved in here about three years ago and feels in full charge of the yard around my cabin. His mate, Silent Susie, is not so forward and ranges where the brush begins. She is a shy dame, and if she loves Sam, she certainly doesn't appear too demonstrative about it. Sam suns himself on the steps during cold days.

Very active during the warm weather, Sam hibernates during the other months. Once last winter I accidentally dug into where he slept. He stuck his head out of the hole, looked up in sleepy fashion, recognized that it was I, or something like that, because he seemed to shrink back slowly and when I covered him up he went to sleep again for three months.

I have to be mighty careful about the trees I have planted here, because they don't take too kindly to the desert, so under each of them I bury empty five-gallon square oil cans. I punch holes in the bottom to let the water out and cut an extra hole in the top to put water in. This waters the tree slowly and lessens evaporation.

Yesterday it was hot and Sam, hunting a cool place to take a siesta, went down through the top of one of the cans and coiled his five-foot body for a nice nap, unbeknown to me. At noon the tree looked wilted, so I took a bucket of water and poured it into the oil can. No sooner did the water hit bottom than Silent Sam put his head out to investigate the situation. As the water continued to go in, Sam continued to come out. I watched him to see what he would do next. The tree was small and bushy. So I stooped over, pouring water, my head low and close into the leaves.

Before the water was all out of the bucket, Silent Sam was all out of the can. He climbed quickly into the tree and got his head about a foot away from mine. Well now, my Eastern Friend, you must believe me, he looked me right in the eye, opened his mouth, showed his black forked tongue like he was licking water from his upper lip. Now I can tell you he looked mad clear through, and that tongue clicking against his upper lip made him look madder, like someone who ought to be stamping about and yelling his fool head off.

Yes, sir, Silent Sam's manner sure was very reproachful.

Yours from out in the desert where water to drink is carried in a canteen, Cabot Yerxa

[Article 123: November 19, 1953]

To the desert over the years have come many different men connected in some way with the show business, starting with Bob Carr, Ford Beebe, and Walter Woods, who at the time were all working with Mack Sennett, famous producer in the early silent days. E. O. Gurney, still very prominent in Hollywood movie circles, Lucienne Hubbard, both [a] writer of note and [a] producer, Warner Baxter, who was beloved by large audiences everywhere, Alexander Conion, better known as "Alexander the Great," who had toured the world with his own shows, George MacAnnon, with a past that reaches from the legitimate stage in New York City to Hollywood, Ed Cartwright, that developed a series of religious plays here and is showing them in other parts of the country, Jerry Storm, the famous director, whose name was in top places during the days of silent black-and-white pictures, Julius Nathanson, who has owned and operated theatres in large cities and done much acting himself, Charlie Tipton, famous as top bucking horse rider with the Buffalo Bill's Wild West Shows, [who] traveled all over the U.S. and half of Europe before he came to this desert to take life more easily. . . .

Well, a very long time ago in homestead days, two men of the show world came down to this desert to rest and bask in desert sunshine. They could have gone to Palm Springs, where accommodations were much more comfortable, but they chose rather to occupy a small wooden cabin out on the desert near what is now D.H.S. They were not campers by nature, but looked upon batching in the desert as a new and novel experience.

[Article 124: November 26, 1953]

A homesteader brought them a barrel of water in a wagon drawn by a team of burros. In the wagon also was a box of simple groceries which had arrived by Southern Pacific R.R. freight at Garnet.

We will call one man Tom and the other Jim. Of course these were not their real names, but will do for the purpose of the story. It was the winter season. They gathered dry wood from the desert round about and each evening enjoyed a cheerful blaze in the open fireplace after dark. They had books and magazines, so were quite comfortable in the one-room small wooden cabin. This was in an isolated location; some mornings they could see a curl of smoke on a homestead far away--that was all.

Like all men of the theatre, they had each purchased a diamond of excellent quality during prosperous periods, each of which cost quite a lot of folded money. Diamonds are always a basis for loans or can be converted into cash quickly if needed. Also they add to prestige and give a touch of affluence.

Tom's diamond was set in a heavy gold ring which he was careful to remove when he washed his hands or when it was his turn to clean the dishes. This was always placed very carefully on the mantel shelf over the fireplace when not on his hand.

Jim's diamond was mounted beautifully on a large-fold stickpin, which he wore at a jaunty angle in his necktie. But if no tie, it was thrust sometimes in his shirtfront, where it gleamed and sparkled as good diamonds do. At night Jim methodically placed this pin alongside his watch, also on the mantel over the fireplace. As an extra precaution for safety, the pinpoint was thrust through several links in the watch chain.

Each man had a folding cot to sleep upon. One was inside the cabin and the other just outside at the door, on a small ramshackle platform of loose boards, which served as a porch. In addition to the cot, this porch would hold two chairs, from which there was a splendid view of the desert and mountains. Here they often sat in late afternoon to watch the sun's decline. They reminisced of the stage, the many cities they had visited, and the world in general. They were quite contented, and life was tranquil.

However, one morning Jim's stickpin was missing from its place on the mantel, and he asked Tom about it. But Tom disclaimed any knowledge of the missing pin. Breakfast was eaten in silence.

[Article 125: December 5, 1953]

At the noon meal Jim said, "Look here, Tom, I want my diamond pin. This practical joke has gone far enough. That pin cost me plenty of dough, and I want it back."

Again Tom repeated that he knew nothing of the pin. Jim mulled over the situation during the rest of the day and at intervals during the night. At the following breakfast, he blurted out, "Tom, there are just two of us in this cabin. My diamond pin is gone, and I want it returned. This thing has proceeded too far to be funny."

The pancakes were unwatched and burned up. The coffee boiled over into the fire, which sputtered and then went out as the men quarreled. Tom, red in face and angry, left the table and walked to the mantel for his ring, preparatory to taking a stroll in the desert to cool off. But his ring was gone.

In a rage he turned to Jim and exploded in a torrent of words. "I did not take your pin, but you have taken my ring, because the ring is gone, and I left it right here last night.

Tom continued, "First you accuse me of taking your pin, and now you have stolen my ring. I am not going to live in the same cabin with a guy like you. But before I leave, I want you to hand over my ring."

Jim countered in high tones, "Me take your ring--not at all. No one has been in this cabin but you and me. Neighbors are miles away. I want my diamond stickpin now. You are not going to get away with that."

By now both men were scuffling on the loose board porch. Blows were exchanged, the chairs tipped over, one man was thrown down, disarranging the old boards. Thus was disclosed under the floor a packrat's nest. This consisted of miscellaneous bits of brush, greasewood stems, leaves, cactus, some small stones, and pieces of paper.

Glad of the distraction, one man said, "Let's clean out this rat's nest, and perhaps they will stay elsewhere." With a shovel he was moving the trash away, when he let out a shout of excitement, for there were both the diamond pin and diamond ring, close together, shining in the sunlight among all the small litter. Desert packrats had carried the two pieces of diamond jewelry to this nest. . . .

[ARTICLE 126: DECEMBER 17, 1953]

Over the years I have examined large numbers of packrats' nests in or around buildings and out in the desert. . . . I have found in their nests babies' shoes, nails, screws, bottle tops, small pairs of scissors, thimbles, spools of thread, spoons, needles, forks, small knives, chalk, pencils, cloth, paper, buttons, playing cards, broken glass or pottery, clothespins, curtain rings, hairpins, pieces of wood, leaves, roots, twine, corks, cactus spines, and many small stones.

In one nest were 17 nails of 20-penny size, which is large and must have been difficult for them to carry. Another rat carried off 24 cakes of dry yeast and had them placed evenly around a circular nest. Near a building was another nest with 15 or more pieces of quarter-round, one inch in diameter and from 10 to 16 inches long. Still another rat got into a homesteader's cabin, chewed a hole into the clothes closet, and cut off every single button from all clothing, which buttons were later found in an extensive nest. . . .

Out on the desert these nests are often found to be three feet across, made up of sticks, stones, pieces of wood, and cactus thorns by the hundreds. Usually they are formed in roots of brush, but in some instances they dig holes into banks and live underground. The nests are kept clean; all bones and refuse are taken outside. The spot where the animal sleeps is filled with fine ravelings of any material at hand. The nest has several entrances, so that if chased it can enter or leave in a hurry. The collection of cactus thorns discourages snakes, coyotes, and other enemies.

[ARTICLE 127: DECEMBER 31, 1953]

One year here at the Pueblo, I secured a lot of prune plums in Banning. The desert sunshine dried them into prunes like you buy in a store. These were then stored in the top of the building, but the clever pack rats found out about them in some way.

They climbed up on the outside of the wall to the top of the first floor, walked 75 feet on that roof, then climbed to the top of the second floor roof, crossed that, then up the walls again to the top of the third floor roof. They crossed this roof, then down the wall, still on the outside, and entered the second floor room through a small hole they made, into the room where the dried prunes were stored. The busy rats then had to retrace their trail by the same route to a large nest some distance away.

We desert people get to be very observant. One day I found a prune in the sand, where no prune ought to be, and by investigation found this all out, but every prune was gone. 120 pounds with 60 prunes to the pound makes 7,200 prunes, and the rats had to make 7,200 trips to complete this task. So you know they have patience, time, and persistence.

Out in the desert these little animals have many enemies. Hawks, owls, and other birds watch from the sky. Coyotes, skunks, foxes, and badgers are ready to snap them up on sight. Rattlesnakes and other varieties hunt them slowly and in silence. Yet amid all these dangers, rats must hunt food, build nests, and carry on their life. Of all locations, they like best to be located in a patch of thick cactus, preferably cholla or jumping cactus. Here they construct crooked paths which make it very difficult for coyotes and other animals, even snakes, to approach the nest. But of course owls work best during the night-time, so the rat in the open is just one jump ahead all the time. Perhaps this is why it is so anxious and ready to move into buildings that we humans make on the desert.

[Article 128: January 7, 1954]

[Louis Sobol, in his "New York Cavalcade" column, is quoted:] "This has not been the happiest world lately. Bitter cold has brought hardships to millions of people all over the world. Finns are fighting desperate battles for their very existence. Germany, England and France are tightening their belts, preparing for a war to the finish. Horrible tales come over the wires of atrocities against minority races. In the midst of turmoil and tragedy of the world arrives a letter which concerns itself with nothing more important than the struggle of one man to build himself a home. It is so full of peace and cheer that I devote most of this column to it--and I shall be the first to read it again, because it takes my mind off more pressing problems.

"The writer is my friend, the artist hermit Cabot Yerxa, of the desert land of Garnet, California. Again he invites me to pay him a visit. 'The day you come to my place,' he writes, 'we will go up to the Eagle's Nest Cabin and talk by the fire. This cabin is dug into the hill back of Two Bunch Palms. It is near the top, about 200 feet above the desert. I built it many years ago so as to be able to live there and enjoy the wide view of the desert floor and the ever-changing colors in the mountains.

"'The idea was good, but its fulfillment required much labor. I had a burro called Merry Xmas. The burro carried one sack of cement on its back, and I carried another sack on my back. There were no roads then, and the burro and I made one trip a day to the Garnet R.R. Station, seven miles each way, 14 miles. A sack of cement weighed 100 pounds.

"'When the cement was all at the base of the hill, two sacks for each day's walk, then came some necessary lumber and the roof materials. Merry Xmas and I carried all these things uphill to the top. Then patiently we carried sand, rocks, water, and tools. The burro was then turned loose to graze, and I alone started construction single-handed. Of course Merry Xmas carried additional sand and water as needed, but it could not help much in the building.

"'Very slowly--I can't begin to tell you how slowly--after months of work the cabin was completed. The walls were of stone 12 to 20 inches thick, more than seven feet high, and the building is 10 x 20 feet. In one end is a fireplace; three windows are in the north to give ample light for painting. And a door to the east lets in the first rays of the sun to reach the desert."

"'Merry Xmas was no ordinary burro. It had superior intelligence and seemed to give encouragement to the work. It would range off a mile or two for grass or vegetation to eat. Then [it] would return and stand around to watch me as I labored with rocks and cement. At meal time it drank half my coffee and ate half my bacon. The pancakes were always counted out evenly, share and share alike, because I always treated it like a man.

"'When at last I moved in and settled down to live, the burro selected the spot exactly in front of the door as the proper place for it to sleep, although there were 15,000 acres round about without any fences. So to get in or out of the door, I had to climb over the burro. But the cabin represented home and food to both of us and we were both happy.

"'Merry Xmas never learned to smoke, but it ate one-half of my tobacco and would beg for cigar and cigarette stubs from strangers. It also learned to drink water from a bottle, because I put sugar in the water. Adios, Amigo, Cabot Yerxa'"

[Article 129: January 14, 1954]

[Letter to Louis Sobol, originally printed in his "New York Cavalcade" column, concludes in article 130:]

"We have recently had our presidential primary election out here in the desert, just like in more settled parts of these United States. But did you ever consider how different this might be from usual conditions in New York City, for instance? The voting place was just a cabin somewhat centrally located, but we who served on the election board traveled 14 miles. I walked 14 miles, but Merry Xmas, my burro, carried the lunch to serve and canteens of water. (In those days all men carried their own drinking water.) Our voting precinct lies out in the desert and comprises roughly 350 square miles of territory, more or less, and mostly more."

[Article 130: January 21, 1954]

"Scattered over this country live some 85 voters, and a large proportion of them come under the classification of miners, homesteaders, cattlemen, Indians, and pioneers in general. . . . 35 people came to vote, and I knew them all but one, so I inquired where he lived and found out it was in the far end of Lost Horse Valley. This man had driven a car for 67 miles over very poor roads from his cabin to the voting place. We had some Indian voters, too. They used to all come on horses, but this time they, too, mostly came in cars. . . .

"Our precinct is rather good size, but other things are also on a generous scale. Joshua Tree National Park, a half mile from my cabin, contains one million acres. And our two deputy sheriffs have 1400 square miles of desert over which to maintain law and order. . . .

"Yours with a view of 35 miles and nothing in the way, Cabot Yerxa"

[Article 131: January 28, 1954]

Let us pause for a moment and consider the greasewood, which is all round us in the desert. Its other name is creosote bush.

This familiar shrub averages from three to five feet in height and can well be a symbol of the great Southwest of this country. It grows far up the sides of the mountains and down into the Salton Sink area much below sea level. It welcomes rain and moisture, yet can exist in the driest desert regions where rain seldom falls. It resists strong, ever-blowing winds and heat of burning sunshine, maintaining a green appearance in strong contrast to its often gray surroundings. It has, as you notice, very small leaves in pairs, which face each other. In damp weather they spread open to absorb moisture, but in dry times they close together like a book to conserve moisture and prevent evaporation.

The welcome shade of greasewood is a haven for the few desert birds at noonday and offers a resting place for lizards and snakes. In its branches birds nest, and in the tangled underbrush desert rats make their homes and drag in many cactus thorns to discourage molestation by coyotes, foxes, and other desert marauders bent on their capture and destruction.

Homesteaders and miners gather greasewood roots for their cabin stoves, which is often the only material to burn in very many miles.

In periods of extreme dryness, jack rabbits will cut the ends off of new greasewood branches during the night hours and stand there several minutes to get the slight moisture of the wood thus exposed. During this time their ears are very erect and alert to detect any danger.

In the brawling days of the old western frontier, lonely hunted men fleeing from the law traversed desert regions by foot or horseback. They crouched by small fires of greasewood to do their simple cooking or to allay the chill of night in windswept open country.

Indians have long made healing medicines from its leaves and roots, thereby curing many ills which made a drugstore necessary to a white man.

And, at last, many adventurers and pioneers--men, women, and children, saints and sinners, both red and white--have had but a few greasewood branches on their hastily dug, crude graves, because it was the only green vegetation at hand in the far-flung southwestern lands of rocky soils and gray shifting sands.

So greasewood is a living symbol of the desert country that we all love.

[Article 132: February 4, 1954]

[The *Desert Sentinel* editor notes: "Back in 1914 Cabot Yerxa wrote:"]

Yesterday it rained for the first time in nine or 10 months, and the desert was drenched. Just a steady, slow rain without any blustering wind. The sandy soil absorbed the welcome moisture completely and none ran off. The greasewood bushes opened their leaves, which are folded close together for protection during dry weather, and the damp air was full of their clean, haunting fragrance. All the sparse desert growth of bunch grass and small plants, usually quite brittle, were as limp and soft as though made of pretty colored rubber.

The few birds and small animal life scurried for their own type of shelter. A half-dozen song sparrows cheeped at me from under a palm ramada. The lone shrike sat bedraggled on his usual perch in the rustic building we call Indian Camp. Lizards got under boards or rocks and shivered the time away as best they could. The eagle took to the high mountain crags and the security of big timber. The owls, no doubt, went to the protection of the Two Bunch Palms, as I have seen them do in other spells of bad weather. Rabbits . . . hunt a depression under roots or [sit in] silent discomfort about half below the surface of the ground, but hunched up on their strong hind legs ready to spring into immediate action at any unknown sound approaching. The coyotes slink around with wet feet, fur dripping with rain and drooping tails, as ever on that ceaseless hunt for food. Coyotes are always out in all weather, because they are endlessly lean and hungry.

Overheard one solitary single goose flies strongly with head and neck outstretched through the murky rain. He was headed as straight for Mexico and warmer weather, as an aviator could with a compass. The goose was flying low and honking very mournfully at regular and frequent intervals. I heard him minutes before he appeared in the mist, and I heard him minutes after he was lost to vision. His heart was troubled because of separation from his flock. I might have shot him, but I did not try.

What took me out into the rain? My rattlesnakes. You see, so much rain made their quarters in the snake pit a little uncomfortable. So I put on plenty of storm clothes and went outdoors in the weather to make the rattlers a better home. Into a wooden box of good size I put 10 inches of fine, dry, soft sand, which was in the workshop waiting to mix up for a plaster job. Then I constructed a heavy wooden lid, covering this with tin. When all was ready, the box and sand were moved down into the snake pit. I then lifted the rattlesnakes carefully and placed them in the nice dry sand, covering them with a piece of warm quilt from the cabin, then replacing the water-tight lid. The snakes seemed very happy over the change into their new home, and when I returned to the fireside in the cabin, I was happy, too.

[ARTICLE 133: FEBRUARY 11, 1954]

. . . When you walk into the desert, do so quietly and slowly. Then you will see much of small life about you that you would not ordinarily have seen. Sit down sometimes and be very quiet. Before long, desert life will resume their natural activities. As long as you are moving, many sharp eyes from hidden spots are watching you carefully. But when you are still, fear is allayed.

A pair of field glasses is well worth carrying and will disclose the details of much that you can observe round you. Buy a small magnifying glass and always carry this with you on your walks. With the help of this glass, a tiny insect or small rock will become worthy of study. The smallest of flowers, when enlarged, show colors and patterns of such richness and intricacy that it seems impossible that they exist in anything so tiny. Little bugs and insects appear as important as very much larger things. . . . People who ride in automobiles on a cushion and never get out to walk, never suspect and do not know what is in the living desert. Neither do they have proper appreciation of desert vegetation nor enjoy the majesty of mountains, because they sit on a cushion and skim over the sands with too much ease. . . .

Only to the person who walks are all desert secrets revealed. . . .

[ARTICLE 134: FEBRUARY 18, 1954]

[The *Desert Sentinel* editor notes: "Cabot Yerxa tells of what one sees on a walk in the desert:"]

The graceful ant-eating lizards will continue their hurried search for more ants, because nothing else do they eat, and many must be found during the day. Small lizards that eat only flies sit very quietly and motionless, but watching sharply for a fly to light in their range, whereupon they spring to action, and never miss the capture. This friendly little fellow will climb about your clothing, if given opportunity, and wait for flies to come near. There are several other lizards very entertaining. Some can climb sand banks by use of webbed feet; others have claws and can quickly scale trees. One or two have bright colors and make quite a gay display against a gray sand background. One fellow can run on its hind legs while keeping its front legs out of use, like a man with his hands in his pockets. Then there is the villain! One lizard is a cannibal and will eat other lizards. The largest one here is the desert iguana, nearly white with many brownish spots. It is vegetarian and eats only green leaves, grass or flowers.

But to me the far most interesting one is the chuckwalla. It is very large for a lizard and has some intelligence. By much time I trained some to play dead, to [hold their] front paws up while sitting down, say their prayers, . . . climb up my clothing, nibble my ears, sit on my hat, . . . also to eat out [of my hand,] come when I called them, to jump into my outstretched hand from a rock shelf, etc. They have a loose skin which they can inflate at will and deflate as they desire. They run between rocks when chased and inflate their skins; thus they cannot be pulled out. When danger is gone, they deflate and back out the way they went in. That takes intelligence. They come with scaly skins of different colors, from pure white in large areas to straight black. Some are spotted or tan, sometimes brown, and red appears occasionally in patches. These are found in the desert mountains, never in low ground. They will sit for an hour on a rock in the sun, sometimes asleep. But at other times [they are] just as alert as a sentry on duty. They are surprisingly quick in movement for such a clumsy-looking creature. . . .

[Article 137: March 11, 1954]

Very recently the last of the Old Ranch House at the east end of Miracle Hill has been demolished. The main building was burned in January of 1952 while being occupied by General Alexander and his 20-some wolf hounds. Thus another landmark of early days disappears.

I came to this desert in 1913 and just had time to prove up on my homestead of 160 acres and then volunteer into the Army for World War I. It just so happened that I was placed under the then-Lt. Col. Dwight D. Eisenhower, serving as his mess-sergeant and later as the adjutant's chief clerk.

Out of the Army in 1919, I was postmaster and had a general store at a crossroads location near Blythe on the Colorado River. Here were spent six years of life under very Western, pioneer-type conditions, amid cowboys, ranchers, Indians, and miners from the mountains nearby. Daily life was often interspersed by shootings, hold-ups, opium smugglers, Chinese and Mexican border jumpers, moonshiners' activities, revenue officers, and F.B.I. investigators. These six years will make another book of campfire tales.

In January of 1925 I left Blythe and the Colorado Desert. I drove back into this familiar desert with my bedroll in a stripped-down Model T Ford auto. This was painted a bright yellow, and on each side of the hood over the engine was painted a scorpion nearly three feet long. The Mexicans all through the Blythe Desert always called me "El Alacran," which is "the scorpion" in Spanish. This Ford I still have.

Returning to my original homestead location, which included Miracle Hill, close to Desert Hot Springs as it now has become, I dug a hole 8 x 10 feet and four deep in a clay bank near that well. Several railroad ties that cost only 20 cents each were split into as many pieces as possible. With these a framework was constructed and partly covered with palm fronds from the native desert palms at the Two Bunch Palms oasis. This provided necessary shade, but was not any protection when it rained.

[ARTICLE 138: MARCH 18, 1954]

The crude shelter I fashioned at Miracle Hill had no door, no windows, no floor, no stove, no table, no chairs, and was open to the free entry of all desert wildlife. Thus came into my dugout rattlesnakes, as well as half-a-dozen other kinds of snakes, all varieties of lizard, many rats and mice, tarantulas, scorpions, centipedes, and all other small things living in the open desert. They crawled about my blankets and food during the day or at night. I looked my blankets over before getting in and shook my shoes out in the morning. In such cases it is well to turn your sox inside out before putting them on. Scorpions can be anywhere, and snakes like to crawl into blankets.

 I slept on the ground, cooked food on the ground, and ate my meals sitting on the ground. Living this way, in a few months you will learn that much of civilization which causes complications and expense is not necessary for health or happiness.

 I lived in this fashion until May of 1925, when I left for a year of walking adventure and a life in art schools of London and Paris. This also included travel in Europe, Central America, a trip through the Panama Canal, and other places.

 Thus it was during the spring of 1925 that I built the Old Homestead buildings just recently destroyed. I lived alone and worked alone at construction. . . .

[ARTICLE 139: MARCH 25, 1954]

On my homestead there was the original cabin and a small barn for burros, with a chicken shelter. These I tore down and moved the lumber with the small Ford auto to the new house location at the east end of Miracle Hill. All nails were carefully saved, patiently straightened out and used again, because money was scarce.

 The cement foundation for the new building was 25 feet square and later enlarged by an addition. With the auto I slowly gathered in much sand from the desert for cement work, many rocks of all sizes, and filled some barrels with water which had to be pulled out of the well with a bucket tied to a rope. All cement mortar was mixed up by hand in a home-made wooden box and alone. I was up at daylight and carried on work until dark. Often my supper fire was the only light to be seen in all this part of the desert. I was very happy and never lonely—perhaps because I have spent much of my life alone in different parts of the world.

 Birds of many varieties came to sing for me from small bushes near where I worked. Hummingbirds attracted either by the bright colors or the moisture came and examined my wet clothes when they were washed and hung up to dry.

 Many lizards of the several different kinds became accustomed to my presence and were around during daylight hours. Two large, brightly-colored chuckwallas made regular daily inspection tours, in their slow clumsy way, of all lumber and rocks which were piled up ready for use as needed.

 One carnivorous lizard with its dull green, active body, covered by many bright spots, was always on hand at noontime and enjoyed part of my lunch each day. It liked best small bits of meat or bacon scraps. These I tossed to him and quite often he caught them in the air. This one resembles a small baby alligator, [with a] large head, strong neck, and generous mouth with small teeth. Roadrunners strutted about some days with their important-looking movement of head feathers and the so-quickly-waved tails. They always reminded me of some very officious clerk in a store or an old fashioned floor walker, always in evidence when entering important department stores of long ago.

[Article 140: April 1, 1954]

Two Phenapeplas, a variety of flycatchers and always friendly birds, built a nest nearby. In due time small birds appeared, which had to be taught to fly. This is a very trying ordeal to the parent birds and only accomplished after days of loving instruction to the young ones.

Snakes often slithered round about or were found under boards and rocks. They like shade during the middle-day hours. On the real living desert you need never to be lonely, nor to lack things of interest to watch.

Into the new ranch house went not only my own small buildings, but the Bob Carr cabin from its place in the mesquite hills, which I purchased and took down board by board and hauled home. Also the Hilda Gray cabin with its small barn, once used for her two burros and chickens.

With much patience I laboriously completed the foundation walls, toiling long hours alone. Never did any person come by where I was, nor could I see anyone, even at a distance. It was a very wonderful experience to be living and working day after day all alone under a blue sky and in an unspoiled desert. I felt sorry for all those millions who live in cities, surrounded all day long by a press of other people, and who at night lock themselves into small rooms to sleep a few fitful hours, so as to be able to struggle through another day of unnatural living.

This new building of mine was to be a story and a half high, which was quite a project for one man and a hammer. And this brings up a story. There was no ladder. So one day I spent hours getting a fantastic pyramid of boxes and empty barrels together. Carefully I climbed to the top of this insecure pile, meanwhile balancing one end of a ridgepole 25 feet long in one hand, hammer in the other, and my mouth full of nails. The whole thing was like a brainstorm of Rube Goldberg. I was 14 feet up in the air and nothing to hang onto. Just at this time I dropped the hammer, the pyramid collapsed, and everything fell to the floor. It took all of another day to get back up to the same spot 14 feet above the ground again. Had there been one man to help me, it would have been easy.

[Article 141: April 8, 1954]

Very gradually I fashioned the miscellaneous 2 x 4s and odd pieces of lumber into a new building and with much satisfaction . . . There was a patch of welcome shade available for short rest periods, and under which I could eat my lunch of cold beans and pieces of often very tough rabbit.

I drove many more nails than carpenters usually do and made use of strips of tin and galvanized iron, which were nailed securely where they could strengthen the structure against earthquakes. During my years on the desert I had experienced several strong earthquakes, so [I] figured on the next.

Each Sunday I drove the Model T over to what is now Desert Hot Springs. Ford Beebe had his homestead cabin where Addingtons now have the Idle Hour Café. Across the road behind the Babin and Simone location, Walter Woods had hired some of us to plant about two acres of black figs. The little trees stood up bravely against the adverse weather, but the venture was never carried to a conclusion. Some tamarisk trees were also planted at the same time and a few yet remain at that corner.

To this location came on Sunday Jack Riley, Mike Driscoll, Walter Woods, Bill Riley, Ford Beebe, Joe Bonhorn, Bill Anderson, Scott Farris, Frank Houghton, myself, and a few others at times. We exchanged bits of news, if any, reported on the dispatching of rattlesnakes, their size and number of buttons. Newspapers were loaned back and forth, and magazines eagerly examined.

The condition of the fig trees was noted in great detail. Always someone started on the very attractive arithmetic problem concerning fig trees. It went like this. If a man had so many fig trees, and they produced this number of pounds per tree, and were sold for such a price, then the net profit would amount to such a sum. We all had many acres, and all knew that the Indians in Palm Springs actually sold the very first ripe figs in the whole U.S.A., and at a very fancy price. So all of us departed for our lonely cabins out in the desert in very high spirits. This in spite of the fact that not one man present could change a five-dollar bill.

[ARTICLE 142: APRIL 15, 1954]

As time passed Bill Tarbutton, Charles Tipton, R. H. McDonald, Orr Sang, Wilbur McCarger, and a few others came in to add interest to the gathering. For several years this meeting place ran a close second to the post office at Garnet as a source of news. Occasionally Frank DeLong, from T-cross-K Ranch, a cowboy from the Talmage Ranch at Whitewater, Indians from Mission Canyon, or someone from Morongo Valley would ride in on horseback looking for lost and strayed animals, or rumors of their whereabouts.

Bill Anderson was homesteading just north and across the street from the present L.W. Coffee Foundation bath buildings. It was he who planted the trees that are still growing there. One time I helped Bill to plant tamarisk trees on each side of the road down to the present Pueblo market location. We spent many hours watering these and were elated when they put up sprouts and looked healthy. But when we were away one summer, they perished for lack of water.

Well, Bill saw me getting behind on my cabin[-building] program and came over for a couple of weeks to help me out. With him came a large Indian from Palm Springs. I do not remember his name, but what he lacked as a carpenter, he made up by being very strong.

Together we made progress. Much time was lost in hauling water, so Bill one day suggested that we should drill a well--and in the cabin, because he said he did not like to be going for water after dark in a rattlesnake country! Just that day a large red diamondback rattlesnake had crawled in the front door and came to rest under the table.

There was by now a cement floor in the house, so we broke a hole in that and started a well inside the building. We had a posthole digger, and by some inventions of our own we attached lengths of pipe to this. An opening was cut in the roof to allow for a pulley, and also to let the long pipe protrude into outer space.

We were getting along quite satisfactorily with the hole in the ground, until we struck a big rock in the bottom. What to do now? Another hole would not be the solution, because the earth is full of rocks. Therefore, after some discussion, we lit a fuse on one stick of dynamite, dropped it into the hole and dashed outdoors. We ran outside the building to await results, and they came fast. There was a big explosion; mud and water and debris were blown all over the place, together with some shingles off the roof.

After things got quiet again, we resumed operations and eventually found water of 108 degrees temperature. With this bountiful supply, we could all take baths, clean the windows, wash the dog, and throw water on the floor. It was a great day to have water in a well, and the pump handle in the kitchen. No other cabin in the desert could boast of this convenience.

[Article 143: April 22, 1954]

In May of 1925, I nailed boards on the windows and started on a journey that was to take me to art schools in London and Paris, through different countries in Europe and Central America, Cuba, to Panama and the Panama Canal, as well as some other places. I traveled not in comfort, not even as a tourist, but with my 20 pounds of belongings strapped to my back. If weather was good I walked; if too tough, then on trains or buses. I took passage on freight boats, lived with native people where possible, and had many adventures. I wrote travel stories for some magazines and newspapers. The interlude from desert living took about a year.

I carried credentials from three small magazines and four newspapers to show that I was a special writer for them. This saved me entrance money for many visits to the British World's Fair in England and the French World's Fair in Paris, both running that year; also various museums. By much economy I made the whole trip on less than $700. People who have covered that long a journey do not believe that it could be done with so little money. But neither would they have traveled on such a small expense account as I did, nor put up with its hardships.

For instance, I went from Los Angeles to Guatemala in a boat filled with Chinese coolies, direct from China, "bound-out" for three years' work on coffee plantations. We all traveled in the steerage, and I ate with them for many days, as it was a slow boat. Great bowls of rice [were] served at every meal, little else.

In Panama my budget was one dollar per day to cover living expenses for a couple of weeks while waiting for a freight boat loaded with copper to come up from Peru en route to England. It cost 50 cents to sleep under very trying conditions in the native quarter. 10 cents spent for green coconuts was my breakfast, 30 cents bought a meal with some Spanish-speaking natives at noon, 10 cents invested in bananas served as supper. Some days, to vary the monotony of this menu, I would skip breakfast entirely and eat a little better meal at noon for 50 cents. This necessitated going without any supper at all, in order to hold within the one dollar per day set as allowable expense. This sounds rather strenuous, but for many years I had wanted to visit Paris, attend art schools, also to see a bit of Europe and other places. Therefore I was very happy to endure any discomfort.

[Article 144: April 29, 1954]

In Ireland I made my home with a very poor Irish family in order to learn how the lower class lived. Their main meal of the day was fish and small white potatoes, boiled together in a large black iron kettle hung over an open soft coal fire. The food was stirred with the same black iron rod used to break up the lumps of coal. Therefore the concoction was always nearly black in color. There was no fruit, no vegetables, no dessert, but sometimes bread and black tea, with a little jam or cheese.

In England, Scotland, and Wales I walked most of the time. I stayed, in France, on the left bank of the River Seine in Paris, where the real French people live, and all the artists, students, etc. I ate at least one meal, sometimes two, in small cafés, if money stretched that far. Otherwise it was bread and milk with cheese or jam in my room. The room had no heat, but did have one electric light bulb. Water had to be carried up three flights of stairs. There was one window which looked out at a moldy stone wall 300 years old. Do you wonder that I often thought of the desert in California?

On ships, accommodations are rated as first class, second, third, tourist, and "deck." Often I traveled deck, and that was just what it means. Such passengers sleep on the deck, [with] no mattress, no bedding. I have even slept on the deck in the rain. But of course such travel is cheap. Therefore, by this and other economies, I made the trip of nearly a year, paid all transportation and living costs, visited 17 different foreign countries, bought some clothing, attended art schools, all on less than 700 dollars!

Traveling on such a meager expenditure of money is very uncomfortable at times. However, . . . one has many adventures. . . What happened to me in a year would more than fill a book.

[Article 145: May 6, 1954]

Once in Panama I was in a crowd of 2,000 Negroes. Every person was black as far as I could see. Then, right in front of me, I saw a very black woman turn a dusty gray and she collapsed-- either fainted or died. So part of the blackness is blood circulation.

On one ship, smallpox broke out among the steerage passengers. The dead were promptly wrapped in canvas, lashed full length to boards with a heavy weight at the feet, and then dropped into the sea. On one northern boat trip the only chance to bathe was under a shower of salt water pumped right out of the ocean, and there was some ice in the sea. That was an experience of cold and chill.

The Atlantic Ocean looks mighty big and lonely. Yet there is always something to watch--birds, great fish, and sometimes other ships. Once we were in very heavy, thick fog for many hours, the speed cut to less than half. The whistle continuously sounded at very short intervals. The precaution seemed rather unnecessary out in the middle of the Atlantic, yet after a while another distant whistle was heard, and then all at once a ghostly ship loomed up in the fog and we passed in the gloom, not too far from each other.

Leaving a harbor in France just at dark one night, there was a dull greenish light over the bay, making everything look a bit unreal, and the churning propeller brought a human corpse to the surface. This weird thing was caught in the swirling waters, which threw one arm up above the head grotesquely for an instant, and then the body sank again into the muddy water. The hand was the last to disappear, as if clutching life.

I climbed the Eiffel Tower, visited Edinburgh Castle and many others, the Tower of London, [the] British Museum, art galleries, famous parks, etc, and was lost one whole afternoon in the Catacombs under the city of Paris. There, under the city in stone caves and passageways, with water dripping from the ceiling, repose the skeletons of many thousand people. All is in very complete Stygian darkness. The escape into outer air was a relief.

[ARTICLE 146: MAY 13, 1954]

On the island of Jersey, off the French cost, I walked among many time-worn headstones of an ancient graveyard. It was close at the side of a moss- and ivy-covered stone church of great age. On a number of these gravestones was chiseled the name of "Cabot," and often "Chabot," which is the French spelling. These were my ancestors, or at least distantly old relations, because in the year 1050 the King of England gave to a certain knight named Cabot a commission to proceed forthwith to the Island of Jersey, and there to construct a fort and a church in the King's name and for England. And from that day to this the family name has persisted on the island.

Well at last, of course, the trip was over, and my fun and adventures became only memories. However, when finally I again set foot on U.S. soil and saw the American flag of stars and stripes floating in the breeze, it was with pride and gratitude that I realized that this was my flag, my country.

The very first thing I did when I was finally in California was to come down to this desert. I rested in the shade of the palm trees at Two Bunch. I climbed thoughtfully to the top of Miracle Hill, which has been [the] center point of my life since 1913. From this familiar spot I again observed the grandeur of our desert panorama and took long breaths of clean, dry air. Later I made a campfire and cooked bacon and coffee, just like we did in the homestead days. As darkness closed about and the mountains became obscured, I spread my blanket on the sand and enjoyed the solitude.

Only by comparison can be best realized what a very wonderful place this Desert Hot Springs area really is. All the rest of the people can have all the rest of the world if they want to have it, but this desert is, in the last analysis, the best place of all. I was very happy to be home again.

[ARTICLE 147: MAY 20, 1954]

[Letter to Louis Sobol, originally printed in his "New York Cavalcade" column, concludes in article 148:]

This is now a late March morning, and the sun is edging over the Little San Bernardino Mountains, which have been a Maxfield Parish blue since daylight dragged them out of the darkness. Only the tops of San Gorgonio and San Jacinto glisten in the first rays of the sun, and the rest of the mountainsides look old rose in color, and the lower levels of the mountains shade off to dull purple.

The desert spring is underway. Sand verbenas still remain in bloom from the surprise rain of the winter season, as showers have fallen at intervals during the intervening weeks. Renewing activity is also noticeable among the birds and animals. Desert chipmunks, which hibernate during colder weather, are now scampering about their own business and flash their tiny white tails like small flags in a snapping breeze.

On my last trip to the post office, a week ago, in the seven miles I saw three horned toads, which blinked at me in friendly fashion. And on my return trip, at a distance of 30 feet, a large eagle got lazily into the air clutching in its claws a small rabbit. It flapped along beside me for a few hundred feet and then with seeming disdain for my earthbound helplessness, it soared upward and with greater speed disappeared into the blue sky toward the snow-covered crags of San Jacinto.

[Article 148: May 27, 1954]

Living alone, one becomes very observing of the wildlife round about. In nesting boxes built to the peculiar requirements of my feathered friends, some 16 have taken up permanent residence. They all leave, however, in the summer heat, except two shrikes. These two birds raise always a family of about three. The young ones fly away in time, but the old birds stay with me, and often when we three are the only ones in this part of the desert, they will come and sit on the porch wall. They drink water from their dish not four feet away, and if I am quiet they will sometimes sit on the back of my chair. And during the hours when I work alone, they will come and sing cheerful notes. If their water dish gets empty, they let me know in a way that we both understand. Adios, Amigo, Cabot Yerxa.

[Article 149: June 3, 1954]

. . . The first man to live on our side of this desert valley of the palms seems to have been an old prospector named Dutch Frank. He drifted in here shortly after the year 1900 and made his main camps either in the mesquite brush at Two Bunch Palms oasis, or down at the Seven Palms waterhole a few miles to the south. Sometimes he camped at Willow Hole, where there is water, but also too many mosquitoes in different seasons for comfort.

At all three camp spots there was good forage for his burros, which is of first importance, and dry wood for campfires. Frank took much time to arrange a camp, and they were always good models of convenience, neatness, and showed expert ability to make use of natural surroundings. His harness and camp equipment were old, but in good repair. He worried not at all about rattlesnakes, and in early days there were many. Trade rats and other small desert life ran freely over his few belongings. He brushed spiders, ants, and scorpions out of his blankets, listened to coyotes howl at night, and protected his food rations from wild cats, foxes, and lynx.

[Article 150: June 10, 1954]

About 1910 another typical prospector by the name of Old Man Coolidge drifted into this area and joined forces with Dutch Frank for a couple of years. But by 1912 Coolidge was too old to make the long, hard desert treks, and so he homesteaded a piece of ground in front of Two Bunch Palms. Frank would have none of homesteading; he wanted no land, no cabin, no family. All he wanted was a chance to roam the desert over, camp where he pleased, and always be on the lookout for mining ground. He spent years in this desert, over into the Mojave, in the Santa Rosa mountains, the Little San Bernardinos, and on out towards the Colorado River country. But in time he came back here to Two Bunch Palms, and to the T-cross-K Ranch in Mission Canyon, which Frank DeLong and his wife started [as] a cattle ranch about 1912. In those days cattle ranged this desert very freely.

Some men carried revolvers, and it was quite the usual thing for all men to carry a rifle or shotgun when traveling about the desert . . . Quail, jack rabbits, or cottontails were welcome food items, and a gun quickly took care of rattlesnakes. Sometimes it was possible to secure a coyote or lynx, and the money for its hide was spent for many needed items by the homesteader. In every cabin was a Sears Roebuck catalog, with little papers to mark the spot where things were pictured and described in great detail, which some member of the family yearned for. Children wanted toys; women looked in admiration at articles of clothing, or at least hoped to get some new dish for the meager assortment in the small one-room cabins. I wanted a 22 caliber rifle and read its description in every new catalog they issued, but was never able to get the few dollars in hand.

[Article 151: June 17, 1954]

About that time a circular came from Chicago describing rifles used by the Union forces in the Civil War, and loaded shells at bargain prices. I had some coyote hides and sold them to a dealer in St. Louis by mail, which made it possible to secure the Civil War gun and some shells. [The shell] was a big slug of lead protruding from a solid brass jacket. The gun would shoot one at a time, and the hammer was a large, crude affair on the outside of the barrel, but it worked, and the resulting explosion was terrific. All these things were packed in a heavy wooden box, which came by R.R. freight to Garnet and then to the ranch cabin on the back of Merry Xmas, the faithful burro. Bob Carr was there when the box was opened and offered the disturbing idea that perhaps [the] gun, after all the years, would not stand the explosion. It might burst the barrel. He had read of such an occurrence, and the owner was killed. So I put in one of those big brass shells, fastened the gun to a greasewood bush, tied a cord to the trigger, and crouched down behind a clay bank for safety. The noise was pretty awful, but except for kicking backwards, the gun was all right. Thereafter I could shoot jack rabbits, and they never ran away, if hit! Once I came upon a large range cow with a broken leg, and coyotes were eating the distressed animal while it was yet alive. So I killed the cow with the Civil War gun and mailed a letter to the cattle ranch owner, giving brand marks with color description.

Old Man Coolidge was tall, slow-spoken, and angular; his black hair was quite long, streaked with gray, and he always had a beard. He was not a burro man. Nor was he a good cook. Dutch Frank was a good burro man and an efficient camp cook. To be a good burro man, you must be patient with animals and have the knack and ability of being able to pack a lot of miscellaneous items securely upon the burro's back. This must be done in such a way that none are lost, and the animal is comfortable.

[Article 152: June 24, 1954]

In the desert every burro had a name, because they differ in temperament and ability as much as people do, and they were mentioned in our conversations by name as casually as that of any person. Dutch Frank traveled with three burros, of which he was very proud. He talked to them and of them, just as naturally as he did to Old Man Coolidge or any other man.

Frank's largest burro was called Jimmy Barley Hay, and the next one answered to Captain Jack. The third burro, with its pack, was always lagging behind, thereby attracting to itself much profanity in mixed German and English from Frank. Its name was "Joppo the Devil." Frank explained with affection that it was just a colt and would learn better ways later. However, it was seven years old at the time I knew it.

Joppo the Devil was mischievous. It could untie ropes, get into food supplies, eat up prunes and pancake flour or rice, tip over canteens of water, and tangle up harness. It seemed to do all these things just to hear Dutch Frank expound and try first in English and then in German to tell Joppo what kind of a burro he was, where he might be going, and what his ancestors were.

Joppo would listen without much attention, but in his brain, beneath those tremendous ears, he was even then planning something else. When not properly staked out, or if [his] stake pins loosened, Joppo would lead the other two burros off on a skylark trip out of camp and into the open desert. Sometimes it would take Frank all day to patiently trail the three runaways into a clump of thick brush or down in a gully where they were hiding out. Frank said, "Joppo, he eeze the devil."

Dutch Frank was a very short man with bow legs. He was small, but active and quick. All that he did was with that German careful thoroughness. He could patch clothing as good as a woman, repair tents and harness skillfully. Meals were well cooked, and if a forge was available, he could make burro shoes or do iron work.

[Article 153: July 1, 1954]

Frank wore a black felt hat, the crown high, the brim stiff, and [it] appeared rather narrow, as desert hats usually are wide. Always a large red handkerchief was tied loosely about his neck. Thrust into his clenched teeth was a short-stemmed black wooden pipe. The bowl might be up or down; it did not seem to be important. Sometimes he put tobacco into this ancient pipe and could light it with one match. Just as easy in heavy wind. But during waking hours, Frank had the pipe in his mouth, even while chopping wood or preparing meals. Also another peculiarity about this man was that, except at mealtime or asleep, he was always astride one of the burros. Frank never walked, perhaps because with his short bowlegs this was very slow and difficult for him. He rode while hunting firewood; he did so to carry canteens to be filled with water, even though the distance was very short. And when he came to visit homesteaders, he sat on the burro near the door, and we would always go outside of our small cabins and talk in the sunshine, while Frank sat in the saddle. He wore blue overalls, blue shirts, faded but washed clean, and heavy types of shoes which had the soles and heels filled full of Hungarian hobnails, the small round-headed ones.

His burros, when packed for traveling, had all camp equipment expertly secured into place. Canvas covered everything, and this was tied down by ropes in the diamond-hitch pattern.

On top of all [their loads,] on one animal was a pick and a shovel, but [on] another was a small hand axe and a black coffee pot. This was the camp companion of years and many smoky fires in the oven. Frank was never in a hurry. Anytime during the day he would stop, take the hand axe, make a fire, prepare coffee. Of necessity and by habit, it was black and strong. Should the burros appear hungry, he stopped, unpacked, and let them eat as much desert vegetation as they wanted to.

Dutch Frank carried no watch, received no mail, never knew the day of the week or month. He never worried about time or weather. On his three burros he had all his worldly possessions, and could set up camp in a few moments. Perhaps he had something we strive to attain and fail, because he had found peace of mind and a happy heart under any and all circumstances. Adios, Dutch Frank!

[ARTICLE 154: JULY 8, 1954]

Old Man Coolidge was quite the opposite from Dutch Frank in many ways. He very seldom, if ever, wore a hat, even in all this brilliant desert sunshine, but like Indians [he] received some protection from his thick, tangled black hair. His clothes often needed patches, and he never owned a burro, but walked everywhere. He walked very slowly, and it was his custom to use a staff, just like you see in pictures of ancient men in Bible times. It was not a cane, but a staff about seven feet tall. This aided him in walking uphill and down grades and through soft sand. When talking, he would stand and lean upon this staff, thoroughly relaxed, until the conversation was over; then he would slowly plod along in the sand with his staff and soon disappear amid the desert brush. He talked in slow monotones, never shouted, never swore. Meeting with rattlesnakes or other desert small life, he would push them out of the way with the staff. He never had a gun and never killed anything.

His camp was a very crude affair and very uncomfortable. While he was homesteading land in front of Two Bunch Palms, he lived in a very small ragged and torn A-type tent, not large enough to stand up in. This had no floor and no door. But it did create some small amount of shade over his blankets and limited number of camp dishes. For water, he had two canteens which could be filled at the water hole under the palms. This was quite a task for him, as he was at this time quite old and not vigorous. . . .

Often as we were out and about the desert searching for lost burros or hunting rabbits, we would come upon Old Man Coolidge lying sprawled upon the desert sand. The first natural thought of course would be, "Oh, oh, the old man is dead," but on seeing some small sign of life, we would awaken him and ask if he was all right or needed help. His stock answer was, "Oh, I just got tired and thought I would rest awhile."

After his homestead period he moved to Whitewater Canyon and entertained a visionary plan of raising trout for market, which was too impractical. But in time, he too died and has gone to join the many. Forty years ago I painted a portrait of him and it was a good likeness, but it was stolen from Eagle's Nest while I was a soldier in World War I.

[ARTICLE 155: JULY 15, 1954]

This land of ours--this part of the desert in which we now live and call Desert Hot Springs--is a new land. There are those among us who can remember its very beginnings, because the first coming of people here to live in this open desert valley is only a few years back. And we all ought to thrill with the uniqueness of this situation, because in Europe it is nothing unusual for towns or communities to be a thousand years old and more. But here, all about us, everything is new and clean, and the future is ours for the making. New houses appear in a short time where no house has ever been before; paved streets and roads open up the desert lands which never had need of highways until now. Electric power, running water in pipes, postal service, and many other things contribute to make desert living comfortable and enjoyable.

We are all a part of this and should be very happy that we have been able to escape from the congestion and confusion of cities. Hot days! Sure, but they are healthy. Windy days? Sure, but they are healthy too. Desert-minded people love the desert. . . .

[Article 156: July 22, 1954]

In all new countries and among all pioneer peoples, one of the early problems is schooling for the children. So this was the case here too.

The rare picture of the first public school in the Desert Hot Springs area was taken by its first teacher in 1912, and she had the only Kodak in the desert at that time. She was then Miss Ethel Rouse, and now Mrs. C.E. Stockton of El Toro, California. She was followed by Miss Webster and later by Miss Wiley [in] 1916-17-18.

Children were few in those days, and so sometimes one or more had to be borrowed from relatives in the city and sent here to live on [the] desert in order that school enrollment could be kept at least near the minimum required to keep a school open.

In the early schoolroom there was one Edwards boy, one Hicks, three or four Schlicters, one from the R.R. station and four McCargers, John, Aleta, Mercy, and Wilbur.

The Hicks and Edwards came the farthest. They had three burros named Jack, Pooy, and California. After school these three burros were driven seven miles in Mission Canyon to obtain water for the family needs. Sometimes, in season, the children gathered cactus blossoms, which were cooked to add variety to desert meals.

Ethel Rouse, the first teacher, was a very young and a very small person. But what she lacked in size was more than made up in quiet courage, enthusiasm, cheerfulness, and ability to overcome difficulties.

She was hired in the city to come down and teach school here on the desert. Her arrival at the Garnet R.R. station was in one of those real blustering sandstorms which sometimes sweep out of nowhere with such fury.

The station agent helped the McCarger boys load the trunk into a small wagon pulled by two long-eared burros. And thus the journey was made over the several miles of sandy roads to the McCarger cabin, where she made her home with the family for the school year. Not a house was passed, not a fence, not a tree--all was just open natural desert of sand and rocks. The burros plodded on slowly; the speed was one mile per hour, but in short stretches of better roadway sometimes two miles per hour was possible. The wind howled and kept the small cavalcade in a cloud of moving sand. Such was the initiation of this young city girl to her first teaching position in the desert.

And then! Only next morning was she informed that there was no schoolhouse.

[Article 157: July 29,1954]

There was a hurried meeting of the very few scattered neighbors, and a location and a plan decided upon.

Jack Riley, when first arrived on the desert, did not have money to obtain lumber, and there was then no way to move lumber over the desert, even though it had been at the R.R. depot. So he therefore dug a hole in the ground and placed over this a patchwork of miscellaneous materials for shade. Just recently he had started a very small cabin nearby.

Therefore it was decided to enlarge Jack Riley's dugout and let him live in his unfinished cabin. Jack drove two burros hitched to a very small, home-made scraper, and the new school teacher and Mrs. McCarger, between them, managed to fill the scraper with earth on each round trip and to dump the load of earth onto the open desert. In this fashion, slowly the dug-out was enlarged enough to make a small schoolroom.

The various neighbors contributed time and materials as the work progressed. The dugout was nearly three feet deep into the ground. A roof was constructed overhead. The side walls between the ground level and the roof were filled with a miscellaneous collection of old boards of various sizes and descriptions. A few sheets of battered, corrugated galvanized iron and pieces of rusty tin were found along the R.R. tracks when lumber gave out. After all the materials were in place and still open walls remained, armloads of desert brush were stuffed into the openings.

There was no floor of any kind. No real door. Up on top of the roof, more desert brush was placed and held in place by rocks. This brush helped to tone down the effect of too much sun and made the dugout a little cooler on hot days.

One small window was found and placed in the north wall. Next to the window was an opening, which never did have a window, nor was there ever a screen there.

The one entrance and doorway was to the east. At the northeast corner was a rough pole from which bravely flew a small American flag. To create some warmth during inclement weather, there was a small sheet-iron stove, which burned desert brush in the southwest corner. There was a six-inch tin stove pipe, which went straight out through the wall and then turned up outside the building.

Wilber McCarger acted as janitor. It was his duty to take out part of the sand which blew into the place during storms. Also to look the floor over for snakes and other desert wildlife that had easy access through the makeshift walls. But you can say the dugout had good ventilation.

Each child brought his own canteen of water, as well as [a] cold lunch. Those lunches were of necessity unexciting. Cold pancakes, pieces of cold desert rabbit, sometimes homemade bread and beans. But never were there fruit or vegetables or things from stores and, of course, no milk ever. . . .

[Article 158: August 5, 1954]

The children had only a piece of 1 x 12-inch board for a desk, and they sat on a crude, made-on-the-spot, rough board bench. All unpainted.

Ethel Rouse, the teacher, obtained from somewhere a wooden packing box, which served as her desk. She sat upon a smaller box and never did have a chair. These, of course, were also lacking in any paint. That first year of school in the old dugout lasted from September, 1912 to June, 1913. The boy from the R.R. depot at Garnet had to cover [the] miles to school as best he could. And the Hicks-Edwards children [had to cover] several miles. Some days they walked, while on others they came in on burros.

This first schoolroom did not even have a blackboard, so Ethel Rouse scratched words and problems in simple arithmetic on the ground. She also made use of stones to illustrate addition and subtraction.

There were scorpions or spiders in the shelves, and sometimes small animals or sidewinders in the brush. During windstorms, dust sifted over everything in the place.

Also during that school year, unfortunately, a burro dragged one of the small McCarger girls by its stake-out chain through some rocks and brush, thus breaking the child's leg. There was no doctor closer than Banning. So the little girl, in much pain, was transported on a burro wagon to Garnet, then in the baggage car of a train to Los Angeles. Mrs. McCarger had to accompany her. Therefore during the next four weeks Ethel Rouse had to keep up the home for herself and the three other small children, meanwhile still be the schoolteacher.

In 1914 the county officials, sensing that there would be more children to be schooled here, arranged to build a wooden school building on one acre of donated land near the B-bar-H corner. This served for the next several years, but eventually burned down.

[Article 159: August 12, 1954]

News of the promised carpenter-built school to be constructed out of real lumber was welcome information to all households having children. But just at this critical time the Schlicter family, with all its children, moved to Morongo Valley. This decreased the number of youngsters to the point where there were not enough left to justify a school under county laws. Therefore frantic appeals were made to relatives in the city to send out some children to live here on the desert, so that the school could be kept open. This was done in time. And the new school building was completed, serving its purpose well. It also was the meeting place for picnics, a few dances, and other gatherings. . . .

[*Desert Sentinel* editor's note: "Here follow parts of letters written by Cabot Yerxa years ago and printed in the New York Cavalcade space by Louis Sobol. . . . " The letters continue in article 160.]

This summer I am making a larger snake pit. It will be 12 feet square and five feet deep. In this I will gather rattlesnakes during the summer to have next winter. I will keep them down in the pit, and when visitors come, I will go down in the pit, open a box, lift out the snakes and show their good points and reactions, etc. The rattlers will make me nice pets for the summer. They are quiet and will be company, as very few people ever call in hot weather.

[Article 160: August 19, 1954]

The first rule of the desert is quietness. Some well-meaning person sent me a duck once. But I had to get rid of him to stop all the noise! Round-the-year guests near the cabin now are two red racer snakes, shaped like buggy whips; one was on the step yesterday getting warm. They can travel with amazing speed when in a hurry. Also [I] have two bull snakes, larger and slower because of [their] heavy-type bodies. But best pet of all is the California pink boa. It has a smooth, slick body which feels like rubber. No scales. You can handle [it] without fear of being bitten, and it twines gently around your arm or rolls into a ball in your hands.

I haven't seen a newspaper in two weeks--must walk the seven miles down to [the] railroad [station] and find one.

P.S. Today it rains. In any other country that would not be worthy of comment, but here on the desert it is a real event. I have just tended to all [my] animals--the goats, chickens, large pet lizards, chuckwallas, tortoises, and the varied snakes in the pits. The rain makes the air chill. I have brought in a large box of dry firewood gathered off the desert floor. With this, the old stove now glows and the cabin is warm again. I wish you might pull up a chair and join with me in several hours of smoke-talk. We would be separated and apart from a world torn by tragedy and uncertainty. It is warm within--

there is a storm outside--and it is on days such as this that we of the desert are repaid for the many hours of work and lonesomeness. . . .

I send you greetings from a warm cabin on a rainy night. Cabot Yerxa

[Article 161: August 26, 1954]

. . . Tiddles is a very large, good-natured cat with dark tiger markings, having very generous patches of pure white fur, which are kept surprisingly clean at all times.

This cat is not one of those present in the pioneer days of this desert, but however is deserving of a place in [the history of] local animals. It belongs to Mr. and Mrs. Stanley Jones, whose Seven Palms Rancho is among desert sand hills heavily overgrown with gnarled mesquite trees and thick tangled thorny brush of many different kinds. During the day Tiddles ranges freely out of doors in this massed vegetation and comes back often with trophies of the hunt to receive praise before eating its quarry. At night the cat lounges in the house before the open fireplace, because during the hours of darkness, coyotes and lynx prowl outside in the deep shadows. Being safely inside, if a coyote howls, it merely yawns.

But when anyone picks up a gun to go hunting, Tiddles shows excitement and feels that it is expected to go along, too. It follows at the gunner's heels like a well-trained hunting dog. After the shot is fired, this strange cat runs quickly into the brush and drags the rabbit to the feet of the hunter with the gun, knowing well that its reward will be the head and all four feet. Tiddles never attempts to chew the main body of the rabbit, because it knows that a portion of it goes to the family kitchen.

[Article 162: September 2, 1954]

Various traps are set about the buildings of the ranch for rats and mice. And when those traps are inspected, the cat walks along too with evident interest. Sometimes it will go alone to the traps and drag a trap and the victim to the back door of the house, call for attention, and to have the trap detached.

Now it just happens that Arthur Stanley Jones, being of a very mechanical type of mind, arranged one of these clever metal door mats at the rear entrance which effectively electrocutes troublesome flies and bugs that come into contact with it.

One day Tiddles proudly brought a trap containing a large mouse to this door for customary praise and to get the reward. By accident the mouse was dropped onto this electric mat and was quite well burned before it could be taken off and tossed aside. But the cat, whom they had forgotten in the excitement, was watching the procedure, recovered the mouse and much to the beholders' surprise ate it greedily.

Now comes the astonishing part of this story. Since that time, when Tiddles captures a mouse or rat in the desert, it brings the dead quarry to the house and deposits them on the iron mat. Of course the hair burns off at once and the resulting smell is pretty awful. Any member of the family detecting this very unpleasant odor dashes to the electric door mat and, with special tongs, picks up the badly singed rodent, then gives it to the patiently waiting and expectant Tiddles.

He named his homestead Eagle's Nest, ca. 1914-1918.

Studio portrait of Cabot during homestead period. ca. 1914-1918

Cabot's first wood frame homestead cabin, ca. 1914-1918.

Cabot holding baby Rodney in front of homestead cabin, 1914

Mamie and Rodney outside homestead cabin on Miracle Hill

Cabot's first wood frame homestead cabin on Miracle Hill, ca. 1914-1918.

Cabot, his wife Mamie and their son Rodney in his box made so he could be carried by Merry Xmas, ca. 1916-17

Rodney posed before Eagles Nest cabin, ca. 1916-17

Bob Carr holding Rodney while Cabot digs his first hot water well.

Family activities in the desert, ca. 1914-1918

Cabot, Merry Xmas commune over campfire, ca. 1915-1918

Two friends gathering firewood, ca. 1915-1918

Mamie riding Merry Xmas with homestead cabin in background.

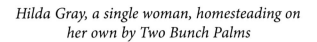

Hilda Gray, a single woman, homesteading on her own by Two Bunch Palms

Neighbor woman with protection, ca.1914-1918

Hilda Gray with her chickens and dog Trixi

Rileys' eventual above ground cabin

Garnet train station with a palm plantation, looking west

Dutch Frank, desert prospector

Carl Eytel by his cabin in Palm Springs, with outdoor cot where Cabot may have slept. (Used by permission: Desert Magazine, The Desert Sun.)

Old Man Coolidge with his staff, date unknown

Dutch Frank with his burros before the Desert Inn, Palm Springs, date unknown

Two Bunch Palms Oasis; second bunch at distance on left.

Neighbor woman, probably at Two Bunch Palms Oasis, ca. 1914-1918

[Article 163: September 9, 1954]

[This article reprinted from the Palm Springs *Villager* continues in Articles 164-167:]

The great southwestern deserts have claimed the lives of many people. Mostly because they were ignorant of or disregarded the known safeguards for desert conditions. . . .

Over 30 years ago, I lived for six years on the desert near Blythe. Every summer there were deaths in the deserts round about, when people ran out of water or became lost. They died because they were not equipped to survive. Some perished of thirst near desert cactus, completely ignorant that it would provide enough moisture to sustain a life.

Here in the early days of [the] Desert Hot Springs area, one man got lost and perished while walking to Palm Springs across the Whitewater Wash in a blinding sandstorm. Another man also lost his life walking from the Willow Hole Sand Hills to Garnet on a very sultry afternoon against the advice of desert men. He was from the city and ignorant of desert conditions and risks.

The following story relates the fate of a Metropolitan Aqueduct survey party which ran out of water 20-odd years ago. The eight men became exhausted and collapsed from heat prostration on the Coachella Desert between here and Blythe. They had no tent and so were at the mercy of the summer sun.

Three lines of survey were made starting in 1930 to determine the most practical route for the Metropolitan Aqueduct to follow, by which to bring water for the Los Angeles area from Boulder Dam.

The intervening country is mostly all natural desert or barren mountains in character. Roads are few, with water only to be found at irregular intervals. The summer months are very hot and rattlesnakes often a menace. So the men forming those survey parties endured many real hardships or privations, and a few lost their lives.

[Article 164: September 16, 1954]

On one mid-summer day 20 or more years ago here in [the] Coachella Valley, the sun seemed to rise over the horizon in a burst of fury. The very first rays of the sun struck out with penetrating heat to all that they touched. Soon the whole desert area was shimmering in heat waves like those you see on top of an old-fashioned iron cook stove.

There was not the faintest evidence of a breeze. Leaves hung motionless where trees existed in this parched land. The few melancholy birds stayed hidden in the scanty branches of scraggly bushes. Even lizards peered out at the world from hidden holes under rocks and ventured out not at all. Of snakes there were none in sight, because no snake could travel on sand or rocks so hot. . . .

By mid-day the sky was pale, nondescript blue. Gradually great thunderheads of high, piled-up white clouds drifted in slowly from the direction of Arizona. Humidity got worse. Still no breeze came, and the mercury in thermometers climbed steadily, making the day unbearable for man and animal alike.

Farmers quit all work and retired to whatever shade there was at their ranch homes. Villagers in Indio stayed within doors and resorted to fans of any description. Children stopped their play and sat listlessly beneath any available tree. The streets in Indio on that day were practically deserted. The few autos were either going to the ice plant, or returning with a tell-tale trail of wet drops in the road dust. . . . All agreed that this was the hottest day of the year. None could remember a day that was worse.

Alfred, the druggist, stood under the awning in front of the store, admiring his new auto, all new and shiny with its bright fresh paint. . . . Inside the drug store it was too hot to live, and few customers had appeared all day. They had mostly wanted salt tablets to put in the drinking water, or solutions to discourage insect bites.

[ARTICLE 165: SEPTEMBER 23, 1954]

. . . Just then the [druggist's] phone range noisily. It jingled in the sultry, empty store. He picked up the receiver. The speaker on the other end was the deputy sheriff at Desert Center, halfway to Blythe. Rapidly and in an authoritative tone, the voice continued, "Word has just reached us that eight men have collapsed with the heat and are near death in the open desert, without any tent, some miles north of here. Will you come out at once and bring both doctors with you? You must hurry. Without proper medical help, all the men will die." . . .

Alfred phoned his home. Then he placed a quickly-penciled note on the door, "Closed. Emergency. Open tomorrow," and rushed into the nearest doctor's office. They phoned the other [doctor]. Both agreed to go, if [Alfred] would drive the new automobile. All three knew the trip was 125 miles at least, and the temperature was above 125 degrees, and the roads were the most difficult in all the desert round about.

Soon they were on their way to Mecca, then out into a one-track road over the desert bound for Box Canyon. The auto seemed only to crawl up the sandy twisting tracks, worming its way uphill between the towering cliffs cut very steeply by centuries of erosion, caused by run-off water from infrequent storms. . . .

Alfred drove the car at the fastest speed possible under road conditions. Sometimes this was only a walking gait, he doing the driving and the two doctors pushing the car in some places. The weather kept very oppressively hot, and their clothing was wet with perspiration.

At last they reached Desert Center--just a couple of small buildings, some tents, and a gas pump. Here the deputy sheriff was waiting for them with an open one-ton truck and a driver.

The two cars left immediately for the scene of the stricken men. . . . The trail led down steep banks, into washes, over patches of rocks, round boulders of large size, skirting bushes, and through deep sand.

[ARTICLE 166: SEPTEMBER 30, 1954]

Finally they arrived where the small group of men lay sprawled about the cold ashes of a campfire. Some were unconscious or delirious. All were in desperate condition because of thirst and exhaustion from excessive heat and exposure to burning sunshine. Pitifully they begged for water, but the doctors ordered that none be given to them. Instead their mouths were moistened with wet cloths.

Hastily all were loaded into the truck and the return journey made to Desert Center as quickly as possible. During this trip every man, in his frenzy to be cooler, stripped himself of all clothing and threw it away on the desert. When Desert Center was reached, every man was nude without one stitch of clothing, except for one man. He still had on one shoe because the lace was knotted, and he could not get it off.

A makeshift hospital was arranged in one of the buildings, and the two doctors took charge of six men in one larger room. They delegated the druggist to watch over the other two men in a smaller room. This had one window and one door opening out on the roadway. The sun was nearing the western horizon, but still there was no letup in humidity or high temperature.

One of Alfred's men was a surveyor and intelligent, who understood the seriousness of the situation. The other man was a Mexican laborer who never stopped begging for water.

The doctor's orders were followed closely. Alfred gave his men water in a teaspoon occasionally for a period. Then later a glass was held to their lips, with the strict injunction that the water was only to cool the mouth and must be spat out. To make sure of this he kept his left hand at the patient's throat and swore he would choke him if he swallowed any. The surveyor was co-operative, but the Mexican had to be choked at times to keep him from trying to swallow any of the water.

Needing more water, the druggist left his two men for a moment. When he re-entered the room, he was horrified to see through the open door that the Mexican laborer had left his cot, gone out the door, and taken a water bag from an automobile.

He was even now standing unsteadily, with the bag above his head, gulping water as it gushed over his face and down over his body to the ground. By the time Alfred reached the man, the bag was empty and both lay in the dust of the road. A small patch of mud was evidence of the spilled water.

Shouting for the help of the doctors and the sheriff, the Mexican was then placed on a small mattress. Over this another mattress was placed, and then all was quickly tied into a bundle with small ropes. The unfortunate man was then stood upon his head. This was in a vain attempt to cause him to disgorge the water he had drunk. The effort was to no avail, and in 15 minutes the Mexican was dead.

[Article 167: October 7, 1954]

The surviving seven men were moved to Indio when able to make the trip, and eventually recovered.

The underlying theory about people suffering from very extreme thirst is that water, if taken suddenly and in quantity, swells the stomach walls. This cuts off the blood circulation, causing death in a short time.

Alfred the druggist, with 42 years of experience, remarks that in days of extreme heat or when excessive perspiration takes place, "If you eat salt and drink hot tea, you will never have heat exhaustion. High temperatures will be more comfortable, and the desert heat will never get you." . . .

[Article 169: October 21, 1954]

[From a letter to Louis Sobol, originally printed in his "New York Cavalcade" column:]

This week I picked up a large red diamondback rattlesnake and put it in a screened cage. It was very nervous, irritable, and hungry, but not a rat or a mouse could be found on the place. This angry snake would rattle and buzz menacingly when anyone walked within 10 feet of its cage.

Then I happened to remember reading that certain snakes in India will drink milk, so I put a cup of milk in the cage as an experiment. In the morning it was gone, and the snake was calm, contented, and peaceful. It will not get mad or rattle. So perhaps continued milk-feeding will change its character and disposition. After keeping rattlesnakes as pets off and on for 30-odd years, this is the first time I ever fed one milk--so there is always something to learn, even about snakes.

Let me tell you, rattlesnakes make novel pets. They can teach the observer calmness, patience, and relaxation. They make beautiful loops and curves and are always graceful at all times. They stay where you put them and make no noise, and now that the experiment mentioned proves that they will drink milk, the feeding is simple. They could be kept in city flats. . . .

By the way of general information, rattlesnakes do not like noise, confusion, or quick movements. Therefore maintain a quiet, unhurried, and polite attitude at all times. Rattlesnakes will much appreciate this.

Adios, and you can have your cold city drinks in bars, but the best drink of all is warm water from a canteen which has sat in the sun out on a real desert. Cabot Yerxa

[Article 170: October 28, 1954]

Forty years ago many men were still chewing tobacco. The railroad conductors and engineers on the small train that came once each day into the desert, stopping at the Palm Springs station, would get a drink of water from the faucet under the palm trees and then get a fresh bite of plug tobacco. On this slow train was a smoking car in which passengers gathered to smoke, talk, or chew tobacco. Here on the desert, too, a plug of chewing tobacco was in many a man's overall pocket.

What has become of the ancient and honorable profession of expert tobacco-chewers? You of the older generation can remember a time when nearly all men chewed tobacco to some extent.

As a boy I can remember my grandfather would cut off a small, neat plug of tobacco, put it carefully into his mouth, and never chew it. This small piece of tobacco would be renewed during the day, but no one suspected its presence. No tobacco was ever used on Sunday. That was one type of chewer.

The second type was represented by Ed Shirk, a typical horseman. I worked for him when I was only 16 years of age in Alaska during the Gold Rush in 1900 to Cape Nome. He chewed tobacco steadily all day, but not much at a time. Seldom did he spit, but could hit any cuspidor accurately, even 10 feet away. This feat of expertness was not done often. However, he never missed and [his] unusual ability to hit any designated spot intrigued me--so I started chewing tobacco. But I never could equal his distance, so gave it up. If 10 or 12 feet sounds easy to you, just try it some time.

[Article 171: November 4, 1954]

The third type of tobacco-chewer was the messy individual who always seemed about to drown in tobacco juice. Such a character was a round-up cook on the desert back in the open cattle-range days shortly after 1900. He was known as Charlie. Charlie always carried a large plug of chewing tobacco in his left hip pocket. It might be Climax, Star, or Horseshoe, but always one of those three brands then so popular in the frontier West. Over the years he had saved enough of the little tin bags attached to each plug to obtain as a premium a large jackknife. With this knife he would cut off generous portions of tobacco and thrust them into his mouth. By sheer will power he kept his lips tightly pressed together. Meanwhile his cheeks always puffed out. Tiny beads of tobacco eventually dripped from the ends of his drooping mustache. Then after some more moments of vain struggle, he would spit a lot of tobacco juice on the ground, "Ker-plop." Charlie talked very seldom. No man could talk while chewing tobacco his way. Once he sneezed while reading the only newspaper in camp. It was turned so brown that no other cowboy could read any more news in that paper.

    Charlie was a very efficient outdoor cook. Short and stout, it seemed easy for him to sit on his heels by the campfire while preparing meals. Bacon and eggs were watched closely and taken out just at the right moment. His Mexican-style beans, beef stew, and fried steaks were the talk of many cow camps.

    He could do rough blacksmithing, too, and so was never out of employment. But Charlie never accumulated enough money for his own saddle horse or other cowboy trappings. On paydays he gambled his monthly checks. His mind was not clear and his judgment poor in everything except cooking. Some men said he was born that way. Still others maintained that he was once thrown from a bucking horse and lit on his head, which affected his thinking.

[Article 172: November 11, 1954]

In the early days on the desert, many cattle bearing different brands roamed this area from Banning to Indio. Among them were Frank DeLong and his T-cross-K brand, Talmage Brothers, Covington, Bill Keys, Mission Canyon Indians, and several different Indians near Palm Springs.

    One year during the annual round-up to separate the cattle and to brand all new calves, Charlie was in charge of the chuck wagon. He cooked all the meals for all the assembled men. It so happened one day at sundown, after a long day's work, that all the cowboys, tired and hungry, were lounging about the wagon. Charlie was very busy with his pots and pans over an open campfire. He was in his glory: plenty of food, and a dozen men hungry and ready to eat. He was determined that every man would remember this meal as a specially good one. He crouched in the wood smoke, watching [as] everything in the blacked pans . . . simmered, boiled, or fried under his supervision, giving off very appetizing odors. Charlie's cheeks were stretched to capacity as usual. He had no time to spit.

    Then all of a sudden this tranquil scene was rudely broken by two very large bulls pawing the ground and then charging at each other head-on, not far from Charlie and his pots and pans. The resulting crash of bulls' heads was tremendous, and the slowly cooking food was showered with sand and dust.

The bulls, each from a different herd, then retreated some distance, pawed the ground in fury, then came bellowing down at each other again. The impact would once more be near the campfire. This indignity was too much for Charlie to take another time. He quickly grabbed an enormous frying pan by its handle, snatched up a long heavy iron spoon, and before the astonished cowboys could stop him, he dashed in between the maddened, charging bulls. Meanwhile he was beating the fry pan vigorously with the heavy iron spoon. Somehow he was able to spit out the tobacco juice on the ground, "kerplop," and yell at the top of his lungs to the bulls, "Hey, you so-and-so's, quit that, you are getting sand in the supper." That Charlie would be killed was certain, but there was no time to do anything to save him. The foreman wondered quickly what could be done with the body.

However, the two bulls were so taken by surprise that they slid to a stop with barely room for Charlie to stand between them, still beating on his frying pan. Then, snorting defiance, the bulls returned each to his own herd, where cowboys quieted them down.

Charlie took out a plug of tobacco, cut off a large piece, thrust this into his mouth. He again crouched down upon his heels and busied himself with the pots and pans.

[ARTICLE 173: NOVEMBER 18, 1954]

If the winter season is normal, we have always a three-day rain every year during the middle of January. At such times the desert changes much in appearance. The barrel cactus gets very red in color because of the thorough washing by rain. Cholla cactus becomes bright yellow, beavertail and deer-horned, likewise for the same reason, show up suddenly green. Greasewood branches and most small brush appear to be nearly black. Indigo bushes, burro sage, and others of similar types are strongly contrasting grays.

There is also a difference underfoot. Scattered bits of brush which litter the desert floor do not crackle and snap when you walk, as it does in dry weather. When you step on small rocks after the rains, they sink into the wet earth, and there is no sound of crunching as formerly. . . .

The January storm gathers slowly. First a soft, moisture-laden wind comes up from the southeast. Clouds drift into the valley, wet mist forms, followed by slight showers. This is the first day and night. During the second [day], steady rain falls, soaking well the ground. Thick, low-lying clouds completely blot out surrounding mountains. You and your cabin are alone in an unfamiliar world; there is a complete hush of all sound. The pale bluish smoke from the chimney hangs close to the cabin roof, as though reluctant to leave. Water falls freely from the wet shingles, and the smell of wet wood is strongly noticeable.

During the third day precipitation tapers off to many short intermittent showers. Patches of thick small clouds hang only a short distance above the ground and drift very lazily along the lower foothills. All vegetation is dripping with raindrops. Pungent odors of greasewood, sage, croton, indigo brush, and other plants fill the air. It's a joy to be alive and [a] privilege to breathe deeply.

[Article 174: November 25, 1954]

On one such day many, many years ago, B.A. (before autos), I took Merry Xmas, the burro, and walked over that portion of the desert which is now Desert Hot Springs. There was not a single building to be seen anywhere nearby. But by looking over the broad expanse of desert, I could discern smoke from Hilda Gray's cabin in front of Two Bunch Palms. Then somewhat to the left further out, two tiny trails of smoke indicated the cabins of Jack Riley and the McCargers. Evidently they were all cooking breakfast. Preparing meals in desert cabins was more fun than being served in restaurants today. At that time, in the very early days of this valley, there were no more than 10 cabins scattered three to four miles apart in all this 100,000 acres of land which lay stretched out below my point of view on that wet morning. . . .

[Article 175: December 2, 1954]

On my many long walks over the desert, Merry Xmas, my burro, often followed playfully like a dog. It would nibble and bite choice bits of vegetation and dilly-dally round, letting me walk some distance ahead. Then it would suddenly break into a running gallop and charge in my direction, meanwhile shaking its head purposely to ring the loud-toned bell attached to its neck by a heavy, wide strap. Just before trampling me down, it would set all four feet firmly on the ground and slide to a stop. There it would wait for a piece of hard sugar candy, which I always carried in my pocket.

No other burro on the desert acted like Merry Xmas, nor showed equal intelligence, as I well knew with 11 animals myself, and having observed many more. I was much attached to this burro; it was young, strong, all black in color except for a white nose. Its ears were enormous, and its bray could be heard a long distance. This strange sound was started in a tone resembling the scream of a mountain lion, and then dropped to heavy, low hee-haws, using full lung power.

The going price for any burro was 10 dollars, but several times I have turned down offers of 100 dollars for Merry Xmas, which I refused without second thought. Even though I was often hungry, my one pair of faded, patched blue overalls had noticeable holes in them, and I used flattened tin cans nailed on my shoes to serve as half-soles--but sell Merry Xmas? No sir! . . . .

[Article 177: December 16, 1954]

On this particular day, as on any wet day after rain, the washed sands retained clearly the footprints of desert animals, coyotes, foxes, rabbits, and smaller things, thus leaving the telltale evidence of their meanderings during the night. So there were many interesting things to look at as we walked along.

Slowly and without definite intent, Merry Xmas and I entered Blind Canyon above Desert Hot Springs. And there, in January, I came upon a very large red diamondback rattlesnake, lying all coiled up in open ground. This was most interesting to me, because snakes are supposed to hibernate all winter. Here it was on wet ground, even though there were overhanging rocks and animal holes in which it could have gained shelter nearby.

Quickly I tied Merry Xmas to a large, gnarled cat-claw bush. Then [I] went back to the rattler and sat down to watch it.

The ground was soaking wet, with the air misty, but I had on storm clothes and was quite comfortable. The snake shifted its position slowly so as to be able to watch me fully and easily. And there we sat--the coiled snake and I. Just the two of us in a vast desert. It rattled nervously a little as I sat down close beside it, but soon relaxed into a watchful quietness. Evidently it was not going anyplace; neither was I.

Sometimes I looked at the snake; meanwhile [I] also enjoyed this wide, elevated view of the desert. On that day I dreamed again of a city someday to build on this desert to make proper use of the hot water for health and for recreation. The clouds commenced to break up, exposing the towering mass of San Jacinto Mountain brooding over a rain-soaked world. Occasional spots of sunshine glistened on some new snow lying high upon the mountain peaks.

After watching the snake for about a half-hour, there came a brisk, short little shower of rain. The rattler kept its position and so did I, each somewhat uncomfortable by the change of weather. But I was determined to find out what the snake was doing in the desert during January in a rainstorm. So I waited. Then an amusing thing happened, and I was rewarded for my patience.

[The "amusing thing" was not printed; the article ends here.]

[ARTICLE 178: DECEMBER 30, 1954]

One day after a rain as Merry Xmas, my donkey, and I trudged over the desert, a small covey of smartly feathered quail [that was] crouched under some thick brush did not move until we were nearly upon them. Then they scampered away in a half-running, half-flying manner, twittering and protesting at being disturbed. Of lizards, there were none at all. The birds were in hiding somewhere in shelters of their own choosing. The few rabbits, because like cats they are unhappy if wet, waited until the last moment before dashing away in long fast jumps. I measured one such leap in the clean wet sand of a wash, where water had smoothed everything out. The jackrabbit had jumped 17 feet.

You have often heard the expression, "no more home than a rabbit." But this is not literally true. The rabbit does have a home. The cottontail digs himself a burrow in the ground. Jackrabbits dig a shallow, open-top hole in a thick bunch of grass or brush, but always on the lee side for wind protection. Here it sits upright on its haunches all ready to jump away if danger threatens. Meanwhile its large ears are held erect, fully extended to catch the slightest sound approaching.

Here is some advice for rabbit hunters. It is a mistake to walk noisily and carelessly outdoors looking for rabbits. Take a lesson from the Indians. They would walk very slowly, very quietly, against the wind [and] stop often to look carefully about their location. When you are "desert wise" and learn to be patient, you can often see a rabbit's ears at some distance, as it sits upright in its home or stops eating to listen. Because of blood circulation, the ears will show a spot of pink faintly in the desert background. By close observation I have often shot rabbits just by seeing their ears in mixed brush.

Here is another hunting tip that Indians well know. The jack when frightened will leave its home in a big hurry and dash over the desert terrain at great speed. Its course, however, is a larger circle, and in time, perhaps two hours later it will return to the very hole, under the identical bush from which it started. Therefore, this being so, you can find the same rabbit in the same hole . . . the next day. Yes, rabbits have a home. . . . .

[Article 180: January 13, 1955]

Always take a lunch and a canteen of water [when you walk in the desert]. . . . [L]et me add that a desert man never quite empties his canteen, unless some source of water is readily available. Because if on a walking trip, some emergency might develop where water was very essential.

It will do most people good to get very thirsty. After a few such experiences, they will give WATER some proper appreciation. City-type people drift through life with water, food, and shelter always at hand. Therefore it is good for all of us to know a few of the hardships and conditions under which the older generations of pioneers lived, with particular thought towards the people who came to the West in covered wagons. That was a rugged life indeed.

Of course a knife, matches, magnifying glass, compass, field glasses, and other items are worth carrying too. We all have different interests.

But I wish to mention one more item of equipment, not known to many, but which is very essential and adds much fun to any walking trip.

And that is a walking stick. Not a cane. A cane is not long enough nor strong enough . . . Also it is too straight. If you walk many miles, a straight cane becomes an irritation, because all about you nature fashions things which are not straight. What you need is a walking stick of natural wood, for instance, manzanita, white oak, or perhaps greasewood. This should be longer than the conventional cane. And it must have some natural curves. Remember you are going to walk alone many miles on the desert and carry this all the way. So, the curves in this stick which nature made are pleasing, but a straight cane from a factory is out of place in the desert, and quite irritating after a dozen miles.

[Article 181: January 20, 1955]

A crooked walking stick has many uses. You carry it in one hand or the other, sometimes balanced in the middle, and at others, end-ways like the conventional cane. Carrying this walking stick creates a balance and swing to your walk which greatly lessens fatigue. With it you examine animal holes, overturn rocks, and find lizards or snakes in hiding. It will push away cactus or thorny brush out of your way and permit you to pass through without severe scratches or torn clothing. If a fire is needed, it will pull pieces of wood within reach, and as the fire burns down, [it] will enable you to keep the fire together. When the fire is no longer needed, with this you can push dirt over the ashes.

If you wish to sit down or to sleep, the stick will clean the ground of rocks or cactus thorns and miscellaneous brush. Then on occasion, if [it's] necessary to kill a rattlesnake or to capture one alive, the walking stick is all you need.

Often on a walking trip you will have water canteens, lunch, perhaps a camera, or extra clothing, for instance, not needed for a side-trip of exploration. In this case stand the stick straight up in the ground and tie the neck handkerchief to it as a marker. Then you can safely leave your extra equipment and find them on your return. Things left on the ground in the desert are often very difficult to find again.

I have never figured out just why it is fun and helpful to carry a walking stick on desert trips. Perhaps this is a memory relic of the past, when primitive man carried a club or spear in search of game. Or possibly it serves as sort of a decoration or satisfies a desire to feel important, like a drum major who waves his stick at the head of a band on some city street. . . . If extra clothing, canteens, or other things become heavy or burdensome, then swing them from one end of the stick on your shoulder like a soldier's rifle. For a rest and change, put the stick across the small of your back and then loop each arm over this in the crotch of the elbows. . . .

As you walk, make a game out of it, too. Say to yourself, if you walk half [an] hour without resting, then you can take one swallow of water. When the top of yonder hill is reached, you can sit down and rest. And at noon with the sun high overhead, the lunch can be opened, etc. If this is open country and you intend to retrace your steps, then it is wise to often stop and look backward, and you will never become lost.

[Article 182: January 27, 1955]

[This article originally printed in the Palm Springs *Villager* continues in articles 183, 184:]

IN A CRATE $5.00

During my homestead days on the desert, I acquired some 11 burros, one a small colt colored like a Maltese cat, with thick soft fur. He was bright-eyed and active, with small neat legs and trim feet.

Walter Woods, a Hollywood screenwriter, saw him one day and remarked, "That little burro can be used in a picture we are shooting now in Hollywood. The company will pay you five dollars for him delivered to the railroad here."

Five dollars was a large sum of money to a man like me, marooned on the desert without even enough to eat some days. I agreed to ship as directed, but when I delivered him to the railroad station, the agent said, "The animal must be crated."

This presented a problem, as there was no lumber anywhere to build a crate. The little fellow had been named Malty, for its Maltese color. So I staked him out back of the depot where there was grass to eat, and water ran over from the railroad water tank. I then walked seven miles to my home cabin and hunted for any loose boards, and next day packed them down to the railroad on the back of Merry Xmas, together with nails and hammer, thus walking another seven miles. By searching around the empty boxcars, a few bits of other material were found, and by ingenuity a crate was finally constructed to Malty's measurements.

[Article 183: February 3, 1955]

When all was ready, the depot agent helped me coax Malty into the crate, and this was placed alongside the tracks. Here he waited for the Los Angeles-bound train to arrive from Indio.

At last, down the tracks in the sandy waste appeared a puff of smoke; the train came rapidly closer. It whistled for the crossing, and the colt was scared out of its wits by the shrill noise. When the engine rumbled up, with the heavy bell ringing and hissing steam two yards from the crate, it was just too much for the little dweller of silent places. Malty became frantic with terror and started kicking, biting, and pawing, braying loudly all the while. The crate now started falling apart. By the time grinding brakes had brought the train to a stop, Malty stood in a pile of wreckage which had once been a crate.

The train crew was in a hurry to start on their way, and it looked as if Malty had won and would remain on the desert. They called the conductor, who finally said brusquely: "Put him in the baggage car, and let's go."

Two men lifted the little burro into the open car door among the trunks and boxes. The train pulled out and was soon just a spot on the way to Banning. I needed the dollars very badly, and I still had ten burros left. But at that moment, I would have given the five dollars quickly to get Malty back again.

I walked another seven miles to get home, which made 28 long miles of walking through sand and cactus to deliver the burro. I was depressed in spirits and could not forget the scene at the depot. Malty was probably still trembling in a corner of the baggage car. I could imagine his efforts to keep on his small legs as the chugging train rounded curves and made stops at small stations. It was a "local" train.

The five dollars in my pocket seemed a poor price for losing my little burro.

[Article 184: February 10, 1955]

Next day, I was still thinking of Malty. I wondered if he arrived safely. I knew he was not appreciating the glamour of Hollywood. A week, a month, and a year had passed but still I remembered the little colt. Occasionally I thought of Walter Woods, and several times considered a time to write him to inquire into the whereabouts of Malty. However, I did not get around to posting the letter, and as further time passed my recollections of the fellow became less frequent.

The First World War came up . . . and in the course of time, I volunteered into the Tank Corps, and thus quickly found myself in uniform at a camp near Washington D.C., very far from this beloved desert of ours. One evening I was sitting on a hard bench in an empty, musty, cold warehouse. Some old black-and-white moving pictures were being shown for the entertainment of a few soldiers off duty.

As I sat down with wet boots and my uniform all damp (it was raining outside), on the screen a tramp appeared, trying to steal a long loaf of French bread from the kitchen of a private home. Just as he was endeavoring to crawl under the board fence, still holding the bread, to get out of the yard, a small burro runs up and snatches the long loaf of bread in his teeth. That burro was my Malty!

Desert memories clouded my eyes with tears, and I cannot tell you what happened to the rest of the screen story, because I stepped from the building into oozing mud and trudged in the rain to my tent. Two things, two questions, filled my mind. Why wage wars, and why do people live in a wet, cold, rainy country when there is a real desert out West?

[Article 185: February 17, 1955]

There have been endless numbers of poems written about the desert; however, of them all, there is one which most truly expresses the real feeling of the open natural desert. This one is called "Mornin' on the Desert." It was found many, many years ago, written on the door of an old cabin far out in the desert. The author is not known. I first read this poem 50 years ago, and so its real age is a guess. . . .

> Mornin' on the Desert, and the wind is blowin' free.
> And it's ours, just for the breathin', so let's fill up, you and me.
> No more stuffy cities, where you have to pay to breathe,
> Where the helpless human creatures move and throng and strive and seethe.
>
> Mornin' on the desert, and the air is like a wine,
> And it seems like all creation has been made for me and mine.
> No house to stop my vision, save a neighbor's miles away,
> And the little 'dobe cabin that belongs to me and May.
>
> Lonesome? Not a minute. Why, I've got these mountains here,
> That was put here just to please me, with their blush and frown and cheer.
> They're waiting when the summer sun gets too sizzlin' hot,
> An' we just go campin' in em' with a pan and coffee pot.
>
> Mornin' on the desert--I can smell the sagebrush smoke;
> I hate to see it burnin'--but the land must sure be broke.
> Ain't it just a pity that wherever man may live,
> He tears up much that's beautiful, that the good God has to give?
>
> "Sagebrush ain't so pretty?" Well, all eyes don't see the same.
> Have you ever saw the moonlight turn it to a silver flame?
> An' that greasewood thicket yonder--well, it smells just awful sweet,
> When the night wind has been shakin' it--for its smell is hard to beat.
>
> Lonesome? Well I guess not. I've been lonesome in a town.
> But I sure do love the desert, with its stretches, wide and brown.
> All day through the sagebrush here, the wind is blowin' free,
> An' its ours, just for the breathin', so let's fill up, you and me.
>
> AUTHOR NOT KNOWN

[Article 186: February 24, 1955]

In 1926 I opened a large general county store with a meat market in Ventura County and stayed there 11 years, until 1937. Then I returned to this desert. For over 40 years the desert has always been my point of destination. The purpose of the store was to accumulate money to use for development of plans here.

This store had a tie with Desert Hot Springs, because to it one day came the "right-of-way man" for the Metropolitan Water District, to obtain right of passage for a pipeline to cross some of my desert land. In the building of the [Colorado River] Aqueduct, it was very necessary for the water district to take water out of Big Morongo and then convey it in pipelines for work being done in Little Morongo, Blind Canyon, Long Canyon, Wide Canyon, and other points along the Little San Bernardino foothills.

And to this same store also came L.W. Coffee, with Mrs. Lillian Coffee, to ask me questions and thus learn important facts about this Desert Hot Springs area and water conditions. Without L.W. Coffee and his ability, and without Aubrey Wardman and his vision of the future, it might have been another 50 years before there would have been a city started with residence lots made available for you in Desert Hot Springs. The details of this story will be taken up later.

[ARTICLE 187: MARCH 3, 1955]

In 1937 I sold the store and asked my mother if she would stay part of each year with me on the desert. She would.

Not only was I returning to this desert, but I had large plans all dreamed up to make important developments on the homesteaded acreage. These plans would make full use of the climate and hot water, with Miracle Hill the center of all activities.

There would be swimming pools of different sizes and temperatures. Also there would be a small lake where boats could float, which would be a great novelty on the desert. Boats will float on three feet of water, just as well as on 30 feet.

[ARTICLE 188: MARCH 10, 1955]

Tunnels could be dug into the centre of Miracle Hill, thus making underground rooms available for healthful sweat baths, made possible by natural heat in the earth.

From those rooms an elevator would take guests to a hotel on top of the hill itself. In all California, there is no other spot quite as spectacular as the top of Miracle Hill. Winding roads along the hillside would give building locations for very unique homes. An art gallery, museum, café, golf course, and other outdoor amusement would furnish diversion for visitors.

To start such ambitious plans, of course, took much more money than I had. So here follows the rest of the story, which is very funny. One day I put on a coat and vest which I never used. Thus attired, I drove to the nearest town that boasted the largest bank with which I had any acquaintance. I wanted to borrow money. I reasoned banks exist for two reasons: rich people put money in the banks, and we ordinary people borrow it out.

This bank was in a rich farming area, but the town had only two streets of importance. One goes east and west, and the other north and south. Where they cross in the center of town stands the bank, an impressive stone building on the corner with the best frontage.

Customers of the bank entered a not-too-large door on one side of the building. On the better side was a very large plate glass window commanding an unobstructed view of both streets and all town activities.

Inside this large window sat the chief officer of the bank in lonely and impressive dignity, at a wide, highly-polished desk. He always wore a small flower in his coat lapel. Occasionally he pressed a buzzer button, and a trim secretary entered on tiptoe to take some dictation for letters. Then she withdrew, practically backing to the doorway. Everyone was afraid of the man at the desk.

[Article 189: March 17, 1955]

The bank officer at this desk held the future of many a man and ranch under his control, because it was this bank which made possible most farming operations for miles round. Cash money was always needed to carry on the type of farming followed in that part of the county--money either to put in crops or to hold products after the harvest for better markets. Therefore the bank could hold or advance money as it chose, having the power to do so, and thus make or break farms and farmers.

My auto at the time was a two-seated Model T Ford. The old-fashioned top had been worn out and thrown away. This machine had once been on the desert here. It belonged to Bill Anderson, who homesteaded the land just north of the L.W. Coffee Foundation bath buildings and across the road on Eighth Street. Desert rats had destroyed the upholstering, and the car was in a generally much dilapidated condition.

So that day when I went to the bank to try to borrow money, you can understand why I could not park it right in front of the bank. Therefore I secreted it out of sight in an alley back of the bank. Entering the bank by the side door, I took my place on a hard bench along with some farmers who had mud on their shoes and overalls from irrigating land. All of us [were] waiting to talk to the dignified man with the small flower in his lapel. We had occasional glimpses of him seated at the big desk when the private office door opened to admit callers.

I was ill at ease, tired, overworked, and had waited more than an hour to present long legal papers, which the clerks had given me to fill out in detail. These papers recorded my past, present, and future hopes and possibilities of having (blank) dollars to repay the loan in full and with interest and setting forth various penalties.

[Article 190: March 31, 1955]

At last it came my turn and I was ushered into his august presence. He was cool, calm, and cold, as bankers usually are. He listened to my story, tossed my papers carelessly on top of others over his desk. There was not even a semblance of a smile. He coughed once, cleared his throat, and stated that the matter would be held under advisement.

I then returned to my paintless, topless Model T in the alley. But during my absence, a gang of men erecting telephone poles had obstructed the alley in such a way that it became necessary to drive out in the street and pass right in front of the bank. This I did.

But when just exactly in front of the bank and in full view of the dignified man at the big desk behind the plate glass window--just at that very precise, inopportune moment--something went wrong with my desert auto. Bill's auto from Desert Hot Springs. In fact, several things went wrong all at the same time.

The rear axle broke. Thus the Model T lost both its rear wheels, and the back end flopped down into the muddy road. Then one of the pistons became loose and broke a hole in the crank case, several other things happened at the same time, and the noise was pretty awful. And there I sat on the wreckage of the Model T, in the very middle of the town and in front of the bank, with half the car flat in a mud puddle.

Bystanders gathered. Men drifted out of saloons to see the excitement. The car could not be pushed nor pulled. Idle Mexicans rolled cigarettes and told me in Spanish what to do. But nothing could be done.

A long funeral procession came along and was stalled also in front of the bank. Finally the town marshal appeared. . . .

[Article 191: April 14, 1955]

The banker looked at all this confusion while safely seated in his swivel chair, but did not even smile. He adjusted the flower again in his coat lapel and continued his dictation to the trim secretary. After many years of life and borrowing most of the time, I doubt much if it is at all possible for a banker to smile.

I phoned an auto dealer in another town who sold used cars, and he sent me a battered Chevrolet pickup. When it arrived, I transferred my personal belongings to it and boarded this ancient machine. And with many "Adios, Amigos" from my Mexican well-wishers, I departed with no dignity at all. This was one of the low points in my life.

The loan was refused. And the super desert plans perished this day, along with the Model T Ford.

However, in that year of 1937, I did return once again to the desert. I started a trading post and art gallery of very meager importance in the shadow of Miracle Hill.

The B-bar-H Ranch had just recently been opened to the public, and their guests always came over to see the trading post, because it was such an unusual place to find out in a desert.

To Lucienne Hubbard this whole desert owes very much appreciation for having established the B-bar-H Ranch in our locality. This ranch and its visitors have published our desert all over the U.S.A. and spread the knowledge of Desert Hot Springs, with its marvelous hot medicinal waters, far and wide. Every time the name of Desert Hot Springs gets into print, it is a boost for our community.

Lucienne Hubbard was no ordinary man. He was a professional writer of note, war correspondent, and contributor to *Reader's Digest*. As a writer and producer of plays in Hollywood, he was known from coast to coast in movie and theatrical circles.

[Article 192: April 21, 1955]

Quite early in the history of this desert, [Lucienne Hubbard] obtained 2 or 300 acres of raw land. On this he drilled wells and planted many acres of dates. This was mostly for a place of relaxation from the whirlwind life that is Hollywood. But his many friends begged for invitations to come down to the peace and quiet and cheerful sunshine of the desert.

Therefore, finally to please everyone and make more accommodations available, it became necessary to open this ranch to the public. Gradually all temporary buildings were replaced by very modern and deluxe structures. A swimming pool was added, wide stretches of grass soon covered desert sand, and very gorgeous beds of flowers delighted guests.

The accommodations and comforts of this B-bar-H Guest Ranch became famous, and guests came from every state. From New York, Chicago, Philadelphia, San Francisco, Hollywood, and other large population centers came the great and the near-great to stay a week, a month, or the season. Bankers, financiers, men prominent to political life, big businessmen rubbed elbows with movie stars, actors from the legitimate stage, famous writers, and well-known musicians.

[Article 193: April 28, 1955]

The B-bar-H register bore the names of such famous persons as Mary Pickford, Warner Baxter, Ronald Coleman, and his wife, Bonita Hume, Phil Harris and his wife, Louis Sobol, the top columnist for the New York *Journal American* and syndicated papers, Si Seadler, the MGM representative for the eastern coast, Max Schuster of the famous publishing house of Simon and Schuster, Sol Lessor, the producer of the Tarzan pictures and others. On the register also was written Jack Krindler, who originated the 21 Club in New York City, Lionel Barrymore, John Barrymore, and many more . . .

Everyone registered at the B-bar-H Ranch came once or many times to my small, crude trading post, and so I knew them all.

Because Lucienne Hubbard was an outdoor man and an expert rider and horseman, the atmosphere of the place was entirely western in character. Overalls or khakis and cowboy shirts of bright colors or wild patterns were worn at all times. Many went in for expensive, high-heeled cowboy riding boots. The ladies also planned all-out for informal western clothing and had many most attractive outfits.

In the dining room often would be groups of happy people dressed like real cowhands, and at the next table might be people just down from the city all decked out in swank evening clothes. But if they stayed long on the ranch they "went western." After the first day or two, all guests called each other by first names, and so when they came to my place at Miracle Hill, I too called them by first names, no matter how many millions they had or how much space in the newspapers was devoted to their name. We all had fun.

The desert is not a place where much dignity can be held. Old San Jacinto Mountain cuts all men down to a reasonable size. You can shout at San Jacinto, or swear at it and the weather, but there is no response. It cannot be threatened by force nor impressed by money or reputation. In the desert all men are equal in importance.

Charlie Bender was the active host and manager of the B-bar-H Ranch of those days. He, with his wife's help, organized picnics, campfires, and riding parties for nearly every day. Of course they visited Seven Palms, Willow Hole, various mountain canyons, along with trips to Two Bunch Palms, that beautiful oasis so close at hand. And often [they] came to my homestead ranch on the east end of Miracle Hill. These rich, sophisticated people seemed to get a great kick out of visiting my first crude trading post. They would buy my desert sketches to take back to cities and browse round among the strange things that I then had for sale . . . There were some women's high-buttoned shoes, corsets, coyote traps, small arms ammunition, fans from Cuba, jewelry from Europe, women's hats, groceries, tobacco and smoking materials, cloth yardage, candy, women's veils, nails, soda pop, cough syrup, horse collars, pins, ribbons, needles, and dynamite, etc. This trading post offered them novel amusement. And in the cabin where I lived were desert paintings, human skulls from Alaska, Indian relics, desert artifacts, animal skins, various articles used by Eskimos on the Arctic Circle, dried deer meat, or rabbits freshly killed, hung up for the next meal. . . .

Outdoors near the gate I kept a lot of snakes and chuckwallas as pets and would lecture on them if they were interested. They thought it strange that a man would keep rattlesnakes just for pets. Then I had trapdoor spider nests, and many had never seen one of these. So we all had happy days.

They came on horseback and tied the animals to three hitch racks of long poles securely fastened to upright railroad ties deeply set into the ground. Always visitors were surprised to find a man way out in the desert that could talk to them about England, France, Mexico, Cuba, Central America, Alaska, all cities of the U.S.A., Canada, and many other places. They bought Coca-Cola and soda pop, but drank it without ice, and we all had a wonderful time.

Mostly they came in groups, but occasionally a lone rider would come over to talk for a time with me. These talks were quite often about the desert, but in some instances they involved personal problems, and the visitor wanted a complete outsider's viewpoint. I discovered that people that were rich or on the front pages of newspapers also had problems like the rest of us sometimes. Those having problems were about equally divided between men and women.

[ARTICLE 194: MAY 5, 1955]

One cold, windy day a man came alone and tied his saddle horse to the hitch rack, which was under a shed roof, and we threw the horse an armful of hay so that it would be contented in the shelter of the trading post. Then the stranger and I went into the cabin and sat by the small sheet-iron stove. Into this we kept shoving gnarled desert roots and chunks of mesquite, so that we were warm and comfortable. No matter that the rain blew against the window and dripped from the roof.

We talked of many things, as men will, and covered nearly all the subjects, politics, war, history, books, plays, women, the desert, Europe, art galleries, religion, life experiences, some quite personal, re-incarnation, life after death, all these and many more. We talked for hours, and found in each other a good companion for a rainy day. We had a very happy time.

When at last he arose to go, I said, "And what is your name?" He smiled and said, "I am Lew Ayres."

Those of you who have read newspapers in the yesteryears can remember when Lew Ayres was one of the most talked of actors and personages in the U.S.A.

Among other things in the trading post were 12 exact authentic copies of the first plates ever used at Harvard, and much prized by many people. Cousins in Boston had given me their sets.

One day John Barrymore and John Decker came over and safely remained the afternoon talking with me, and we had a very enjoyable time, just the three of us. He was quite intrigued by the Harvard plates and bought a couple. He and his friend looked at the snakes, trapdoor spiders, and asked many questions about the desert.

In Palm Springs at the time was a famous newspaper reporter from New York, and he heard the story from John Barrymore, so the reporter came over to investigate for himself, if all he heard was true, and to see what a desert hermit looked like. Herewith follows his story as printed in the Palm Springs *News* . . .

[ARTICLE 195: MAY 12, 1955]

[This article by an unnamed reporter, originally published in the Palm Springs *News*, continues in articles 196, 197, 198:]

REPORTER MEETS NICK, A TRAPDOOR SPIDER ON MIRACLE HILL

When John Barrymore and John Decker became lost in the desert some weeks ago and fell into a sand pit together, they brought back some weird tales. One of them was about a gent named Cabot Yerxa. Barrymore said this man lived on a place called Miracle Hill in the desert and sold 30-year-old corset laces, and he had all about him little desert beasties called trapdoor spiders.

Figuring the Great Profile had hallucinations, the editor this week sent the Manhattan Reporter out to find Yerxa, corset laces, and trapdoor spiders. . . .

Stiff-lipped, the reporter left. After wandering two days half lost through galleta grass, burro weed, and daisy bush in the wastes between Desert Hot Springs and B-bar-H Ranch, Yerxa was found piling up rocks in the sun to build a house.

"Howdy," said Yerxa simply. "Where's the trapdoor spiders?" the reported asked rudely. The sun was very hot.

Yerxa smiled and said he had 'em and he'd show 'em.

"You get any beer here?" asked the reporter.

"Nope. I just drink water," said Yerxa, adding he had marvelous water on his homestead. In fact there were 15 hot-water wells on his land. One had 180-degree temperatures, which was enough to hard-boil eggs and make tea. Another well near his house was so hot it heated up the cabin and he could walk round on his cement floor at night in his bare feet and not even sneeze. In fact a person could sleep right on the floor if they cared.

[Article 196: May 26, 1955]

RATTLESNAKE PEN, AND HAPPY CHUCKWALLAS JUMPING ONTO NET

"You got any 30-year-old corset laces here?" asked the reporter as they walked toward Yerxa's house.

"Yep, that's in the Miracle Hill Trading Post. I've also got about everything else there from hair- clippers and beads and curios to real Harvard plates."

Yerxa then explained the Harvard plates were rare and valuable to people who attended Harvard. Yerxa himself knows New England well, says he's a direct descendent of John Cabot. He looks a little like Norman Thomas. His eyes are a desert-sky blue. His nose aquiline, his face tanned and his pate somewhat sparse of graying hair. He is in his 50s and walks slightly pigeon-toed at a fast gait, saying he travels best through sand that way.

As they passed through the front yard of his house, the reporter looked in a pen and saw a bunch of rattlers and chuckwallas. The latter were climbing up ladders and jumping into nets of gunny sacking. They seemed very happy.

[Article 197: June 2, 1955]

HOUSE A MUSEUM AND YERXA AN ARTIST

The house was really a museum of oddities Yerxa had picked up in his world travels, working as seaman, stagecoach driver, newspaper man, cook, dog-sled driver, prospector, and other things. Sealskin boots, Indian buffalo shields, and even a Chinese fly-chaser hung among the many curios on the walls.

There were also many paintings, all done by Cabot Yerxa. There were pictures of White Russians done when he studied at Juliens in Paris, he says. Swarthy Eskimos done at Cape Nome and Red Indians done here hung along with desert scenes. Everything is for sale, but Yerxa mainly lives on revenues from his paintings.

"Yes, but where's your trapdoor spiders?" asked the reporter, somewhat desperate. Yerxa nodded Okay and rose. "I think it is a fake," [the reporter] added.

Out into the sun they went, the reporter belligerently.

"I'll show you a special one," Yerxa said, pointing to a box filled with dirt.

"I don't see any trapdoor," said the reporter.

Yerxa chuckled and took his knife point, gently sticking it into the top dirt clump. And sure enough, a trapdoor opened. It was set so finely, there were no visible markings when it was closed.

"Nick might come up and see what's doing," said Yerxa.

"Who's Nick?"

"Nick's the spider's name."

"How do you call him out?"

"You don't. He comes up when he feels like it."

[Article 198: June 9, 1955]

TRAP DOOR OPENED

Out into the sun the reporter and Yerxa went. Then Nick, a little grey spider, came to the hole opening and peered out at Yerxa and the reporter. When he saw the reporter, pencil in hands, he slammed the door shut.

"He's temperamental to strangers," said Yerxa, adding he often comes out at night, stranger or no.

The reporter waited round that night to see Nick. Something unexplainable happened in the desert moonlight. The two struck up [a] great friendship. The reporter has taken up property near Yerxa and is currently digging a hot water well.

Last word received as the *News* went to press was, the reporter was some 30 feet down into the ground with Nick the Spider. He claimed he was near, very near hot water, because he and Nick had already sighted steam.

[Article 199: June 16, 1955]

The snake pit was about 13 feet square, with a cement floor in order that nothing could dig out or into it. The four sides sloped inwards so that snakes trying to crawl over would lose balance and fall backwards, which the larger ones often did.

There was a sign, reading, "Ten cents to see the snakes," but people often gave me a dollar if I would go down into the pit and handle the reptiles and lecture on the rattlers and others.

As a rule there were from 12 to 25 snakes of all kinds in the pit, with diamondbacks and sidewinders in the greatest numbers, because people were more interested in them.

Rattlesnakes prefer live rats and mice to eat, so it was quite a task to feed them. Also I kept chuckwallas, a few horned toads, and some desert tortoises, which are very curious and interesting creatures peculiar to desert regions. Sometimes, too, there were desert chipmunks for visitors to look at.

One of the most loveable men that ever came to the B-bar-H Ranch was Si Seadler, who self- styled himself, "The Broadway Cowboy." He it is who represents M.G.M. for the full Atlantic coast and has to deal with many problems. But somehow he used to arrange things so that he could come to the desert for a couple of weeks each year. He always borrowed the wide-brim hat of Lucienne Hubbard, so this added to his own outfit of western clothing and made him look quite authentic as a cowboy.

He took long horseback rides and gloried in all the sunshine that he could get. If Lucienne was here, they rode together. Long rides--Mission Canyon, Long Canyon through the mud hills to the east, Wide Canyon, and other rather rugged days on horseback, with a light lunch tied to the saddle--but days spent in this desert do a city man very much good, and the desert will always welcome Si Seadler back again, because he is one city visitor who loves the desert as it is under natural conditions.

On some of his trips out here from New York, he was accompanied by his wife, a very charming lady, who was known affectionately among their friends by the nickname of DoDo. My mother always enjoyed their visits to the desert very much.

[Article 200: June 23, 1955]

June is the month for moth millers, flies, ants, grasshoppers, and many small bugs and insects to appear. Some of these are a nuisance, many are interesting to watch, and a few are harmful to a degree. Centipedes and tarantulas are not often seen; they look bad, but the bite does not amount to much and is not serious.

Scorpions will come into the house if it is not properly screened. They sting with a sharp hook on the end of their tail, which is painful but not at all dangerous.

However, in June there is one among the bugs which you should look out for and kill when seen. This is called the kissing bug, assassin bug, or walapai tiger. It is attracted somewhat by lights, therefore will come into the house if it can do so.

This one is a very dark brown to the point of being black in color, with a faint one-stripe pattern of lighter color on its back. In size they are from one-half to one inch in length, and the shape is like an elongated narrow triangle. Its very slender, narrow head protrudes forward and sharply downward with bug eyes and prominent cutting proboscis, with which it cuts a hole in its victim's skin to suck out blood. The Kissing Bug frequents rat nests and is also found around small animals. Its food is warm blood. Therefore careful screening of houses is important.

In daytime this insect will hide under rugs, quilts, blankets, or in dark corners. They move fast and are difficult to catch. At night they will climb walls, curtains, ceilings, or be seen near windows. Look for them. This is June and their month--we have killed seven in the Pueblo this week.

The Kissing Bug lives on the blood of warm-blooded animals and so might bite a human also. They do not attack people, but come and bite when they are asleep. Sometimes [they] are able to take blood without awakening the sleeper. The area about the puncture quickly swells [and] turns red over a surface one to three inches or more in diameter, which becomes feverish and inflamed. There is a strong itching effect. . . .

This small insect and the black widow spider are the only ones to call for any concern. All the other bugs and insects are very interesting and practically harmless. Adios, Amigos.

[Article 201: July 7, 1955]

Warner Baxter, Ronald Coleman and his wife, Bonita, were very congenial friends, and they were interested in bird-life or other denizens of the desert. Therefore when they came over, we four would take short walks round the cabin and investigate what was going on in the desert.

There were some trapdoor spiders living in their tiny underground homes in a red clay hill just across a dry wash. And we would try a few moments to see if we could find locations of others to add to those we knew. During sunny days we could see horned toads or lizards hunting for food. Now and then a snake, and they were curious concerning its name and character.

Desert plants and vegetation were the cause of many questions as to the common name and uses made of them by Indians . . . For instance, different plants' leaves will cure colds or throat trouble. Some cause hair to be lustrous and healthy, still others can be burned as incense. Also dyes can be made of pleasing color from common plants, and another bush makes [a] healthful drink. Hours on the desert can be happy hours, when far removed from jazz music and cushion-seated automobiles.

In the yard I had placed several small boxes to encourage birds to nest in them. Some did. And to these bird boxes we would give our attention from time to time.

Under the roof of palm leaves on the large ramada was a nest made by a pair of shrikes, sometimes called "butcher birds." This bird, the "shrike," is very active and strong. It is a fighter and chases all other birds out of its domain. These shrikes of mine would fly into the desert, kill lizards and small snakes, and then hang them on a barb-wire fence near the ramada. Then as food was needed for the young birds in the nest, the parent birds would tear off pieces of meat with their strong beaks from the visible supply hanging on the fence. That is a system.

[Article 202: July 14, 1955]

Another bird activity that interested Warner Baxter was centered around a heavy birdhouse made of one-inch lumber, resembling in shape a rural delivery mailbox eight inches square inside, 24 inches long, and with one end entirely open to the nest, so that birds could come and leave at any time, no matter what the weather. This box was unoccupied for a long time. It was too big, I guess, for most birds on the desert are rather small.

However, one spring two yellow-breasted woodpeckers came and looked the box all over carefully. They would each take turns in entering the box from the open end and walk around a bit, then dive out the front straight down at a sharp angle for the ground. But just in time, they maneuvered their wings and swept upwards and came to rest on top of the box.

Two days of this investigation seemed to satisfy them both that the place was suitable for a nest and [to] raise a family. Their actions were the same as two real people talking things over. But now the unexpected thing happened. One of the birds started at daylight the next morning to peck a hole in the bottom of the box from underneath. It would cling to the side of the supporting post and peck upwards at the bottom of the one-inch board forming the bottom of the nest box. Very slowly by steady application and persistent expenditure of energy, the two birds finally had a hole chipped out of the bottom of the box so that they could enter and leave with ease. Then, and not until then, did they start to build a nest and later lay eggs. Young birds were raised successfully.

Always they entered and left [by] the hole in the bottom of the box, thus entirely ignoring the full open end to the east. When they left the box, they literally dropped head first down the hole, but before hitting the ground, they opened their wings and sailed off over the desert in safety.

[Article 203: July 21, 1955]

Now I understand the reason for all the preliminary flying about the box before they started to peck the hole in the bottom. The male bird had dived off the box several times; then he evidently told the lady bird, "You can do that too." And when they found that they both could dive from the box and yet have time to spread wings and zoom upward, they decided that it would be practical and safe to dig a hole in the bottom of the box to use as an exit. Those birds were not so dumb after all.

The cabin yard was divided quite definitely. The shrikes chased the woodpeckers back from the ramada, and the woodpeckers kept the shrikes well away from the wooden box on the heavy post.

Warner Baxter, at his home in Hollywood, had a very large glass case which was full of extra-size ants. He said he would be pleased to give this to me, if I would drive in and stay over a day and bring it back to the desert. But I never had time to go. My trips to the city were often two or three years apart. . . .

[Article 204: August 4, 1955]

There never has been a ranch quite like the B-bar-H as it was in the early days, and there never will be another. During the 1930s and 40s it was a place out in the open natural desert, with luxurious living accommodations to which celebrities and interesting personalities came for days or weeks. Under the ownership of Lucienne Hubbard, the ranch atmosphere was very western, friendly, and informal.

On the register were such names as John J. Raskob, Joan Crawford, the Marx Brothers, playwright Sidney Kingsley, Tyrone Power, Darryl Zanuck, Walt Disney, Marlene Dietrich, Wendy Barrie, publisher Schuster, Si Seadler, Robert Taylor, Eleanor Powell, Beatrice Kaufman, Warner Baxter, Ronald Coleman, Sol Lessor, Jack Krindler, and many other prominent people.

Jack Krindler it was who originated the world famous 21 Club in New York City, one of the best known eating places in the U.S.A. Every winter he came to the B-bar-H Ranch to stay awhile, and came often to the trading post to see me. He was young, very athletic, good-looking, and always togged out in the best cowboy trappings. An excellent rider, he rode only the most spirited horses in the barns. In the saddlebags were always expensive dates, candy bars, or peanuts to give the horse. It pleased him to have the horse follow him around to get the candy.

Jack's business made him plenty of money, and he was a free spender. His saddle had been specially made for him and heavily trimmed in silver at a cost of $4,500. One of the cowboys, when he first saw this saddle, remarked, "Danged if that ain't the first all-silver saddle trimmed with leather I ever seen." The bridle was hand-carved of thick leather and with silver doodads all over it, for which he paid $250. Then he had spectacular silver spurs that dragged on the ground when he walked.

[Article 205: August 11, 1955]

Round his neck Jack wore flaring, bright-colored neck handkerchiefs of large size. They were pure silk and of heavy material.

His riding boots were of black leather and polished, showing much decoration. Made carefully to order for perfect fit, the bill was $250. Every day he wore heavy silk shirts of different colors, hand embroidered and trimmed with white leather fringe. He purchased several at a time and they cost $85 each. Jack had several hats hanging in his room, but preferred a large black sombrero, silver-trimmed, that cost $150. He carried beautiful gloves of real buck string with much fringe to wear if needed.

So you can see that Jack Krindler had the best and most expensive cowboy outfit that has ever been seen on this desert. Unfortunately he has joined the other cowboys in the sky who have also gone west, or I am sure he would still come to this desert every winter season. His business was in the big city, but he was at home and happy when on this desert.

In my memory I still see him riding over our desert in the sandy stretches between cactus and greasewood. This in the days before auto roads were made, or Desert Hot Springs was advertised. Adios Jack, hasta la vista.

One day he nearly fell off his horse with surprise. It happened like this. Jack rode up to bid me farewell. He said, "I'm flying back to New York tomorrow. I like you, and you have given me much of your time. Therefore when I reach New York, I will send you a dozen bottles of the best whiskey in the U.S.A. What is your favorite brand?" I smiled and thanked him for the gesture. But I replied, "I never drink anything stronger than goat's milk, and even then I must know the goat."

I was teaching him a few Spanish words, which he liked to toss around in his expensive restaurant for the confusion of New Yorkers, so therefore we exchanged parting greetings in Spanish, and he was gone to New York and the big city, and I, to pick up dry sticks to cook my next meal on the desert.

[Article 206: August 18, 1955]

Sol Lesser liked to have a group with him, both men and women, so he always encouraged others to come along too. He was always talking business, the show business. So I listened in to many details of the screen world, actors' salaries, box-office sales, and the problems of the producer in general. Sol Lessor produced very many of the Tarzan pictures. . . .

I have been on the desert for 42 years, and much of that time have lived alone for different periods, and so was a hermit of sorts. During a couple of years once, I wrote nearly every month a letter about this desert. These letters were published first in the New York *Journal American* in the space called "New York Cavalcade" by Louis Sobol, the top writer for the Hearst papers, so they had seven million readers after they were reprinted in other papers.

This is a reprint from the Louis Sobol space, years ago. . . .

"Perhaps you wonder what a desert hermit does all day? Well, at this time of year he sleeps out of doors on a cot. Advancing daylight awakens him at a few moment after 4 a.m. So he first looks under the cots to see if a rattlesnake may be also sleeping there. Then he methodically shakes out each shoe to make sure that no scorpion or tarantula has nested therein during the night. Stockings also are turned inside out, just in case."

[Article 207: August 25, 1955]

[Letter to Louis Sobol, originally printed in his "New York Cavalcade" column, continues in articles 207, 208:]

First order of the day is pumping by hand 25 buckets of water and carrying them to some trees around the cabin. The eight chickens are fed and watered, also the pet rattlesnakes in their pit, and a dish of fresh water put out for the birds who depend on it.

Next, the different traps, which have been set for various pestiferous small animals, are attended to. Mice and kangaroo rats go into the snake pit. Trade rats are thrown out for the two brown owls to pick up during the night. Rabbits provide meat to be given to the chickens daily.

Coyotes the hermit does not trap, because he likes to catch occasional glimpses of them on the desert and to hear them call in the quietness of the night. Rabbits are the number one nuisance where any attempt is made to grow things on the desert, and coyotes help to keep them in check. As one homesteader says, "Rabbits will eat fence posts if they are painted green."

The two brown owls have been here nearly a year now. They stand almost 15 inches high and spread their wings not quite a yard. One morning there was an owl with its foot in a trap which had been set for a rat. It glared at me with full round yellow eyes, ruffled its feathers and bit with a sharp beak as I released it. I wore heavy gloves. It walked slowly away, stomping its feet in great indignation, like an old man with a cane and a limp.

[Article 208: September 2, 1955]

Fully a week later I was in about the same spot when out of the blue came a whirl and a fury of feathers. It was the owl. It stopped three feet above my head as I threw up my walking stick for protection. Screeching, it gave vent to full owl displeasure and owl profanity. But it retreated before the menacing stick. We do not credit ordinary birds with memory, but this owl surely in its mind connected me with the trap experience.

Now it is time for the hermit to make a cup of coffee and eat cold rabbit. This being finished and as it is seven o'clock in the morning, he would ordinarily go to work with a shovel, making roads or mixing concrete. But as this is Sunday, he writes this letter, then takes up paints and brushes and a square of canvas and paints a desert picture during the best daylight hours.

To you in New York City, I send greetings, you who have millions of people but a few stars. I have millions of stars and no people. Adios amigo, Cabot Yerxa. . . . .

[ARTICLE 210: SEPTEMBER 15, 1955]

100 years is a long time. But let it be known that 100 years ago, a U.S. surveyor named Henry Washington came to this desert where we now live, in 1855, and surveyed sections 30-31-32 Township 2 South, range 5 East, SBM. He was a relative of President George Washington.

Then the next year, in 1856, another U.S. surveyor named J.G. McDonald arrived and surveyed sections 28-29 and 33 to tie in with the sections surveyed by Washington. I can take you today to some of these stones placed on this desert 100 years ago. No other surveys were made here until after another 50 years. 100 years ago there were no railroads, of course, so those first survey parties came down from San Francisco on horses with all camp equipment carried by pack animals.

The reason for this very early survey of only a few sections of land was because gold was discovered in California during 1849. This made the need urgent for communication between the East and the West, together with transportation of freight and passengers. There was much excitement and confusion in Washington. Overland routes were planned along different trails, then traveled only by trappers and other pioneers.

One such route was planned to pass through this desert and to use Two Bunch Palms water holes as means of supply for men and animals on the way to Los Angeles. The oasis at Two Bunch Palms was one of the few places in this vast desert region where water could be obtained easily.

However, as history tells us, Two Bunch was never used for this purpose. The route used was over the Borrego Desert, then to Warner's Hot Springs in [the] Santa Rosa Mountains, and so on into Los Angeles over more friendly terrain, with better roads, more water, and safer climate. But we did get the early survey of a portion of [the] Desert Hot Springs area.

[ARTICLE 211: SEPTEMBER 22, 1955]

. . . Hilda Gray was a single woman of good education, and weighed not over 110 pounds. Yet she lived alone, cleared land with a mattock, gathered wood from the desert, and carried water all during her four-year homesteading period, as well as most of the men.

Her original cabin was of single-wall 1 x 12 pine boards, with bat strips on the cracks. Like the others on the desert, it was 10 by 12 feet, with a black felt paper-covered roof, which made the interior hotter than hades, except on cold days.

Later this cabin was made somewhat more livable by the addition of a lean-to. Kerosene lamps were burned for lights (candles melt in desert heat). Cooking was accomplished on a wood stove. The wood she had to gather on the desert and carry home in her arms, no matter what the weather.

[ARTICLE 212: SEPTEMBER 29, 1955]

. . . But Hilda Gray went through all this cheerfully and with rare courage. Her cabin was one mile out on the flat desert southwest of Two Bunch Palms. Every day she had to walk those two miles, one out and one back, to carry enough water home to last over one day's needs. Then the next day, walk and carry again. And the next, and the next. Because every day, water is the first necessity.

For the first two years of her stay on the desert, she made daily trips for water and carried home two gallons, which weigh 20 pounds. That was the limit of her strength. Sometimes strong winds blew, which added to the effort. Occasionally sidewinder rattlesnakes lay in the path.

Of course she made these trips in daylight, because at night it would have been unwise to leave the cabin.

Burros at that time cost 10 dollars. So after the first two years she was able to finance a small burro, which then afterwards carried 12 gallons of water--two five-gallon square kerosene cans and two one-gallon canteens. There was an iron drum at the cabin for water storage now, but if the daily trip was not made to Two Bunch Palms, then the burro drank four gallons from the container of precious water reserve.

[ARTICLE 213: OCTOBER 6, 1955]

The water hole at Two Bunch Palms was just that and no more. By this time (1914), Riley, Carr, Yerxa, etc., had cleaned the hole out until it was six feet across, surrounded by heavy brush and about eight feet deep. Water very slowly trickled in from a sandy bottom until the water level was five or six feet from the top.

A ladder with round rungs rested on the bottom [and] gave access to the water. Going down in the dark hole on the ladder and holding on to one rung with the left hand, it was then possible with the right hand free to force a canteen into the water until it bubbled full. The five-gallon cans had to be filled by repeated trips with canteen, because five gallons of water weighs 50 pounds.

When Miss Grey first arrived in the shadow of palm trees at the Two Bunch Palms, she filled a tub with water and bathed alfresco out in the open. Her small dog, Trixie, would have barked had anyone approached, but no one ever did, because there was no stranger on the desert. The two or three neighbors who knew the procedure would stand still if we heard the dog bark and wait for a cheery shout from the palm trees, "O.K., you can come now."

After bathing, she washed all the clothes from the cabin and hung them on a wire stretched between two trees before proceeding to fill the water cans. By the time they were filled, all clothes were dry. And the return journey made to the cabin out in the desert sand, that one mile, she said, often seemed like a dozen on hot days or windy ones.

[ARTICLE 214: OCTOBER 13, 1955]

Burros are all different in temperament and intelligence, and the one [Hilda Gray] had knew less than any animal in the world, and was quite the most worthless. But because it carried the water, she was very fond of it and would sometimes tie a bit of ribbon to the straps. She named it "Babe."

Sometimes this burro would become frightened at a snake in the path, or for pure meanness it would run and jump until all the water was spilled, and the cans [were] on the ground. This was a wonderful reason for much profanity, but Miss Gray was not that type. So she merely gathered up her belongings, returned to the waterhole, and refilled all the cans again.

In the year 1915, Mr. Chapman, who had a desert claim on 80 acres of Two Bunch, together with Orr Sang and Dana, his father in-law, combined to do some cement work at the pool. They made a shallow reservoir into which the small overflow from the waterhole spilled lazily, and this in turn spread over the low side of the new tank and promptly sank out of sight in the thirsty sand. The idea was all right and meant to be helpful, but the levels were wrong and the plans not practical. So it never worked properly and caused a hardship on everyone who came there for water.

Wild cattle that roamed the desert in those days came in to drink and then lay down in the water tank. Soon, and continually, the water was all fouled up, covered with green scum, the outlets filled up, and soon the water from the cattle tank flowed back into the original water-hole, and the whole situation was one grand mess. Dead leaves, green scum, dead rats or snakes, cattle dung, mud flies, and wind-blown sand. If you had to get drinking water out of such a place, you might cave in.

But not Miss Gray. She always took a leading part in clearing the place up. We helped, but sometimes she was alone in the desert and had to do all this by herself.

[Article 215: October 20, 1955]

Then she had the same problem about mail, as we all did. From her cabin to Garnet and back, to mail a letter was about 12 miles . . . , and on a hot day, or a heavy windy day, that is quite a journey. When I passed her place on my 14-mile walk to the railroad, she was very glad to have me mail them, and I always carried 10 gallons of water on Merry Xmas for her iron barrel, after I had dug a well at my homestead. A trip to mail a letter in those days took all day long, so we should all pause sometimes and appreciate the many varied things we have in Desert Hot Springs to make life easier and more enjoyable.

. . . Hilda Gray came to this desert to stay on her homestead claim in October, 1912, and was the first woman to ever live in the Desert Hot Springs area. She had a very pleasing smile, and so much intelligence shown in her eyes that she was quite attractive. Even though many of her daily tasks might be described as man's work, she never wore overalls or any article that could be classed as men's apparel. Her clothing was always feminine and somewhat frilly. A straw hat tied on with ribbon gave protection from the sun. Her shirtwaists were always freshly starched and with long sleeves. A khaki skirt neatly patched, where torn by desert brush, reached only half-way from knee to ankle, because it is unwise for a woman to wear long skirts in the desert, which might hide from vision rattlesnakes, spiders, scorpions, etc.

Always she had tightly laced canvas leggings extending to her knees as protection against rattlesnakes. And there were many in those days when we first came to this desert. During my walk to the railroad for mail, it was quite the usual things to kill from three to seven rattlesnakes on every post office trip.

[ARTICLE 216: OCTOBER 20, 1955]

After she completed her four years of homesteading and fulfilled the other government requirements, she moved to Arcadia, settled on a one-acre piece of ground and resumed her vocation of stenographer in a lawyer's office. She has since departed this world. Hilda Gray was a most unusual woman. She filled a very obscure niche in the scheme of things, but filled it well, with great courage and optimism. May we all do as well.

I purchased her buildings and odds and ends when she left the desert, including that worthless burro, which by then had a colt of even less intelligence, if that were possible. One day these two animals wandered down to the Southern Pacific railroad tracks west of Garnet. They stood perfectly still in the middle of the R.R. tracks, paying not the least attention to the onrushing train or shrill whistle blasts, and so were killed outright.

During the summer of 1916 I would drive a team of burros hitched to a small rickety wagon from my cabin on Miracle Hill down to the Gray homestead on the flat desert. Then all day I worked alone taking the buildings apart. Using a nail-puller, every nail was saved and straightened for future use. Each night some boards were placed on the wagon and hauled home. Most of them now are part of the Indian Pueblo. . . .

[ARTICLE 217: NOVEMBER 3, 1955]

Miss Gray was a very methodical person and a tireless worker. There were little piles of scraggly desert wood here and there which she had carried home, when the weather permitted, for fuel. In the cabin everything was in perfect order. Dishes, very clean, rested on paper-covered shelves. Small bits of string were coiled or rolled into balls and stored in small cotton sacks. Other sacks and boxes contained patches of cloth, clothespins, jar tops, corks, nails of several sizes, not over a pound of each, and other miscellaneous small articles--all things were segregated.

On the east side of the cabin was a small space of sandy ground, protected by box boards thrust endwise into the soil to form a low fence. In this tiny plot she had raised a few struggling radishes, onions, small weather-beaten leaves. . . .

Miss Gray could not conceal her pride and felt somewhat repaid for the time and effort those tomatoes represented. She had spaded up the ground, constructed the fence alone, set rat traps every day, chased rabbits and birds with sticks, and had carried the water from Two Bunch Palms to moisten the very dry, sandy soil. And here one day were tomatoes in the middle of the desert as a reward for her perseverance and lonely work. She was as happy as a woman with orchids.

The cabin had wooden batt strips nailed on the outside to cover cracks. Inside she had made flour paste and concealed them with strips of newspaper. Knot holes were covered by tin can tops, all of which made the place more livable and helped greatly in keeping out the wind-blown fine sand, which searched any opening to enter buildings. . . .

"Proving Up" on a homestead claim under the old laws in vogue 40 years ago was quite an ordeal. We had to appear on the second floor of the post office building in Los Angeles with several witnesses on the day which had been advertised for some time in advance. For all [of] us to arrange to be there starting from the desert was very much involved with many details. Burros, dogs, cats, chickens, and children had to be moved round or provided for in some way. Transportation on the desert and to the city had to be carefully arranged. Travel costs were very serious expense items which must be surmounted by the person "proving-up," and appeared to us as big as the national debt. . . .

[ARTICLE 219: NOVEMBER 17, 1955]

Well, anyway and at last, the momentous day [for "proving up"] would arrive. Promptly at nine o'clock in the morning the grass land office door would open, and we few desert people would file in and stand awkwardly before the high, long wooden counter. Back of this were the clerks. Many questions were asked, and a handful of legal papers filled in on both sides.

Those city clerks were always well-dressed, and by contrast we desert people felt ill at ease because our clothes were old, patched, and faded by many washings and drying in the sun. Shoelaces were always a problem on the desert. They broke so often we would reach the city with one black lace and one brown one. And if no lace was to be found, then to improvise, it would be a piece of common string or short piece of wire.

. . . A popular hat with men on the desert at the time, and practical because of its cost, was one of braided strands of palm leaves from Mexico. A peon's work hat, it cost 25 cents. These lasted two or three years and sometimes, if there was no other hat, they were worn to the city on a short trip.

The women had on miscellaneous pieces of clothing that had outlasted the four years, or which they had made without a sewing machine or dress pattern, or perhaps had borrowed for the occasion.

[ARTICLE 220: NOVEMBER 24, 1955]

We all, both men and women, were suntanned to a color as dark as Indians or Hindus. We also showed the lack of proper food and were noticeably dehydrated from the desert clime under our strenuous living conditions. We were lean and thin, as a group.

Homesteaders in those early days never had money to buy proper foods, and there simply was no place to get fresh things, even though money had dropped out of the sky. So much less could we buy presentable clothing. That was impossible to all.

To us, the one and only goal in life was to somehow live out the four years on the homestead and "prove-up" in order to get a title. This was a common purpose, well understood and shared by everyone alike.

During those early years there was almost no work at all, except in small amounts and at rare intervals. When we worked for each other, it was returned in kind. When this was not possible, then payment was at the rate of 20 cents per hour. Riverside County gave some pick-and-shovel work at times on section lines to rough out a roadway. This paid 25 cents per hour and was sought after.

Carpenter work brought 25 to 40 cents per hour. Well-digging, because of its danger and know-how, scaled 40 to even 50 cents per hour.

Once Jack Riley and I took a contract from the county to break up piles of many rocks that used to be in the way between Rolly's windy corner and the Southern Pacific

R.R. depot. I was paid 25 cents the hour and Jack 50 cents the hour, because he had to shoot the big rocks with dynamite.

[ARTICLE 221: DECEMBER 1, 1955]

Now, to set up a dynamite charge, you cut off enough fuse to give you time to run for safety when lit. No one wants to be a sissy, so this is always cut a little on the short measure. And a fast run is necessary after lighting. The next thing you do is gingerly take off the copper gadgets [and] slip the hollow sleeve onto one end of the fuse.

So far so good. But here comes the man of know-how, and his job is to "bite" the copper sleeve and pinch it to the fuse. If not bitten hard enough, the sleeve will not be properly pinched and the dynamite stick will not explode. If you bite too hard, the cap explodes in your teeth and off goes your head.

After pinching the sleeve to the fuse, it is thrust into the soft dynamite stick and you are ready to lay the charge. So light the fuse and run for cover.

On this job Jack and I took turns in "biting" the dynamite. He was paid to do so and I, because I always try to learn how to do new things.

[ARTICLE 222: DECEMBER 8, 1955]

Gee, the [previous] story makes me think of something that I had forgotten. Under my bed, outdoors where I sleep, is a bundle of dynamite caps wrapped in a piece of woolen cloth to act as a cushion. It has been there for 18 years.

You see, I have always been looking for a mine in the Little San Bernardino Mountains, and they would be needed in such case. Also I thought that I might hand-dig another well some day and would use them if rocks were in the way.

Funny place to keep dynamite caps? No, not at all. If they were stored on a shelf in the house and fell off, they would blow up the room. If left in the workshop and a man dropped a hammer on them, the man would be blown up. Therefore, the only safe place was under my bed, and they have been there now for 18 years. On the desert, time is not important and so slips away without notice. . . .

[ARTICLE 226: JANUARY 5, 1956]

. . . Years ago in one Sunday issue of the New York *Journal American*'s magazine section, my desert letter [to Louis Sobol] was featured along with a color picture of Marlene Dietrich, dressed for her role in MGM's "Kismet" production. My page was under the heading: "HERMIT GOES TO TOWN."

"Cabot Yerxa, my hermit correspondent from the desert of Garnet, California, writes that for the first time in seven years he hiked off to the big city to see what was going on. This is what he found:

"In seven years styles have changed, but the people have not. Going to a bank, the pens were chained to the desks. On the desert we leave valuable tools out of doors for weeks at a time. And calling on friends in an apartment building, I noted the doormat chained to the concrete wall. Out in the desert one day an Indian sold some cattle. The buyer offered a check, which the Indian refused and demanded cash. So the next day the buyer returned with $1600 in currency. The Indian was busy irrigating a small garden, so he put a rock on the bills to keep the wind from blowing them away and went right on irrigating the garden." . . . .

[Article 228: January 12, 1956]

[From letter to Louis Sobol, originally printed in his "New York Cavalcade" column:]

"City men wear coats, collars, ties, cuffs, and hats, changed for the season. They are pressed, polished, and styled up until no comfort is left in them. And a very considerable part of each man's [income] is expended for clothing. Not because it wears out, but because fashion dictates a change. Men of the great outdoors dress for protection from the weather and so are comfortable at all times.

"Another nerve-wracking habit of city people is the continuous turning-on of the radio. The art of conversation has all but been destroyed by the loud and persistent voices of the tin-pan radio announcers, cutting into all personal talks.

"You city people go to the zoo and look at all the funny and queer animals, birds, and fish in their different cages, occasionally. WELL! I have been to the city and seen people just as funny and queer. So I am glad to be back home on the desert again, and look out the door and see 35 miles of open country and no people at all.

"The day I returned, I went down into the snake pit to visit my pets and rest my soul. The rattlesnakes seemed to smile widely in welcome. The chuckwallas climbed gleefully over my shoulder and nibbled playfully at my ears. And in the eyes of the desert tortoises I seemed to see tears of joy (maybe it was moisture in my own eyes). Anyway, even a hermit is welcomed back to the desert. And the desert rewards all those who dwell therein with peace, health, and happy hearts.

"Adios Amigo, Cabot Yerxa, Out in the desert where summer days can be found in winter"

[Article 229: January 26, 1956]

. . . Three years ago out in the desert near the Old Indian Pueblo, I heard the weak cry of a cat. There was just a fleeting glimpse of a tiny black kitten as it ran away to hide in thick brush.

That night I carried a small saucer of milk to the spot, but saw no cat. However, in the morning the dish was empty. This went on for over a week before I discerned the small fellow to be watching one night as I again placed the saucer of milk in the accustomed spot.

It took more than a month to break down the kitten's distrust and get it to come to the goat corral for its milk. Even then, if I approached within 10 feet, it would back up and spit with all fur raised along his back. Fully two months passed before it could be petted.

Someone had thrown this tiny kitten away on the desert when it was so small that it could curl up in a cereal bowl. Weak, thin, and scared, it distrusted all humans. However, after three years it has become large and strong and is a very important part of the Old Indian Pueblo. Now he acts as though he owns the place.

[ARTICLE 230: FEBRUARY 2, 1956]

Because this cat is black with gray shades, we named him Smokey. He is no ordinary cat. His fur is very thick and much longer than usual; also he has a very large, pronounced, noticeably gray ruff round his face and neck like that of a lynx. He walks proudly with his tail straight up in the air. It is much too long to be like other cats--in fact, it measures 15 inches, and the end has a curl just like a question mark. He keeps curling and uncurling the last 5 inches of his tail as he walks.

After trying all the different canned cat foods, of which he took small interest, we tried a can of dog food. This he likes. Presumably he considered cat food too sissy for a cat that lives out-of-doors all the time.

Often he rolls in desert sand, getting his fur full of it. At other times he just lies in the sand, flat on his back with all four feet up in the air, if the day is warm. This is also the custom of a lynx.

He is never allowed in the house, but has many various dry, comfortable hiding places round the buildings to his liking. He sleeps all day and prowls the buildings and surroundings during the night, thus keeping the premises free of rats and mice.

To see this very large black cat walking on the various rooftops of the Old Indian Pueblo or sitting quietly on broken adobe walls in the moonlight is an eerie spectacle and makes you think of witches and haunted houses. Smokey still runs from strangers and so far has eluded coyotes, who often come close to the buildings at night. . . .

I sleep out-of-doors and occasionally see them. One night I awoke to find a full-grown coyote standing 15 feet away looking at me. On another occasion a coyote snatched a rooster by the neck as he was making the first crow for daylight and scampered up the steep bank near my outdoor bunk.

[ARTICLE 231: FEBRUARY 9, 1956]

This Old Indian Pueblo has 65 doors, and it is possible to enter or leave the building by any one of 17 doors. So therefore in the morning when I first go out to gather the milk from the goat, Smokey the cat never knows which door will open. At first he was much frustrated and would come screaming in protest for his breakfast if a strange door was used. But Smokey now has this situation all figured out. The Pueblo has 30 different roof levels, and it is his custom soon after daylight to sit on one of the high levels and listen intently for a door to open. Then down he jumps from one roof level to another, finally to the ground to claim his breakfast.

This cat Smokey looks so very unusual that I searched a book giving the history of cats. From the book it seems that his ancestors came from Abyssinia. These were the sacred cats of old Egypt and were believed to have psychic powers.

Occasionally Smokey makes hunting trips all by himself into the small canyons back of the Pueblo and stays out from three to five days. Back in those canyons there is much small life--desert rats, field mice, kangaroo rats, lizards, snakes, rabbits, etc. So he has a very exciting time, no doubt.

Sometimes he brings home with him to the Pueblo rat tails, rabbit ears or feet as proof of his prowess and hunting success. These he deposits always under one certain tree in the yard.

He drinks milk out of a blue bowl, always the same one. One day this was being washed, and his milk was put in a green one. He refused to drink it. I went into the house and changed the milk into his regular blue bowl. Then he drank the milk.

Is he color-conscious? I do not know. Because it is difficult to explain everything that animals do.

When I work outside about the buildings, mixing concrete or making repairs, Smokey comes along and sits down to watch what goes on. He accompanies me on the short walks to burn papers out in the desert and follows closely at my heels as the milk goat and various desert tortoises are fed and watered for the day.

If we leave by auto at night, he comes out of hiding to watch us go, and many times when we return from the village, Smokey will slither out of a dark corner and walk up sedately to be petted. If boxes, blankets, or bags are in the car to be unloaded, he jumps up on the hood and sits down to watch this operation.

Sometimes Smokey comes in with battle scars and bleeding cuts from fights with desert rats, some of which are large. He watches closely for dogs or coyotes and makes fast runs for the Old Indian Pueblo. He then scampers up broken adobe walls and gains the safety of high rooftops.

When he sits down on his heels in quiet contemplation, he wraps that extra-long tail all round his four feet and purrs very quietly. During such times he keeps flexing the claws in his front feet. The sharp claws are fully extended and then retracted. This goes on for many minutes.

His eyes are sometimes yellow and at other times appear to be green.

Yes, Smokey is a very unusual cat.

[Article 232: February 16, 1956]

[Letter to Louis Sobol, originally printed in his "New York Cavalcade" column, continues in articles 233, 234, 235:]

This week it was necessary for me to walk a dozen miles over the desert. At the break of day I left the cabin. Billie the owl screeched at me, questioning my early departure. Billie and his family live underground during the day, but at night they patrol the vicinity of my cabin for rodents.

As people come into a new country, wildlife disappears. Some native palm trees stand like military guards beside a small, muddy, scummed pool of water at their base, which this morning was deserted as I passed by. But in days gone by this pool was much frequented by wildcats, lynx, foxes, coyotes, and smaller animals. Many birds of different kinds came from a distance for water. Sometimes mountain sheep or a lion came in for a drink.

Leaving the brushy places amid the low hills, I was soon out upon the level valley floor. Greasewood bushes, sage, bunch grass, and other desert vegetation were still green and thrifty-looking from the scattered winter rains. Between plants, the sand was blown floor-smooth by recent winds.

On this clean, dry sand was recorded the passing of many small desert creatures, even the delicate tracery of the ambling journey of the small black circus beetle, which will stand on its head for minutes if you touch its back with a twig.

The trails left by many various kinds of lizards differed sufficiently to determine that they were fly-catchers and -eaters, or meat-eating leopard lizards. An occasional desert iguana had dragged its leisurely way in open places, and horned toads had left tiny marks here and there.

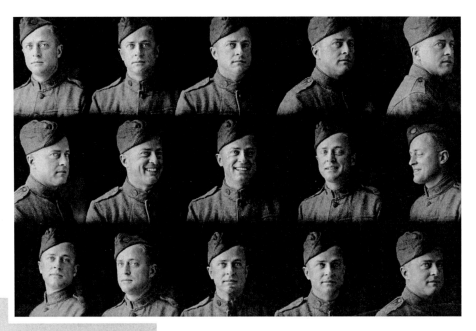

Cabot in his Army uniform wearing 15 expressions, ca. 1919

Cabot holding his niece, Jeannetta, next to his brother Harry. Cabot's wife, Mamie, and their son Rodney in front, ca.1918

Cabot and son Rodney in uniform, ca. 1919

Cabot's Fertilla store and post office near Blythe. Cabot is on the far right, his mother Nellie at left-center, ca. 1920-1925

A studio portrait of Cabot, perhaps during the Fertilla years

Cabot's Moorpark home; "We left it in August, 1937," wrote Nellie.

Cabot's Trading Post on Miracle Hill, in business from 1937-1941

Cabot and Nellie, Moorpark 1936. He seems to be wearing a grocery store coat.

Cabot in front of Trading Post on Miracle Hill, ca. early 1940s

Cabot's second wife, Portia Fearis Graham, sitting in front of the Trading Post; the sign beside her reads, "Ring Bell for Storekeeper."

Cabot's "Ranch" near Miracle Hill Trading Post, Cabot second on the far right. A frequent gathering spot for family and friends

Harry Oliver, humorist and friend, wrote "Desert Rat Scrap Book." Cabot sold it in his Pueblo, ca. 1944.

[Article 233: February 22, 1956]

Then too, the footprints of the racing lizard were in evidence, and it was plain to see where he had risen to his hind legs and proceeded in high speed, without using its short front feet.

Once I picked up a bull snake and let it coil round my arm in its friendly fashion, then placed it carefully on the ground. We parted friends with full appreciation of each other. Later a beautiful black- and red-banded king snake lay in a spot of sunlight, making a fascinating pattern of contrasting colors. I enjoyed its graceful movements as it slowly moved into a low green bush and turned curiously to look at me.

At another place a coyote trail crossed my course at right angles. The sand recorded he was not trotting freely, as it is his habit to do. He was crouching low and taking short steps.

So I followed the trail and found where he had dragged himself along in the sand, gathering his energies together for the fatal spring upon a rabbit, whose tracks were intermingled with those of the coyote. But Sir Coyote had missed.

In the sand at this point, I could read the rest of the story. The rabbit was sitting lightly on its furred hind feet and nibbling buds and tender bark from a desert willow. He had detected the coyote and left the spot in a great hurry. Some of his jumps measured 15 feet.

He got away that time! The coyote had leaped clean and far, as the sand prints showed, but had failed to secure his breakfast.

In the next dry water course, called Mission Wash, some desert willow trees were in bloom. The leaves [were] slim and pointed, the flowers bell-shaped, with ruffled edges of apple blossom pink, and sweetly scented. My favorite desert flower.

[Article 234: March 1, 1956]

Those desert willow trees have roots of tremendous length and store up water from sudden flash floods, often months apart. They are always growing near some spot where the desert's very infrequent rains give them extra moisture.

Not long afterwards I crossed one portion of Devil's Garden, so-called because for several hundred acres, cactus of many different varieties grow to the exclusion of anything else. In and out among the cactus' thorny plants are small trails of twisted pattern. These are mostly made by rabbits, who, when chased by coyotes or foxes, make a run for the Devil's Garden and thus elude their pursuers by making quick turns among the thickly growing cactus stalks.

Always watching the ground ahead of me, as is the custom of desert men, I saw, neatly coiled, a large desert horned rattlesnake, nicknamed a "sidewinder" because of its peculiar mode of traveling sideways. They will eat lizards if necessary, but prefer warm-blooded creatures. Therefore it is their habit to coil and wait patiently for some small rodent or bird to come within striking distance.

Not being in a hurry, I sat down on the ground close by the rattler to watch it. It moved its coils slowly into a better position to observe me fully. So we communed with each other. And the rattlesnake, sensing no animosity from me, resumed its watch for the morning meal on the trail through the scattered brush. . . .

[Article 235: March 8, 1956]

Oh, yes, I carried a snake stick, as I always do on desert ramblings, and could have captured it alive or easily killed it. But capture was without point, as I did not have a sack that morning, and killing was unnecessary. So I left the snake happy in its life and surroundings.

In handling snakes over a term of years, I have come to the conclusion that it is best to have no fear of them, and also to have no animosity toward them. Because, in some mysterious way, snakes seem to recognize those persons who bear them no ill will. In support of this theory, we often read of babies or very small children being near rattlesnakes and not bitten by them.

Adios, amigo, to you in New York, Cabot Yerxa, Happy to be out in the desert

[Article 236: March 16, 1956]

One of the most interesting creatures to be found in the desert is the tortoise, which is classed as a reptile because it crawls. In the ocean similar creatures, which grow to great size, are called terrapins, and from them turtle soup is made.

All over the U.S., you are very familiar with mud turtles, seen along the banks of lakes and rivers. They will eat meat. But our desert tortoise is a vegetarian and eats only grass or leaves. It cannot swim, but lives its whole life on dry land.

This very curious tortoise . . . is remarkable because its skeleton is brought to the surface of its body. This formation is frequent enough in lower orders of life, like crabs and many beetle-like insects. But in the tortoise, the bones of the chest are formed into sort of a hard, rounded box, which contains within itself all the muscles and viscera. At the will of the little fellow, its four legs and head can be withdrawn into the shell, leaving no apparent openings. Thus it can rest in peace and perfect safety.

Many small living things on the desert tremble in terror when snakes, foxes, coyotes, or large birds appear. But not the tortoise. Let the coyotes howl! Who cares? Not he.

Mud turtles and terrapins are so constructed that they are semi-aquatic in their habits. Their construction makes it possible for them to progress or live much of their life either in the water or upon the land. They even can stay considerable time under water without necessity of breathing. Not so the tortoise. He lives only on dry land.

[Article 237: March 22, 1956]

. . . By examining the inside of a tortoise, we find the front legs to be attached to the inside top of the shell, and the hind ones are fastened in the same manner. There is no backbone within the shell. The front legs are curiously club-shaped, and the rear ones have a noticeable resemblance to elephant legs, with the comical appearance of baggy pants you are familiar with if you have ever been to a circus and looked at elephants. The tortoise's tail looks like the elephant tail in miniature. Both are extremely curious creatures, and are a demonstration of the "big" and the "little" in this ever-intriguing world of ours.

All four feet of the tortoise have rather thick, dull claws with which he can dig slowly, but well. With the front ones, he digs holes in the ground for winter home or to get shade from the desert sun. But the female, when ready to lay her eggs, will dig holes straight down, using only her hind feet. Into this hole she lays several white eggs, somewhat resembling golf balls, and covers them with earth.

Nearly 120 days are required for the eggs to hatch. Then the newly-hatched baby tortoise must scratch his way to the surface of the ground and face the world alone. His elders take no notice whatever of him. This new arrival is so small that it can be hidden under a silver dollar. How they find food and escape their enemies, both from the air and on land, is quite beyond imagination. But somehow enough live to perpetuate the species.

[Article 238: March 29, 1956]

Do not think that you can rush out of doors in Desert Hot Springs and find a tortoise in an hour. In over 40 years I have only found three in this valley. You see, a tortoise must have green grass and leaves in order to exist, and in this area we do not have enough rain to make this possible. However, in the Big Mojave Desert there is more vegetation, and therefore tortoises are in happier surroundings.

In captivity they are very fond of lettuce, bananas, peaches, grapes, and other fruits. They particularly also enjoy green corn on the cob, picking off one kernel at a time until all are gone. If lettuce is fresh and crisp, they will bite if off very sharply. However, if it is old or wilted, it is held on the ground with one foot and pieces pulled away with its mouth.

These desert creatures will drink milk or water if thirsty, scooping up the liquid with their lower jaws and then elevating the head, which lets the liquid run down their throats by gravity.

Tortoises on hot days will hunt shade or dig a hole underground. They delight in throwing earth over their backs with skillful movements of the front feet. This lessens the heat of sunrays on the shell. Elephants also throw leaves and trash on their backs in hot weather.

[Article 239: April 5, 1956]

At the Old Indian Pueblo, I keep about 23 desert tortoises as pets and for observation, and have had them for a number of years. In November they go into hibernation and do not wake up until the middle of March. During all this time they do not eat, or drink, or move about.

Once, in my ignorance, I placed a pan of water in their pen after they had gone to sleep. One of them sleepily staggered into it and drowned in three inches of water, not being awake enough to climb out.

A baby tortoise when hatched from the egg has 13 spots on its back. These never change in number, but do get larger as time goes on. After a while there comes one ring round each spot for each year of life, just as a tree gets rings.

About 35 years ago, Mr. and Mrs. L.R. Hayward of Coachella were vacationing in the big desert near Randsburg. While crossing a dry lake in that vicinity, they found several desert tortoises, two of which were extremely large. They brought this group of reptiles home to Coachella and were successful in raising some small ones each summer. A couple of years ago they sold their collection to me, and these tortoises are now part of the Old Indian Pueblo's oddities. The Haywards say that in 35 years there is very little change in the size of the two largest ones.

[Article 240: April 12, 1956

[A couple of phrases are not visible on newspaper copies available to the editor.]

Much controversy exists as to the exact age of the desert tortoises, and their life span is not known. But all observers agree that they attain great age, probably 100 years or so. I myself have had some for 50 years. Therefore my conclusion would be that they eventually reach a grown-up size, after which they do not get much larger. Just as a man reaches full growth at 21 or 25 years, even though he may live many years longer.

A tortoise can make no noise, except that when surprised they [. . .] out their breaths forcibly, making a very noticeable sound.

Males will fight each other, the procedure being for one to try to turn his opponent over on his back. This is accomplished by thrusting the other shell projection under the [. . .] and pushing forward strongly with all four feet. Their fights sometimes last an hour.

If left too long on its back, a tortoise will die. Two or three times each day I look in the reptile pens and turn over any that may be upside down, with all four legs in the air, trying vainly to right themselves.

These denizens of the desert are very slow and patient. If you feel all in a dither, flustered and hurried, just sit down and watch a tortoise for half an hour and you will calm down. Because after all, you have nothing to gain by all the dither. Relax—rest—slow down, and you will live longer. The turtle does. Why not you?

[Article 241: April 19, 1956

[A few phrases are not visible on newspaper copies available to the editor.]

The Indians say a tortoise is not as dumb as he appears. They tell the following story to each new generation.

Once upon a time . . . a fox and a turtle were arguing about who could travel faster and best on the desert [. . .] sandy wastelands. So [. . .] decided to have a race and thus settle the controversy. The point of destination was a flat rock far out in the desert, which they both knew.

The fox licked his chops, took a big breath, and started out in [. . .] at high speed. But just as he passed his opponent, the tortoise reached up quickly and grabbed the fox's tail in his mouth. The fox ran and ran, strong [. . .]. Uphill he went at full speed, then downhill again, through bushes and through [. . .] of sand. He knew that he was far ahead of the turtle, though he could not see him anywhere on the back trail!

At last, being somewhat winded, the fox slowed his fast pace, because his feet seemed to be dragging. However, he kept on until finally he saw the rock. Its flat top was but a little way now! With a last spurt of speed he swung round and stopped to rest with his tail brushing the rock. The tortoise let go his grip on the fox's tail just at the right moment and quickly sat down on the flat rock. Then as the fox turned its head to look about, the turtle asked the fox why he had been so long on the journey across the desert!

. . . This most unique character has a stomach like you and me, but in addition Mother Nature endowed it with a water sack as well. If the turtle comes in contact with water from the infrequent rain, it drinks normally like any living thing and puts water in his stomach. But in its case, later on, days afterward, if it needs water in its stomach and there isn't any available, it can by this strange provision of nature take some water from its water sack and put it into its stomach. This is one of the many secrets by which animals, plants, and reptiles can live in a "land of little rain."

[Article 242: April 26, 1956]

One time quite a while ago, driving home in a Model T Ford from a trip to Garnet for the mail, I saw a coil of rope some distance ahead in the sandy one-track road. When I stopped to pick up the rope, I found it had a head and tail! And turned out to be a thick desert bull snake, between five and six feet long! So I happily picked the snake up and carried it home to add to my collection of desert pets. This was a very rare specimen and was as large as they ever get, so I turned the one I had in the snake pit loose in the yard, because it was only three feet long.

The desert bull snake, Pituophis Catenifer Deserticola (quite a name), is harmless and difficult to find in this area. Average specimens seen are from two to not over three feet, so you can see how happy I was to have found the very big fellow. It had 70 large, dark brownish blotches down its back, and the intervening space was dull yellow. This snake has a loose piece of skin in its mouth, used as a sounding board, with which it can make quite an audible "hiss" when it expels its breath.

The bull snake, as is also true of several others, will not bite if picked up at once, but if any delay or nervousness by the picker-up is evidenced, this snake will bite. It is not poisonous, however, and no harm will result.

In picking up snakes, always grasp them in the middle, never by head or tail, as they like these to be free.

The bull snake has the rattlesnake's habit of rapidly vibrating its tail if irritated or made nervous. Should the tail be among dry leaves, the sound will be just like that of a real rattlesnake. So be observant and give this interesting, friendly snake a chance for its life.

[Article 243: May 3, 1956]

This is spring, and a good time to make a plea to all people in the desert not to kill any of the vanishing small living things about us. This means birds, snakes, and lizards. These small desert-dwellers add much of interest to our surroundings.

I make special mention of snakes because all are perfectly harmless, and friends of man, except the rattlesnake. This one is easily recognized by its triangular head, with wide jaws in which the poison is secreted. The rattles of the tail also serve to distinguish it.

The rattlesnake should be killed if near buildings or picnic grounds. But all other snakes you see, without exception, are harmless and beneficial to man. Do not kill them. If snakes or lizards are seen on the highways, then stop and let them pass in safety.

Remember, they were here first, and this is really their country. Be polite--they are.

To carry this thought a little further, visitors and newcomers should be told that all birds, snakes, and lizards are useful and performing a service keeping rats, mice, and other rodents under control.

Also, let it be known that people who have guns can get just as much fun and practice at shooting at tin cans as they would from destroying living things.

Among the lizards, some put in their whole lifecycle eating nothing but flies, and others eat only ants. Some birds eat only flies and moth millers. All will agree that ants and flies are a nuisance on any picnic.

So let us be friendly and considerate of all the wildlife that remains on our desert, so that those who come after us will find a place as interesting as we find it now.

[Article 244: May 10, 1956]

Many things have gone already forever from the desert, so we must guard well that which yet remains. Even night hawks and ground owls are now a rarity.

In homestead days we had great flocks of wild turtledoves that nested in this area. These very appealing birds take turns sitting on eggs to hatch them. And the one that is off duty and searching for food will fly back from time to time and sing a plaintive song to the one sitting on the nest. This song goes on during the night as well as during the day.

Desert valley quail ran around in coveys of 16 and 20 and chirped happily all the daylight hours. Overhead sailed hawks of different kinds, and occasionally great eagles drifted silently down mountain peaks to take a look over the desert. Small, swift foxes and sleek coyotes made their stealthy way among the underbrush. Badgers, skunks, and other small animals could be seen if you walked quietly. At night, great white owls with wide wingspreads floated close above the ground, without sound, ready to pounce upon luckless desert rats abroad in the night darkness. After a rain, the wet sand sometimes held tracks of a mountain lion, or some mountain sheep down from high places to get its fill of desert galleta grass.

All these fascinating things of the past days are gone, so therefore, let us all have care and thought for that which still remains. Those who have guns, please shoot at tin cans!

[Article 245: May 17, 1956]

Many of you who are observant and take a little time to be out in the desert some days will observe that during the spring season numerous different kinds of birds stay a day or two in our area, on their way north after a winter spent in Mexico. Then, in the fall, these various birds pass through here again on their trip south for the winter. Not long ago the annual group of large black crows spent a day here. Did you see them?

Ducks, geese, bluebirds, robins, orioles, wild canaries, vultures, flickers, and many other migratory birds fly through this desert to rest a day or two and then resume their journey to the place of their destination.

This desert is truly a wonderful place if you observe and appreciate what exists and takes place outside of towns, in the open land where nature is undisturbed by man's heedless encroachment and thoughtless ways. . . .

[Article 246: May 24, 1956]

. . . About the year of 1919, an Indian died in Palm Springs. His name was Pedro Chino, and he was believed to be one of the eldest persons in the United States. He had foretold his death more than a month before. His age of 126 years was vouched for by the fact that he could remember the great meteoric storm called the "Falling Stars" of 1833. This occurred when he was 20 years old. Also, an Indian woman who passed away at the Morongo Reservation that year testified before her death that year that she knew Pedro Chino as a grown man, when she was a very small girl. Her age at death was 121 years.

Pedro Chino lived his whole life in this desert. Once, for a number of years, he lived in a camp at the base of towering San Jacinto. This is the largest canyon in the mountain, and the one which we here in Desert Hot Springs see so prominently. (From this canyon will start the tramway in its dizzy climb to the tree- covered heights near the peak.) From his camp location he could look out over the vast desert and see the sun as it first rose over the edge of distant blue mountains which formed a part of the Little San Bernardinos. . . .

[Article 247: May 31, 1956]

Slowly [Pedro Chino] watched each day as the mystery and spell of desert night clouded out all details, and the stars filled a quiet, open sky.

Back in the canyon were deer, rabbits, and game birds. A small rivulet of water was close at hand, there were enough trees to give ample shade, and grass enough for his burro. This was Pedro Chino's camp, and this place now appears on maps as "Chino Canyon" and was so named after him.

This venerable Indian experienced the simple comforts and a tranquility of life not known to millionaires living in a civilized world.

Pedro Chino was for many years, and at the time of his death, medicine man and a ceremonial chief of the Cahuilla Indians, most of whom lived at Seven Palms Oasis in our side of the valley, and others at Two Bunch Palms. He had been medicine man as long as any of the Indians could remember.

The assembled members of the tribe chanted [the] history of their race over his grave, and the ceremonies were concluded before sunset.

However, the Indians believed that the spirit of Pedro Chino would be earthbound until the coming of the next spring, the season when the greasewood puts forth yellow blossoms and the desert floor is sprinkled with flowers of different colors and renewed growth is noticeable in trees and all vegetation, all evidencing a new life, in a new land, for the spirit of Pedro Chino.

[Article 248: June 7, 1956]

. . . Bill Anderson lived in his homestead cabin just across the street from the [later-built] Coffee Foundation Bath Buildings and open bathing pools. Bill lived alone, except for the company of a small white fox terrier dog named Amie, because it was found lost upon the desert.

Bill at that time had just completed a water well in his front yard, and I helped him plant the trees which have now attained size. These you see on the north corner of Eighth Street and Palm Drive today.

I was then living on my old homestead of 160 acres at Miracle Hill. Frank Houghton, a young man in very poor health, lived in a small cabin on the mountainside near the now-Ryan and Headley Miracle Springs pool situated at the corner of Desert View and Miracle Hill Road.

[Article 249: June 14, 1956]

We were the only three men in the Desert Hot Springs area at that time [the late 1930s] and often met in one cabin or the other to eat our simple food. On these occasions we had ample time to make big pictures of the future in store for this valley and to plan in our minds the development that could be made to make use of the hot water and our ideal climate.

We knew full well that the desert, aided by hot mineral water and abundance of sunshine, could improve the health of all who came to stay awhile, and that absolute cures for some people could be accomplished. All this big talk and visionary planning went on for hours, but the combined capital of all three men was less than five dollars, so nothing concrete could be done by us.

However, Bill and I decided that we could do something about roads. Therefore, at our own expense and unrewarded time, we slowly worked on our road plans. Frank was too ill for hard work, but gave us much encouragement.

We first made a road from Bill's cabin down Palm Drive to the corner of Pierson Boulevard for one-half mile. On each side we planted tamarisk cuttings and watered them as often was possible. They did well for a time, but eventually died because there came a period when neither Bill nor I had any chance to carry water.

Then we made a one-way road from my Miracle Hill cabin to Frank's, and from there down the section line of Pierson Boulevard to the corner of Palm where Addington's now is, but which was then known as the Ford Beebe cabin.

From the central corner of roads we made a hit and miss road, taking advantage of any existing trails, all the way to the railroad at Garnet, a distance of seven miles! (It was there that we all had to go to get mail.)

[Article 250: June 21, 1956]

Our most ambitious activity, and one involving much work and effort, was opening a road on section lines from the corner of Palm Drive and Pierson Boulevard, all the way westward to Indian Avenue, then south on Indian Avenue, also on section lines, to the railroad at Garnet. This is seven and a half miles of road-making.

Bill Riley and his mother had a cabin on Indian Avenue, so he worked some on the road, and his brother Jack also. Mike Driscoll put in time on the project, and so did Joe Baunhorn when he was in the desert for vacation. Other very early homesteaders also were active in road improvements.

It was not for some years that Riverside County appropriated any money for roads here, and then in only very small amounts. We homesteaders made our own roads!

Bill Anderson and I always traveled with a pick, a shovel, and a mattock in our Ford Model T cars, and very patiently and laboriously we worked at removing stones or taking out brush as we traveled about the desert. When we went to the post office, we always worked the road down and worked the road back again. So on mail days we carried cold lunch and worked seven or eight hours on the fields.

Our object in all this unpaid work was partly to make our own trips with less trouble, but also, because we were very poor people, we hoped by making roads into the desert, that city people and investors would come into the country, see what was here, and make developments. We reasoned that if there was activity, there would be jobs, and payrolls, and some acres would be sold, etc.

[Article 251: June 28, 1956]

About 1941, I started the construction of the Old Indian Pueblo. Alone and single-handed, because there was no money for a man or machine, I took a pick and shovel, cut down a side of the mountain, put the earth in a wheelbarrow, and filled up a gulch to make a front yard. This nearly took me a year. Then I put the new building in the hole that I had made, because I wanted the Pueblo to fit into the mountainside. I have now been working for 15 years on this project and have plans for five more years of work. . . .

Here follows a letter written [to Louis Sobol in New York] after the Old Indian Pueblo was under construction . . . "From this vantage point on the side of the Little San Bernardino Mountains, I can see across the desert a cluster of buildings which is Palm Springs. Towering above them is the snow-crested peak of San Jacinto Mountain bathed in the early morning sun. Other mountains round about rim this small desert in flowers and green things at this time of year, quite unspoiled by civilization."

[Article 252: July 5, 1956]

[Continuation of a letter to Louis Sobol, originally printed in his "New York Cavalcade" column; continues in article 253:]

"It is a soul-uplifting experience to roam over the sands alone and to climb about the mountain slopes. Or to enter canyons which, perhaps, have never had a human visitor before.

"At such times I think of you and your millions of city dwellers, who live an artificial synthetic life, doped by your pushbuttons and electric-lighted existence amid high buildings and stuffy paved streets. Streets where the sun shines but for a few minutes during a day's time, or perhaps not at all.

"You herd together in crowded office buildings, jam into restaurants at meal hours, squeeze into tiny rooms to live, and snatch restless sleep. You fight traffic in automobiles and try desperately to make this month's salary pay up last month's bills.

"The next time you come out here for a vacation, we will put blankets and bacon and coffee on a pack horse and then go rambling about this desert and wander into unknown rock canyons.

"Some that I know will be cool and shady. If the days be warm with a brilliant sun high overhead, cool springs of water can be found . . . The Indians found them centuries ago, and this knowledge has drifted down through the years to old-time prospectors and 'desert rats.'

"The term 'desert rat' is an honorary one, only bestowed upon a man who has proven, during a period of many years, his ability to endure loneliness, privation, shortage of food and water, and to have the resourcefulness necessary to cope with the unpredictable emergencies of life in a primitive desert country."

[Article 253: July 12, 1956]

"We will sleep on the ground, eat round a campfire, absorb sunshine, and expand our lungs with clean, pure, dry air a dozen miles from any other human. After all, when you calmly analyze your surroundings and get down to basic facts, the only really important things of life are but three, and they are water, food and clothing. All else, civilized man has added to daily life and thereby made it complicated and expensive.

"Even these three, he has managed to make complex. Water is all the body needs for health, but man has made a thousand different drinks--tea, coffee, beer, and alcoholic curiosities, all a detriment to health.

"Good food is a very simple matter, but man has invented unnumbered varieties, most of which are expensive and harmful in many ways.

"Clothing was meant to protect the body from inclement weather, but not so to civilized man. Its usefulness is always secondary to silly patterns and styles which change with the seasons and year to year in such a fantastic manner that he becomes a slave to fashion. He is always hard-put to have his salary meet expanding expenses.

"I am enclosing a picture of the Hopi Indian building that I am now constructing on the mountainside high above the desert floor. It has 30 small rooms so far, 26 different roof levels and very many variations from your conception of a house. I have worked alone on this project several years already and it may take 20 years to complete.

"Yours for today, with my head in the sun and my feet in the sand, CABOT YERXA"

[Article 254: July 19, 1956]

A sailor when on vacation hires a ride on a small boat in a city park, the postman goes for a walk in the country, but I, being a desert man, have just had two or three weeks' vacation on the Mojave Desert near Barstow. In that area the elevation is about 3,000 feet, and much of the vegetation is green. We killed two diamondback rattlesnakes, and they were a rich strong green in color.

It's characteristic of rattlers that their color corresponds quite closely to the predominant color of the terrain where they are found. For instance, near the Pueblo here, as it happens, there is much red clay, so they are deep brownish tan to nearly red in color. Yet in other parts of the desert where white rock or decomposed granite sand covers the ground, rattlers are very light in color, verging into white. Down in the heavy mesquite growth lands toward Indio and further on to Mexico, these snakes are definitely gray, with just a hint of tan resembling dead leaves.

It is this snake which grows to be very large and therefore is quite dangerous. They attain a size that permits them to swallow small cottontail rabbits, but fortunately this over-size snake is scarce. However, if you tramp through the parts of the desert covered by mesquite, be very watchful. . . .

[Article 256: August 4, 1956]

. . . Snakes cannot hear sounds through the air. So the cobra that sways to the native flute is acting in rhythm to his body motion and is not dancing to music. However, if we have cobras, you can play the flute! I never studied music!

. . . Our own little pink boa in this desert is only about 24 inches long, harmless to man, and will coil around your arm or curl into a ball in your two hands, affectionate in its friendly way. This snake has no scales, and its skin is smooth as rubber. They are quite rare.

[Article 257: August 16, 1956]

. . . During one period I lived on the Isle of Pines in the Caribbean Sea off the coast of Cuba. The largest snake we had there was the boa constrictor, 18 feet long. Its habit was, in some cases, to lie on the limb of a large tree a little distance from the ground and then drop onto a man or animal as they passed underneath. You know something? I always made wide circles round big trees!

The natives on that island lived in small houses made of palm leaves. They kept house snakes from three to five feet long to catch rats and mice. These snakes crawled in and out among the leaves of the roof or sides of the natives' homes, wiggled under beds, round your feet or among pots and pans, as well as foodstuffs, in their search for rodents. They were fed milk in saucers.

Often a snake would be coiled up neatly in a chair! In that case just take another chair! Because they would be quite unhappy if you sat down upon them.

[Article 258: August 30, 1956]

Randall Henderson, whom I first was acquainted with about 1918 in the Chuckwalla Desert, where he had a weekly newspaper, has done a tremendous service in acquainting many thousands of people with the beauties and advantages of the Southwestern desert country through his writings. He is editor and founder of *Desert Magazine,* now being published in its own building in Palm Desert. . . .

[Article 259: September 6, 1956]

10 or 12 years ago Randall Henderson mentioned Harry Oliver, Paul Wilhelm, and myself in the editorial columns of *Desert Magazine*, in which he wrote as follows:

"My friend Harry Oliver of Thousand Palms, California, is building an adobe house, a quaint little replica of an old Spanish Mission. Harry has a formula I can recommend to those who aspire to live to a ripe old age. He calls it his 20-year plan. It is very simple. The first day he makes 10 adobe bricks, good bricks with just the right amount of adobe and gravel in them. It takes three days for the bricks to dry and cure. Harry spends the next three days in contemplation of his handiwork. On the fifth day he carefully lays the bricks in the wall. Then he rests and is ready to start work the following day on the next 10 bricks. And thus the cycle continues.

"Not a very speedy way to build a house perhaps, but Harry's theory is that too much speed is taking all the fun out of life for the majority of Americans. And perhaps he has something there.

"Another desert neighbor with a 20-year plan is Cabot Yerxa, one of the old timers in the Desert Hot Springs section of [the] Coachella Valley. Cabot very recently brought a Texas bride to his desert homestead, and now they are building a combination dwelling and art studio up in a gully at the foot of the Little San Bernardino Mountains. Cabot has been gathering materials for that studio for the last 30 years. He has lumber and chicken wire and rocks and sash scattered all over the landscape. But slowly, one stick at a time, Cabot is putting his house together and it is going to be a work of art when finished, which will be in about 20 years. That is, if he stays on the job and doesn't go gallivanting around with his easel and paint brushes, as these artists are prone to do."

[Article 260: September 13, 1956]

[Continuation of an article by Randall Henderson:]

"Harry Oliver and Cabot Yerxa are speed-demons compared with Paul Wilhelm at Thousand Palms Oasis. Paul already has been on the job 20 years, and his grand plans for the development of a super resort at the oasis are still in the dream stage. At the present rate of progress Paul will need at least 100 years to convert his poetical ideas into cement and wood and window panes.

"But do not get me wrong. I envy those fellows, Harry and Cabot and Paul. Somehow, they have found a way to detour all the zip and bustle and worry that keep the rest of us in a state of demoralization. They are healthy and happy in doing the things they want to do.

"As far as I am concerned, it all adds up to this: we need more poets and artists in this old world, and less chamber of commerce secretaries and super-salesmen." . . .

[ARTICLE 261: OCTOBER 4, 1956]

Landmarks come and go. Time erases everything. Here locally, the first real school building was the center of all desert activities for many years. It burned in 1940 and is now forgotten.

About 1923 a man named Drew Oliver, then living at Seal Beach, came to the desert and was much impressed by the great amount of wind blowing in the pass between Banning and the desert. He also noted its strength and great velocity. To most people, that wind was a nuisance. But to him it was a phenomenon and a great waste of natural force which might be harnessed and utilized.

He had an initiative mind, coupled with a flair for promotion. Therefore by 1925 he had many careful mechanical drawings of his original inventions to harness the winds of our "Banning to desert" pass country. Construction of this large, weird machine was started on high ground just north of Highway 60- 70-99 near Whitewater Bridge. Stock in the enterprise was presented for sale to the public, and money was used to continue operations.

The big talking point was that by having the power of the wind, which cost nothing, electric power could be produced cheaper than in any other way. And in Southern California were millions of people ready to buy and use electricity.

Then, of course, after this demonstrator was up and in use, still larger ones could be built, many more of them, and so on to riches for all stock[owners].

[ARTICLE 262: OCTOBER 11, 1956]

Finally, after much work and delays caused by the very wind which was to be the source of power without cost, this huge machine was fully constructed in details [following] the original plans, and was ready for demonstration.

It was all built of heavy iron and steel, well-riveted and bolted together. It consisted of a very large funnel opening some 30 feet in diameter, which could be turned in any direction to meet the wind by the operator, because all was mounted on a circular iron track. The track itself was fastened onto a heavy stone foundation.

The immense funnel of this strange contraption gathered the wind, which was then concentrated down into a steel pipe three feet in diameter, which reached a length of nearly 120 feet. By reducing the wind from the large funnel to the much smaller pipe, wind pressure had been magnified 12 times. Inside the pipe were aluminum propellers turned at great speed by the pushing air, and designed to operate two generators located just below the turbine.

The first generator used came from an old roller-coaster in Seal Beach. This 25,000-watt generator was turned so fast that it burned up.

Oliver and his electrician tried again, this time with a generator obtained from the Pacific Electric Railroad power sub-station. However, here again was trouble. The 14-inch belt connecting the generator burned up. A chain transmission was next used. Then the footings of the generator gave way, and it was necessary to bury it in concrete.

Oliver had many troubles, both mechanical and financial, but lack of money was the biggest obstacle, and the venture was finally abandoned. During 1942 all the machinery was dismantled to be sold as scrap iron. Now only parts of the foundation remain, in mute testimony of an inventor's dream to harness the wind and make electric power without cost.

Oliver's strange contraption attracted the attention of many people who climbed the hill from the highway to get a closer look. That location has many diamondback rattlesnakes, and a number of visitors were bitten. One or two died. So if you go looking for the remains of this old machine, keep a sharp lookout for snakes.

[Article 263: October 18, 1956]

[*Desert Sentinel* editor's note: "This is the first in a series of articles written by Harry Lawton of the Riverside *Press Enterprise* . . ." Continued in articles 264, 265, 266, 267, 268, 269.]

A carload of eastern tourists pulled up outside Cabot Yerxa's fantastic Old Indian Pueblo at Desert Hot Springs recently to park and stare. Finally the driver got out and stalked up to the leathery-skinned desert rat who has been piling endless units onto the bizarre structure for over 15 years.

"I'm a New York architect," he said to Yerxa heatedly. "I want to say your building is the most sinful building I've ever seen. You've broken every rule of architecture, sir!" He then climbed back in the car and drove off with his passengers, who presumably were so shocked by Yerxa's brand of carefree architecture that they didn't get out of the vehicle.

That's the way Yerxa's incredible adobe reproduction of a Hopi Indian pueblo affects some visitors. Others like it. Others have called it the most interesting structure in Southern California. A large metropolitan newspaper referred to it as a "magician's handiwork." A prominent Los Angeles architect, who specializes in modernistic construction, admitted the older his buildings get, "the worse they look." "That's why I envy you working in any material you want," he told Yerxa. "The battered materials you use look better every year."

Whatever the impression the individual visitor carries away with him, Cabot's pueblo remains one of the unique wonders of the Colorado Desert. Cabot estimates [that] since 1942, over 50,000 persons have driven out to gape at his ever-growing structure, and many of them have paid the small entrance fee for a guided tour of the pueblo, which is a combination trading post, museum, art gallery, desert lookout, and residence.

[Article 264: November 15, 1956]

Cabot Yerxa, who is as sinewy and seared by the desert sun at 73 as a dried manzanita limb, has always looked upon himself as an artist. Several years ago the desert rat began painting American Indian portraits, a number of which are hung in the art gallery of the many-storied Cabot's Old Indian Pueblo at Desert Hot Springs.

"There were 300 major tribes of Indians of the North American continent," asserts Yerxa. "I intend to paint one member of each tribe. I figure I'll be 120 years old when I finish the project.

"But then I intend to live to be exactly 120," he adds decisively.

Cabot has been sketching and painting since he was a child on the Dakota prairies. He once spent a year at the Julian Art Academy in Paris, and between bouts as jack-of-all-trades he has always returned to art.

"I do other things to eat, but art is my main interest," he explains. "Right now I'm studying under Bert Procter, who's been art director of the Laguna Beach Art Festival the past seven years."

There's an aching trace of disappointment in Yerxa's soft-spoken voice when he speaks of art. His paintings have brought him little fame or even monetary remuneration.

[Article 265: November 29, 1956]

The neutral colors of the many-storied pueblo merge into the buff-colored foothill background, and a motorist is practically on top of the pueblo before it springs suddenly into sight. The pueblo is nestled in a canyon overlooking the various colored rooftops of the community of Desert Hot Springs a mile away. Surrounding greasewood trees shimmer like smoke in the sunlight.

Built of massive timbers from mountain washes, weather-stained railroad ties, hand-made adobe blocks, and rusty nails collected from the desert, the weird structure fans out in every direction, room upon room.

There are over 35 rooms ("I don't know how many more," explains the white-haired Yerxa, "I haven't counted them all lately.") There are over 150 windows, no two alike. (One woman, after studying the windows, commented to a companion, "Look at those windows. I wonder if that man knows they don't match.")

There are 65 doors, 30 different roof levels, innumerable winding corridors. There are hidden alcoves, a surprise cavern lurking behind a boulder fireplace, and several secret cubbyholes.

Cabot is always building hiding places into his structure. His wife, Portia, a former lecturer on applied psychology, admits she hasn't fathomed their purpose. But it is these hidden cubbyholes which have given rise to inevitable legends that Cabot has buried treasure in his pueblo. Anyone who knows Cabot knows this is unlikely. If he had any treasure to bury, he'd use it enlarging his pueblo until it swallowed up a few more acres.

The mystery is why?

Cabot's stock answer runs as follows: "The Indians of New Mexico never had time to come to Southern California to make one. So I felt it my duty to construct an Indian pueblo right here on the desert." . . .

[Article 266: December 6, 1956]

. . . Unlike most desert rats, Yerxa is not a recluse. He likes the quiet monotony of desert life, but retired to the sagebrush only after a footloose career as an adventurer. . . .

. . . Yerxa was the first white child born in Pembina, N.D. His father, Fred, was a trader for the Sioux Indians on the Dakota prairies.

Yerxa and his brother Harry grew up with the aging Hughie O'Donnell as their nursemaid. O'Donnell, chief scout for General George Cluster, escaped disaster at the Battle of the Little Big Horn when he left to take a message to the rear.

"One of my earliest memories is of my mother burning buffalo chips to keep us warm in winter," [Cabot] recalls.

"Every season the Indians would camp around my father's trading store," he continues. "I had a dog, and one night they caught it and cooked it for supper." Yerxa burst into tears over his dog's fate. "My dad was too scared to stop the Indians. Each year they cooked my dog for supper. My father used to always say, 'I'll get you a new dog when the Indians leave.'

In 1890 the Yerxa family made a train trip to Mexico, accompanied by George Thompson, then director of [the] Associated Press.

"It was an exciting trip for a boy of seven," he remembers. "We were entertained by Porfirio Diaz, then dictator of Mexico. He showed us the room in Chapultepec Castle where Maximilian slept the night before he was taken out and shot."

En route for California from Mexico, Yerxa said the train was held up by bandits. "There was a lot of shooting, but no passengers were killed. The bandits carried away their own dead."

One morning about daybreak, Yerxa continues, the train stopped in the Colorado Desert at a station called Palm Springs. "It's now called Garnet," he points out.

The conductor let the small boy take a walk outside the train.

"I stood there and looked off across the desert at what is now Desert Hot Springs. It was a wonderful view, and I never forgot it." . . .

[Article 267: December 13, 1956]

. . . The descendant of explorer John Cabot ran away from his home on the Dakota prairies in 1900 at the age of 16 to join the Alaskan gold rush. Some of the souvenirs of that trip may be seen in his pueblo museum.

"I arrived in Cape Nome, and it was a pretty rough place then. They'd kill a man in a shooting brawl every day and sometimes two a day," he recalls.

The youngster soon made a livelihood purchasing newspapers for 12 cents each and hiking miles into the wilderness to the mines, where he sold the papers for $1 each to news-hungry miners.

"I was trying to ford a river one day, and I fell in and got soaked to the skin," he remembers. "I went on until I found two Eskimo tents, and the Eskimos invited me in to get warm." According to Yerxa, he thereupon decided to live with the Eskimos awhile. During that period he learned the Eskimo language.

The following year Cabot returned home and struck up an acquaintance with a New York artist, George Rehse, noted for his sketches of Indian life.

[Article 268: December 20, 1956]

Together they journeyed to Ghost Dance Flats near the Pine Ridge Indian Reservation to watch the abdication of the famous chief, Red Cloud, who was stepping aside for his son, Jack Red Cloud. More than 2,500 Sioux Indians were gathered for the ceremony.

"A New York photographer arrived, and the poor dumb cluck set up a tripod and black cloth to take pictures, and the Indians went at him with clubs. He ran for his life and didn't come back," says Yerxa.

The anti-climax of the affair, Yerxa said, occurred when he decided to risk a similar fate. Hiding a camera under a borrowed Indian blanket, he took numerous pictures of the ceremony, which he still possesses.

Rehse helped formulate his desire to become an artist, and from that time on he was constantly making sketches wherever he went.

Yerxa continued to travel, and meanwhile his family purchased a 100-acre orange grove in Riverside. When Fred Yerxa died in 1910, his son took over management of the orange ranch. The great freeze of 1912-13 wiped out the Yerxa bank account.

"We lost $80,000 overnight," says Yerxa. "I got a job ditch-digging for a while, but I couldn't see getting ahead that way, so I moved out here on the desert to homestead 160 acres. . . .

"I decided one day I'd dig my own well. I had sold one of my paintings that day, so I bought boards and equipment to work with."

[Article 269: January 10, 1957]

"I'd go down the ladder and fill my bucket with dirt and take it to the top," he continued. "At 40 feet I struck water, and it turned out to be 132 degrees hot, and the hole kept filling with steam."

Yerxa could only work in his hole 15 minutes at a time and remembers that the "water was so hot I had to stand in cold buckets of water to work."

"That well was the discovery well in this area for the hot mineral water which has made Desert Hot Springs famous," recalls Yerxa.

World War I interrupted Yerxa's progress with his desert homestead. He joined the Army and after the war traveled extensively throughout Europe. Later he roamed through most of the states in the Union and racked up a career as a reporter, butcher, sailor, teamster, and general storekeeper.

For six years he was postmaster at Frutilla, [now] a ghost town on the Colorado River near Blythe. "My customers were cotton pickers, cowboys, Indians, and border characters," he declares. "Sometimes F.B.I. men would hang around for news of opium smuggling and other illegal border conditions."

Yerxa finally left Frutilla to open a general store in Moorpark. He sold it in 1937 and returned to Desert Hot Springs, where he has lived ever since. His Miracle Hill trading post soon became a regular hangout for desert artists, among whom was the noted landscape painter Carl Eytel.

On one occasion actor John Barrymore and artist John Decker were visiting the bohemian writer Sadakichi Hartmann in Banning. They wandered down into the desert for a drive, became lost, and wound up at Miracle Hill. Barrymore's fantastic account of Yerxa brought him a crowd of curious tourists from Hollywood.

"Believe it or not," Barrymore told his friends, "this desert trader has everything from 30-year-old corset laces to buffalo hide shields for sale."

While operating his trading post, Yerxa began scouring the desert for materials for building a pueblo. "I got the idea suddenly," he explains. "The Hopi never built a pueblo in this desert, so why shouldn't I?"

In 1941 Yerxa began building his pueblo, which is on a site 300 feet above the desert floor. Built over a hot water well, the pueblo has a pump which lifts the water to a tank in back of the building.

Since that time he has set numerous dates for finishing the pueblo, but every time he approaches the deadline, he sees something which needs changing. When Yerxa married Portia Graham, a former lecturer in applied psychology, he told her Cabot's Old

Indian Pueblo was almost done. That was almost 10 years ago. Last week Yerxa announced the pueblo project will be completed in January of 1961.

Portia smiled knowingly. "Just wait till 1961," she said.

[Article 270: January 24, 1957]

There are many new people in the village, and to them we might say that flowers do not come in profusion to the desert every year. . . . When rains do come in quantity, the desert puts on a very colorful show of bright blossoms over its very many wide stretches of open land. Low-lying desert verbenas cling closely to the shifting sands of the sand dunes in the middle of the valley. Encilia bursts into masses of brilliant yellow as it covers the rocky lower slopes of the Little San Bernardino Mountains surrounding our village. The ocotillo with its flaming red tops are worth the necessary miles of travel to see them in blossom. These brilliant flashes of color are at their best in the Borrego Desert Area, located in the mountains called Santa Rosas between here and San Diego, south of the Salton Sea.

Mixed in among the encilia, usually on somewhat rocky terrain, will be found the very noticeably large flowers of the beavertail cacti, . . . These too have spines, but they are very small and completely deceiving in their appearance, or harmless. But they too, in common with all cacti, can cause pain if handled carelessly.

[Article 271: January 31, 1957]

The sturdy barrel cacti, by far the largest in this desert, put forth a single ring of greenish yellow flowers, like a crown, on the top of the spined barrel. Later on, when the flowers drop off, there is a seed pod left, withered and dry, which contains many small, black, hard seeds. Desert rats watch them closely, and when the seeds are fully formed, they climb up the sides of the barrel amid all the spines to the top, cut a neat hole in the yellowish pod, and extract every seed.

Desert rats are abroad about their own business of finding food during the nighttime, and so they are watched by coyotes, foxes, snakes, and owls, which capture them for food. So nature's laws of survival are ever in full operation. It is the barrel cacti from which water may be obtained in sufficient quantity to save one's life if necessary on the desert. To do this, you can break open the barrel and squeeze water out of the pulp. Or this may be eaten to allay thirst; it tastes like a very poor watermelon, being about the same character but only slightly sweet and quite tough.

The creosote, with a more common name of greasewood, is very widely distributed over all our Southwestern deserts. It is extremely hardy and drought-resistant. During March, April and May, if encouraged by rain, it will fill with small bright blossoms which stay on for several weeks. These finally change to small white fluffs containing seed which blow away with the wind, thus starting new bushes elsewhere. The petals drop to the ground and simulate a yellow carpet beneath each bush.

[Article 272: February 14, 1957]

The Indian dye plant puts forth a profusion of bluish-purple flowers which have a very distinctive odor if crushed. They will stain the fingers for many hours. It is this staining quality which the desert Indians used to color basket material, and in some cases articles of homemade clothing and pottery. Desert chuckwallas, that largest and most interesting of all our lizards, are very fond of these flowers and will climb up among the branches of this bush to obtain them.

But when you see a desert indigo bush in full bloom, you will be amazed at its strong blue-colored flowers, which are violet[-like] in shape. No one can help being thrilled with the beauty of this bush. In a good rainy year, these flowers are so thick that when they start to fall, the ground under the indigo bush is fairly like a carpet.

[Article 273: February 21, 1957]

Now I must mention my favorite flowering tree: it is the desert willow. Found only along water courses, dry washes and in locations where ample water comes at least once in a year or two years, it has a very extensive root system, of course, to withstand drought, and much of the root system is concentrated downwards, whereas many desert plants have root systems reaching out laterally.

This begins its growth as a vigorous bush, but in time [it] reaches the proportions of a tree, with a thick trunk covered with adequate bark. The flowers come to this tree in late March and may last until June. They are bell-shaped, often tinted pale pink, and have a faint, delicate, sweet odor very noticeable in early morning hours. This seems to evaporate in mid-day sunshine and warmth.

The leaves are pointed and small, the branches slender and quite limber, so the tree is very graceful and provides welcome shade for small animals, birds, and insects. You too will welcome a rest under its protecting boughs, if you are walking in that vicinity. People on the desert who persist in riding in autos miss very much of the beauty and charm that is here. Do try to walk out into the desert and capture the thrill and quiet peace of the real desert, especially beautiful after rains.

When rains come, all nature in the desert puts forth many variegated flowers, not for the admiration of man, but in order to cause notice by bugs, birds, and insects, which are attracted with bright colors, to investigate them and thereby increase the pollination, which is imperfectly done by the wind. In this way seeds are produced to carry on the growth of new plants into other seasons of future years.

So very many early flowers are colored yellow that [there] is a theory among scientific minds that birds, bugs, and insects are particularly attracted to the yellow in color, because it is in such contrast to the blue of the sky. Blue is the complementary color to yellow.

[Article 274: March 14, 1957]

After rains come, nature will provide very many different kinds of flowers in various colors . . .

There will be desert daisies, beautiful white rafinesque, desert poppies, not as richly colored as those on the east coast but still quite attractive, desert asters, star flowers, thresh plant, desert trumpet, desert sunflowers, evening primrose, wild potato, desert milkweed, coyote melon, palo verde sage, desert mistletoe, Mormon tea, that striking blue placetta resembling canterbury bells, desert sand lilies, and chia.

Do not overlook chia, [a] quite small, straight, soldier-like, single-stem, blue-button type of flower and seed pod. The plant is usually six to 10 inches tall. This produces seeds that are small but of high food value. Indians in primitive times took a small handful of chia seeds and walked from waterhole to waterhole over the desert country for surprising distances without other food.

As the season progresses, one of the late patches of color is the strikingly deep yellow blossom of thick bladderpod bushes, which are of very noticeable size and are most common along dry watercourses. This bush has a strong, pungent odor, and it is better that you look at them rather than make a bouquet.

Should the season be wet, there will be extensive patches of lupine, with its purple blossoms, said to be poisonous to livestock, but the flowers make a bright show and they last for many days, which is in contrast to the flowers of the cacti, which may last only one or two days before starting to fade and wither away.

[Article 275: March 21, 1957]

In addition to the beavertail and barrel cacti, there is pickle cactus and others called deer horn, old man of the mountain, hedgehog, and of course the cholla or jumping cactus, which draws blood from all newcomers to the desert who are deceived by its innocent, soft appearance.

There [are] very small, inconspicuous flowers clinging close to the earth called Nama Demissum, which grow in very flat, small clusters. The color is a bright, attractive pink.

Among the larger growing things to have flowers, you will notice the screw bean mesquite, mountain cat claw, wild tobacco plant, and honey mesquite. Of course, in favored places you can observe the Spanish dagger, yucca, and nolina, which attain a height of eight feet.

All these and many more can be found within a short distance of Desert Hot Springs, if we get those needed rains to keep the growth with some moisture through February and March.

If you enjoy flowers and [the] out of doors, then pull on heavy shoes for short hikes away from the village or your parked automobile. Get out into the desert, kick round in the sand, tramp through brushy places, watch the small life of the desert in its serious search for food. Examine how desert plants and growth lives in a land of little rain.

You will be inspired with a new appreciation of the real desert, learn much of interest, find beauty in many things you never can see while sitting on a cushion in an automobile traveling at 45 to more miles per hours, and you also will attain peace of mind.

But in regard to flowers, remember this: all desert flowers are protected by law and there is a stiff fine for picking them. And anyway, desert flowers wilt extremely rapidly, therefore cannot be transported any distance. . . .

[ARTICLE 278: APRIL 18, 1957]

This week C.R. Browning, who is now a retired consulting civil engineer, visited Cabot's Old Indian Pueblo in Desert Hot Springs. Mr. Browning said that back in the year 1888, his father was an early fruit rancher in Northern California, and that in some way the first land-sale promoters of Palm Springs contacted his father and induced him to come to the desert and buy 40 acres of land near the town site, and also they sold him four lots in the proposed city of Palm Springs.

The family moved to the desert, built a small cabin, and prepared to make the 40 acres into a ranch and home. But when he learned that the Indians owned all the water and none could be had for his 40 acres, he gave up the project.

During the interval, Mr. Browning . . . undertook to carry the mail from a station called at that time Seven Palms, on the Southern Pacific tracks, to Palm Springs twice a week. This old first depot was two miles east of Garnet. He was only nine years old and rode a burro.

When the sandstorms were too bad, he was not allowed to attempt the crossing of Whitewater Wash. Shortly after this, the Seven Palms depot was dismantled and the station and telegraphers moved to the point now called Garnet, somewhat to the west. The promotion of Palm Springs of that era was abandoned, and the area again relapsed into a mere Indian village.

His father gave up title to the 40 acres and moved up north again. Some years after this, he received an offer of $500 for the four lots in the center of Palm Springs and was glad to get some money back, as the desert then seemed to be without future.

This story makes plain the vast difference in conditions of this desert during only one man's lifetime. I would very much like to see our desert at the end of the next 100 years of change.

[ARTICLE 279: DECEMBER 20, 1957]

Newcomers to the desert ask many questions concerning the early history of this Desert Hot Springs area. So this is a short abbreviated rundown on what happened before you people rode in here over paved highways in an automobile and sitting on a cushion. The first pioneers had no autos and no cushions.

In the beginning a few Cahuilla Indians lived in this desert region and on up into Banning Pass country. Never very many.

During the 1820s, padres of the San Gabriel Mission, which is near Pasadena, made occasional visits to the Banning area and eventually established an outpost called the San Gorgonio Rancho, where was built a small cabin and some corrals. Very meager farming was attempted.

About 1845, Paulino Weaver, a native of Tennessee but a citizen of Mexico, made his home with Indians at the summit of the pass. During 1855, Dr. Isaac Smith, with some emigrants from Iowa, arrived and built cabins and corrals north of Banning, farming in a small way. Mostly they gave attention to raising cattle. Also in 1855, a small party of U.S. surveyors reached this end of Riverside County to start selecting primary routes for the Butterfield stages. They worked down the Whitewater Wash, then angled off northerly to what is now Desert Hot Springs. They marked four stones on the corners of Sec. 32-2D

& 5 East S.B.M. It was . . . these stones that I searched for and found in the year of 1913, to make my homestead entry to 160 acres of desert land.

In 1862, William D. Bradshaw started a stage from Los Angeles to Prescott, Arizona, by the way of Banning. Wyatt Earp, one of the most famous characters of the Southwest, was in the group of stage drivers for this line. General Phineas Banning organized a stage line from Wilmington, through Banning and the desert, to old Fort Yuma in the year of 1865. But 1876 was the big year of our history, because that witnessed the first train of the Southern Pacific Railroad to go through this desert. Progress, however, was slow. By the year of 1891, the total population of Banning was only 207, and 94 of them were children.

[Article 280: December 27, 1957]

I went through Banning on the train as a small boy in 1893, and there was almost no town to see then. Three or four homesteaders' cabins first appeared north of the railroad at Garnet in 1912. One at Seven Palms, Bob Belt's (a cowboy), and the others scattered along in the general vicinity of Dillon Road. In . . . 1913, Bob Carr and I came into the desert to file our homestead claims, making us first in what has now become known as Desert Hot Springs. After that came Dixon, Ford Beebe, Walter Woods, and Bill Anderson. Bob and I showed these people where to put up stakes, and their homestead lands are now covered with houses and the paved streets of Desert Hot Springs. Thus started our town.

In those early days all of our friends in the city thought that we had lost our minds to believe in any future at all for this desert. The prospects then were, indeed, extremely slim, and desert life very strenuous and forbidding. But we had fun from day to day, and had hope for the future.

Time passed along for 24 years with no important changes in desert conditions worth mentioning. There is not enough space here to go into details, but finally a passable road was made to Palm Springs, one to Indio, and one to Morongo Valley from Banning.

Then about 1937, L.W. Coffee came to the desert and visioned a town here at Desert Hot Springs, and Aubrey Wardman advanced big money to make paper plans an actuality. The details and local history we will take up at some future time.

Cabot standing before the Pueblo with his canteen marked "1913," 1957

ON THE DESERT SINCE 1913 - EXPLANATORY NOTES

Article 1. Cabot Yerxa was 10 years old in 1893. President Diaz strongly encouraged American business investment in Mexico, and it is possible that he personally entertained groups of foreign visitors, including the Yerxa family, if they made it known they were scouting for commercial opportunities.

2. Robert Van Carr (1877-1930) was a popular Western poet and short story writer, as well as a writer of scenarios for silent films. His *Cowboy Lyrics* (1912), containing 110 poems, was reprinted in 2008. His wife was Estella R. Carr (1870-1973). The couple may have first met Cabot in Sierra Madre, where they lived while he was postmaster.

The federal Enlarged Homestead Act targeted farming areas that couldn't be irrigated. The Southern California desert was officially opened to homesteading in 1910. The program was later blamed for dispossessing Native Americans, though the encounters between Indians and homesteaders described by Cabot are friendly.

7. Rodney Yerxa was born October 5, 1914, in the Queen of Angels hospital in Los Angeles, according to his obituary in the *Desert Sentinel*, though Cabot refers more than once to his son being born in the desert. Rodney died in 1985. When the couple divorced is uncertain, but they separated for good sometime in the early 1920s, while Cabot was keeping store in Fertilla, near Blythe. He was survived by his wife, Margaret, daughter Lauren, and two grandsons, Chris and David Gilland.

Cabot married his first wife, Mamie Carstensen (b. 1885), in 1908. She came to live in the desert with her husband after the birth of their child. When the couple divorced is uncertain, but after Cabot returned from the Army in 1919, he lived alone. Article 88 refers to Cabot taking young Rodney to Seattle by boat. Cabot joined the Army there in October, 1918. The article doesn't mention whether Mamie accompanied her husband and child on that voyage. In fact Mamie is missing entirely from *On the Desert*, though Cabot mentions some other women admiringly: Hilda Gray, Stella Carr, and his mother, Nellie.

9. Carl Eytel (1862-1925) was a noted Southwestern painter. He was born in Wurttemburg, Germany, first came to America in 1885, settled on Tahquitz Creek in Palm Springs in 1898. In an interview with the Palm Springs *Sun* (February 19, 1963), Cabot remembered Eytel.

> Carl was peace itself. He refused to carry a gun because he could not bring himself to kill anything. . . .

> We burro men named him the "aristocrat" because he owned a horse instead of a burro. But Carl used to make long trips into the Arizona desert and New Mexico to paint the Indians, and he never could use a burro, whose top speed was two miles per hour. . . .
>
> Carl told me how he ran away from his home in Stuttgart, Germany, when his family insisted he become a baker. . . . Horses and cattle had always fascinated him, so he roamed the plains as a cowboy until he could lay aside enough money to live on while he taught himself to paint.
>
> He was mostly a pen and ink artist, although he did a few things in watercolors. His sketches were always meticulously accurate and detailed.
>
> He was such a frail man and so very poor. About the only money he earned when he first came here was made by selling his sketches to the few tourists we had.
>
> Finally he did get a break when George Wharton James commissioned him to illustrate his book, "Wonders of the Colorado Desert."

The interview ends with a sensational anecdote. Eytel was mistaken for a horse thief and sentenced to hang. "The only thing that saved him was that the owner of the horse pointed out that the horse which had been found in Eytel's possession was not the stolen animal."

> Eytel was far from being a timid man but an experience like so, so unnerved him that his hands shook whenever he talked about it.
>
> His work required persistence, patience and gentleness. Carl possessed all of these qualities. The Indians loved him, and when he died in 1925 they buried him in their tribal cemetery in Palm Springs, the first time they had accorded a white man this honor.

11. Merry Xmas, Cabot's beloved burro, is described in several articles below.

13. Mack Sennett (1880-1960), the "King of Comedy" of silent films, founded his first Los Angeles studio in 1912. He was awarded an honorary Oscar in 1938.

15. It is said that Walter Woods (1881-1942) wrote scenarios or scripts for about 76 films between 1915 and 1938. Ford Beebe (1888-1978) wrote scenarios and scripts for about 121 films, directed 105 films, and produced 14 films. His earliest screen credit was in 1916. We must imagine Woods and Beebe commuting regularly between Hollywood and the desert.

16. Woods' cabin was built in 1914; L. W. Coffee's bathhouse opened in 1941, burned in 1947; the "new" bathhouse opened soon thereafter.

20. L. W. Coffee, a land developer along the coast, met Cabot in Moorpark (1932) and heard about the hot water aquifer. He seems to have been inspired, and began work quickly. He opened an office at the corner of Palm Drive and Pierson in central Desert Hot Springs in 1933, commissioned the Discovery Well in 1934, and spent the next years struggling to control land in the area. The Dr. Chandler whom Cabot mentions briefly in Article 248 was Coffee's nemesis. (In *Waters of Comfort: The Story of Desert Hot Springs*

[1997], John Hunt describes their legal battle.) Finally, supported by Aubrey Wardman, Coffee was able to begin selling lots and building houses. He died in 1957.

William and Frances Keys ran the Desert Queen Ranch, now located in Joshua Tree National Park. Ranger-guided tours are available.

24. A memorable part of the full Merry Xmas story is not told in *On the Desert*. Here is a version recorded by Caroline Coleman in an interview with Cabot titled "His Burro Saved His Life" (Riverside *Press Enterprise*, March 4, 1960): "One night when the sand and wind blew so thick that you could cut it with a knife, Merry Christmas saved my life. We were crossing the Whitewater Wash between Desert Hot Springs and Palm Springs when I lost my sense of direction. I put my head down on the burro's neck to get protection from the wind, threw my arms around her and said, 'Take me home,' and she did."

42. Old Highway 60-70-99 has been replaced by I-10 in the Desert Hot Springs area.

52. This wooden cabin was the Yerxas' house throughout the homestead period, 1914-1918. It was later taken apart and the materials were reused when Cabot built his new "ranch" house at the opposite end of Miracle Hill in 1925. The stone cabin shown in a famous photograph (included on the back cover of this book) was built sometime later during homesteading days; it stood near the original wooden house and may have been used as a studio and for more secure storage. It was demolished the 1950s after Cabot sold the property.

61. J. Smeaton Chase (1864-1923), born in England, wrote lyrical travelogues of the American West, including *Our Araby: Palm Springs and the Garden of the Sun* (1920). He was interested in California plants, animals, and Native culture. He died at Banning.

Edmund C. Jaeger (1887-1983) was a biologist known for popular as well as specialized writings on desert ecology.

67. George S. Patton, sr. (1856-1927), a wealthy businessman and the first mayor of San Marino, came from a distinguished military and political family in Virginia. Henry E. Huntington (1850-1927), railroad magnate and collector of art and rare books, founder of the institution now known as the Huntington Library, Art Gallery and Botanical Gardens in San Marino, retired in 1916. It is typical of the coincidences that marked Cabot Yerxa's life that he happened to get a short-term job in an office suite that connected him with these two men, as well as the soon-to-be-famous WW2 general, George S. Patton, jr. (1885-1945).

Although Cabot gives the impression that his job in the Huntington-Patton offices occurred sometime during his homesteading period, 1914-1918, in an as yet unpublished memoir he places this job in about 1906, when the Yerxa family first arrived in the Los Angeles area from Seattle, and George S. Patton, Jr., was still a college student. The 1906 dating seems more likely.

68. The angel on San Jacinto: San Jacinto Peak (10,834 feet) towers over Palm Springs. From Desert Hot Springs, various formations can be discerned amid the morning shadows on the northeast side of the mountain, including an angel, a sleeping warrior, and a burro

that reminded Cabot of Merry Xmas. The Angel View Hospital that opened near Cabot's Pueblo in 1961 (mentioned in "Three Days at the Pueblo" in this volume) was named for this formation.

73. Having met the young Patton in Pasadena, Cabot would serve as supply sergeant under Eisenhower in WW1! The future president was promoted to the temporary rank of lieutenant colonel on October 14, 1918. He trained tank crews at forts in the Northeast before they were dispatched to Europe. Cabot's military service lasted from October 23, 1918, to July 12, 1919.

81. Vinegarones, in Mexican Spanish, are a type of scorpion. When disturbed, they emit a secretion that smells like vinegar.

93. Louis Sobol was a Broadway showbiz columnist for Hearst newspapers for four decades. He retired in 1967, died at 90 in 1986. Cabot met him while Sobol was vacationing at the B-bar-H Ranch in the late 1930s. Cabot's letters to Sobol must have begun soon after that, continuing for two or three years. Sobol introduces Cabot's letter printed here as Article 128 by mentioning the Finns fighting and other dark allusions to international affairs. Finland fought the Winter War against the Soviets in 1939.

   Mother Yerxa is Cabot's mother, Nellie, who lived with him during this period.

94. Cabot described the hostilities in Cuba as still going on after his family arrived. Though an armistice was signed between Spain and the U.S. in 1898, American troops did not withdraw until 1902.

95. The duration of the Yerxa family's wealth seems to have been fairly brief, lasting from the 1890s until 1913. It was based on various business successes achieved by Cabot's father, Fred, and his uncles. By contrast Cabot's letters record how poor his parents seemed at the beginning of their marriage, when his father ran the trading post on the Lakota Reservation in the 1880s.

97. This description of Merry Xmas being buried near the cabin is contradicted by Cabot's accounts elsewhere of releasing the burro into the desert in 1918 when he went off to war, and being unable to find the animal when he returned in 1919. The letters to Sobol are written in a more romantic style than Cabot usually practiced, and here the style may have transformed the facts.

105. On living alone: "On windy days I would search out very sheltered spots in thick mesquite brush, build a small fire, and read a book. Oh, I had Marcus Aurelius, Thoreau's Walden Pond, the Bible, Bagavadgita, Omar Kayyam, Epictetus, Leaves of Grass, Typee, Oomo, Emerson, and a few more" (from an unpublished manuscript).

121. June Hill Robertson McCarroll (1867-1954) was a nurse, then a medical doctor employed by the Southern Pacific Railroad in the Indio area. Caltrans, the present-day state highway authority, credits her with painting a white line down the middle of a road and starting a state-wide campaign to adopt the custom. There is said to be a memorial plaque at Indio Boulevard and Flower Street in Indio.

129. Presumably the primary election of 1940. However, Cabot never found Merry Xmas after he returned from the Army in 1919, so the appearance of the animal in this story is curious.

137. The crossroads near Blythe where Cabot ran his general merchandise store from 1919 to 1925 was officially spelled Fertilla, though Cabot sometimes wrote Frutilla or Furtilla.

143. World's Fairs: The *Exposition Internationale des Arts Décoratifs et Industriels Modernes* (Paris, 1925)--from its title came the abbreviation "Art Deco"; and the British Empire Exhibition (Wembly, England, 1924-1925), the largest fair ever staged to that time.

154. "Coolidge seemed to have had considerable education somewhere in his past life"; he "could recite some poetry after he had been invited to a meal" (from an unpublished manuscript).

180. A walking stick shaped by nature: Visitors to Cabot's Pueblo Museum have observed his preference for irregular lines and natural shapes.

185. "Mornin' in the Desert" was a popular poem in the early Twentieth Century that has recently been rediscovered. Various websites give accounts of its origin. It is said to have been "found written on the door of an old cabin in the desert," as Cabot states, though he is not credited as the discoverer. One site claims that it was published in a book of poems by Katherine Fall Pettey, *Songs from the Sage Brush* (1910). It is said the poem was read on the "Death Valley Days" radio show, November 4, 1939.

186. The store in Ventura County was in the town of Moorpark.

191. Lucienne Hubbard and his son-in-law, Charles Bender, bought the B-bar-H property in 1927 and soon began inviting private guests from Hollywood and moneyed circles in the East. They opened the ranch to the paying public in 1937. In 1940 it was sold as a going business to Jay Kasler, who closed it to the public in 1950 and maintained it for his family's use. Cabot entertained visitors from the B-bar-H at his first trading post on Miracle Hill during the late 1930s, and at the Pueblo as soon as he'd completed his new trading post there, sometime in the 1940s.

193. The museum Cabot opened in the Old Indian Pueblo was the climax to some trends from the 1930s. He "staged" his first trading post on Miracle Hill with amusing conversation starters to entertain his visitors from the B-bar-H Ranch, while at his nearby cabin he showed off souvenirs from his travels. Meanwhile he was gaining experience as a lecturer on desert lore. In Article 199 he remembers climbing into the snake pit he kept near the trading post to explain his pets to a paying audience.

194. Lew Ayres (1908-1996) had a breakthrough film role in "All Quiet on the Western Front" (1930). His private life, which he seems to have discussed with Cabot on that rainy day, featured marriages to Lola Lane (1931-1933) and Ginger Rogers (1934-1940), as well as a later marriage to Diana Hall (1964 to his death). Ayres did not serve in WW2, a fact that crushed his box-office standing. Cabot indirectly notes that Ayres' reputation was in

decline in the 1950s. It is intriguing to speculate that the two men may have discussed their views on military service, especially since, in Article 184, Cabot remembers thinking, "Why wage wars?" while he was in uniform.

195. John Decker (1894-1947) was a Hollywood set designer, a portrait painter to the stars, and a caricaturist.

197. The Académie Julian, where Cabot studied art in the summer of 1925, was established in Paris in 1868 as an alternative to the official French art academy. It differed in admitting women, as well as talented amateur artists. But its traditional curriculum still centered on drawing and painting human models, frequently in the nude. Some of Cabot's classroom studies are found in the Cabot's Pueblo Museum collection.

201. Warner Baxter (1889-1951) played in over 100 films, beginning in 1914. He starred as the Cisco Kid in the first all-talking Western, "In Old Arizona" (1929). He won two Academy Awards for Best Actor.

204. Many of these names are still widely known. Among those that have faded, John J. Raskob (1879-1950) was a business executive at DuPont and General Motors. Sidney Kingsley (1906-1995) was a Pulitzer Prize-winning playwright ("Men in White," 1934). Wendy Barrie (1912-1978) was a British actress who moved to Hollywood in 1935. She played opposite Spencer Tracy and James Stewart. Beatrice Kaufman (1895-1945) was a New York poet, playwright, editor, and wit. Her husband was the even more famous George S. Kaufman.

236. Among Cabot's letters to his second wife, Portia, is a tortoise joke, which Cabot calls "desert humor." "Three turtles decided to have a cup of coffee. Just as they went into the café it started to rain, so the biggest turtle said to the littlest turtle, 'Go home and get an umbrella.' So the little one said, 'I will if you don't drink my coffee.' 'We won't,' promised the other two. But two years later the big turtle said to the middle turtle, 'Well, I guess he isn't coming back, so we might as well drink his coffee,' and when he said that, a little voice called from just outside the door, "If you do, I won't go."

241. *The Land of Little Rain* (1903) is the title of Mary Austin's classic memoir about living on the desert around Independence, California. Cabot's evident awareness of her book is striking.

246. The Palm Springs aerial tram rising up the side of San Jacinto Peak opened in 1963.

259. Harry Oliver (1888-1973) was an Academy Award-nominated art director of films in the 1920s and 30s. He retired to Thousand Palms, a few miles east of Desert Hot Springs, where he built an adobe house he called Old Fort Oliver in 1941-1942, at the same time Cabot was constructing his Old Indian Pueblo. Sadly the fort is no longer standing. A local guidebook from the 1950s indicates that it contained a museum. Harry Oliver also published a humorous broadsheet, the *Desert Rat Scrapbook* (1946-1964), which was rather widely distributed. Cabot sold it in his trading post.
    For Cabot's Texas bride, see note to Article 265.

261, 262. Drew Oliver's wind contraption was only a few decades ahead of its time. In 1982 the U.S. Bureau of Land Management and Riverside County cooperated to produce a plan that allowed modern commercial wind turbines in the San Gorgonio Pass. Currently over 4,000 windmills are deployed; the tallest are hundreds of feet high.

264. Bert Procter (1901-1980) was a noted Western landscape and cowboy-and-Indian painter based in California.

265. Cabot's second wife, Portia Fearis Graham, was born November 27, 1884. They met in late 1943 or 1944, married on August 8, 1945. She had been married to a prominent banker in Galveston, Texas, and after his death in 1924 she traveled the Upper Midwest and California, making her living as an inspirational speaker and personal counselor. After she married Cabot, she adopted a new desert life and moved with him into the Pueblo. The correspondence between the two gray-haired lovers is one of the museum's treasures. She died in an Orange County nursing home on April 1, 1969.

266. Emperor Maximillian lived briefly in the Chapultepec palace overlooking Mexico City before he was executed in 1867 by Mexico's republican party.

267. George W. Rehse (1868-1939), remembered mainly as a political cartoonist in Minneapolis and New York City, collected American Indian artifacts; he donated important items to the Smithsonian Institution.

268. Chief Red Cloud's abdication in favor of his son is a documented historical event that occurred in July, 1909. At the time of this adventure, Cabot was officially postmaster of Sierra Madre, hundreds of miles to the south. Cabot's father, Fred, is said elsewhere to have died not long after the devastating 1913 freeze that wiped out the Yerxas' citrus crop in Riverside County.

269. Carl Eytel died in 1925, so he could not have participated in this artists' society in the 30s.

THREE DAYS AT THE PUEBLO, 1961

[In Article 191 of *On the Desert Since 1913,* Cabot Yerxa states that he returned from Ventura County to Miracle Hill and built a trading post near the B-bar-H Ranch in 1937. A reporter's description of that trading post appears in Articles 195-198. In Article 251 Cabot writes that he began building the Old Indian Pueblo, located a mile north of Miracle Hill, around 1941. In Article 253 he refers to it as a "Hopi Indian building" with "very many variations from your conception of a house." Its construction is briefly described by Randall Henderson in Article 259. The Pueblo and its operation as a museum are observed by a reporter for the Riverside *Press Enterprise* in Articles 263-269. The following letter describing daily life in the Pueblo was found among Cabot's papers in the museum.]

Buenos Dias, Amigo   Desert Hot Springs
                          Cabot's Old Indian Pueblo
March 17, 1961   California

People ask us, "What do you do on the desert where there is NOTHING to do?" Well, here is what has happened in the last three days at this Indian Pueblo way out in the Desert.

    Portia's sister Vadus just left after three days' visit. Then came in Jack Reuter, an ex-professional ballplayer and prizefighter, accompanied by his wife. After they left came a cousin of mine from Long Beach with his wife. After they left came a cousin of mine from Long Beach with friends to stay awhile. He has not been here for ten years. As they left, a man from Texas arrived who had flown in to stay three hours; with him [was someone] who had spent years on ships in Alaska bringing canned salmon down to the States. He said one Indian, an expert at the business, made $30,000 catching salmon in one season.

    After a short interval we were glad to see a friend who had driven all the way down from San Francisco just to visit us for two hours.

    Saturday night I had to go to the Jewish church with [the] American Legion to attend some one of the special religious ceremonies. To sleep at midnight.

    During all this time in daylight hours I had to take visitors to the Pueblo through the building and give lectures. Some chew gum, some wear dark glasses, some do not listen, some talk more than I do, the children are misbehaved, disarray exhibits, eat apples, cry, and do not mind anyone.

    Saturday night [there was a] big meeting of County Legion groups, home at 12 a.m. Sunday two friends from Santa Barbara for dinner, this one a movie writer, the other [a] leading lady with E.H. Southern [sic] and Julia Marlow [sic], [who] was the wife of the flyer who carried the first sack of mail in U.S. history in 1911. You will see a commemoration stamp out perhaps with his picture on it soon. A very close friend of Portia's called with friends of theirs to see Smoki Mountain.

Then a salesman called with a most wonderful bible and made a sales talk to Portia, and she has the book and will pay $5 per month from here on to future.

The wind started blowing and made up to many miles per hour, turned over trailers and took paint off cars between here and Palm Springs, temperature dropped way down and we are freezing. Phone rang and people from Chicago will soon call on a yearly visit to the desert.

A woman came with laundry from Morongo Valley and this took some time. Karl Obert, the most famous photographer of California, called with his wife. The phone rang and a schoolteacher will bring 25 children to see Pueblo and wanted to be sure of time. More tourists at the door; got to leave to attend to them. 450 people in January, 483 in February, and 22,000 to date. Whew! I am tired, talking and walking. Just now a woman drove up and left four children, all under seven years. She said, show them the museum, I will call for them in an hour, or hour and [a] half. Gee whiz, I am a babysitter too.

A very distinguished man just arrived with letter of introduction. He is the head of all Gospel Missions round the world, China, South America, India, Italy, Formosa, and many other places too.

And today is dedication day for the Children's Hospital across the street, and 3,000 people expected to that, many will come here too.

In the mail, a letter saying that my son and wife and child from San Francisco will be here very soon to stay a few days.

Things quieted down somewhat, and in walked Chief Semu, with red bandana round his head and wearing western hat, of course, and moccasins, and turquoise. With him his daughter Manesset, both full-blooded Indians, the last of the Shumash tribe with full blood, and with them a very attractive 20-year-old girl from Chile in South America. She spoke very beautiful Spanish as you can imagine. She is in the U.S. to learn English to be a teacher or work in embassy, etc.

Every day there are problems with people. Some have been drinking, some cannot see well, some very old, some off mentally, some deaf, all children present individual uncontrolled problems. Some stumble on stairs and I catch them before they break their necks. Some wear dark glasses and complain that the rooms are dark; some wonder why we make any charge to see exhibits. Some say they want to see the rest of the 37 rooms. Some comment, "What took me so long to build it?"

These things all happened in three days, and so it goes, never a time for rest or reading or to write letters, but this I write in desperation, to explain why there is no time of our own, out in the desert where there is—nothing to do. ----- Adios amigo,

Cabot

COMMENTARY

The audience for this letter is not identified.

Cabot's energy still seems inexhaustible, though he claims to be tired. At least he had enough juice to write this vigorous page on top of everything else he was doing. The tone, a mixture of humor, satire, close observation, and factual detail, shows that his mind still kept its bright edge. He would turn 78 on June 11, 1961.

The attendance figures he claims for his museum are impressive: 22,000 overall, and 450 or more per month that winter. However, his attendance claims during the 1950s varied greatly. In a letter dated November 11, 1952, to the Los Angeles *Times*, he had claimed 10,000 visitors, while at different points in *On the Desert Since 1913* he cites 40,000, even 50,000 who at least stopped to look at the building's exterior.

"We are freezing," he complains, because the Pueblo probably contained only a small heater in the main kitchen with a pipe going up through Portia's second-storey room in one direction, and another pipe to the museum on the other side. The stone fireplace tucked away in the living room would have produced little heat.

According to his obituary, Cabot's son, Rodney, lived in San Leandro (east of Oakland) for the last 30 years of his life.

Cabot's sense of civic duty is apparent in his reference to two American Legion-related events in Desert Hot Springs that kept him out until midnight.

The pilot who carried the first sack of U.S. mail in 1911 was Earle Ovington, who flew from Garden City, on Long Island, to Mineola, New York, where he dropped a bag to the postmaster below. Ovington's wife, an actress, is said here to have worked with Edward Hugh Sothern (1859-1933), and Julia Marlowe (1866-1950), a prominent stage team who performed Shakespearean drama. Ovington's wife is also mentioned in *On the Desert Since 1913*.

Karl Obert (1897-1973) was a prize-winning photographer, born in Germany, who settled in Santa Barbara in the late 1920s. His best-known work is a book, *This Is California* (1957). He photographed Hollywood celebrities, cityscapes and landscapes. The Old Indian Pueblo Museum's collection includes photographs by Obert.

The children's hospital across the street was a rehabilitation facility built by the Angel View Crippled Children's Foundation on Miracle Hill Road. The foundation was inspired by Dr. Robert Bingham, dedicated to helping victims of polio by use of hot mineral water. Today it operates rehab facilities for children challenged by various conditions.

"Chief" Semu Haute (1908-2004), a member of the Simi Valley branch of the Chumash tribe, was actually a medicine man and a long-time friend of Cabot's, with whom he shared many attitudes. Semu's politically-charged wooden sculpture, still housed in the living room of the Pueblo, is called Ah-ha-oh-ta, or Two-Faced-White-Man.

Cabot's Pueblo in early construction, ca. 1942

Cabot working on the Pueblo. Scaffolding on the Pueblo's front tower, ca. 1947

Cabot during the construction years

Tar paper covers the wood frame of the upper stories of the Pueblo with ramp to carry materials to upper levels, late 1940s

The Pueblo nearly complete on the outside, ca. 1948

Portia and Cabot surveying their work, ca. 1945

Cabot pauses for a drink during construction.

Cabot points downhill towards Eagles Nest from the Pueblo, still under construction; note building materials for the Pueblo piled on the ground below him.

The Pueblo (more or less) completed, two of the kachina paintings visible, ca. 1950

Cabot standing before his masterpiece

Cabot showing Alaskan boots inside the museum; Alaskan photos hang beside him.

Cabot with his second wife, Portia, ca 1950s

Cabot sitting at the door of his Pueblo, holding one of his tortoises, ca 1950s

Cabot Yerxa, ca. 1940s

DEATH TAKES PIONEER RESIDENT, CABOT YERXA

[Cabot Yerxa died on March 5, 1965.]

Probably the largest attended funeral in the history of Desert Hot Springs occurred here Tuesday morning when more than 400 persons attended last rites for Cabot Yerxa, 83 year old pioneer, [which] were held at the Eighth Street Community Center.

The colorful pioneer died of a heart attack while reading a newspaper Friday morning in his Old Indian Pueblo Museum home, a project on which he had worked for many years and which was still uncompleted.

The resuscitator unit of the fire department was summoned but he was pronounced dead by Dr. Charles Starr when efforts to resuscitate him failed.

He was a native of South Dakota, but had grown up in Minnesota before embarking on a life of adventure that carried him to the far corners of the globe.

He was a direct descendant of John Cabot, the famed discoverer of Newfoundland in the 15th century.

His life of adventure began at the age of 16 when he opened a cigar store in Nome, Alaska, using funds he had accumulated while working in his father's grocery store.

In the Alaska territory, he was befriended by the son of an Eskimo chief and he then spent two years among the natives there, learning their language and customs.

Then followed the years until 1907 when he at various times owned a pineapple plantation in Cuba, working at various times as a cowboy, sailor, and reporter. From 1907 until 1913 he was postmaster at Sierra Madre.

In 1913 he homesteaded here on 160 acres of land and is credited with discovering the hot mineral waters found here. Yerxa recognized the importance of the discovery, but failed for many years to interest others in its importance or development.

After five years of homesteading, the old urge to move apparently caught up with him and he joined the United States forces in W.W. I, serving in the Army. He did not return here until the 1930s, meanwhile touring the world, studying art in Paris and running a trading post in Blythe.

In 1937 he managed to interest the late L.W. Coffee of Los Angeles in the value of the hot water here, which led eventually to the founding of the small village of Desert Hot Springs.

Back in 1941 he began his major project, the building of the rambling four-storey pueblo, patterned after those built by the Hopi Indians in the Southwest many years ago. The pueblo was used as a combination residence, museum, art gallery, and trading post.

Still unfinished, it is visited each year by thousands of visitors who were regaled by the owner on the history of the area.

Practically the entire building was built by Yerxa himself, adding to it from time to time as his ambition, health and funds permitted.

After the community was founded, Yerxa busied himself with many of the organizations here which soon began to flourish. He was credited with being the founder of the American Legion post here and was a founder and charter member of the Improvement Association.

He also held membership in the Masonic Club and the Senior Citizens Club. Last fall he was marshall of the parade observing the city's first incorporation birthday.

Yerxa was considered an authority on the early days of this community and many times has been called upon to relate his experiences and those of the young community before clubs and organizations.

He has also been the subject of innumerable feature stories in newspapers and magazines and more lately on television. Only about a month ago, his pueblo was prominently featured on the television show, "Happy Wanderers."

He is survived by his widow, Portia, of Desert Hot Springs, and a son, Rodney, living in San Francisco.

The funeral services . . . were conducted by the American Legion post and by the Masonic Club. Burial was in Desert Memorial Park, Palm Springs. . . .

COMMENTARY

This obituary, published in the *Desert Sentinel* on March 11, 1965, is nearly identical with an obituary that appeared in the Riverside *Press Enterprise* on Saturday, March 6, the day following Cabot's death. Apparently his birth year ('83) was mistaken for his age, which was actually 81 years and nine months. He was born in North Dakota, not South Dakota.

The "John Cabot" who discovered Newfoundland was not related to the Cabots or Chabots of the island of Jersey where the Massachusetts Cabots originated. See the Commentary on Cabot's Alaska Interview earlier in this volume.

Cabot met L.W. Coffee and persuaded him to investigate the hot water aquifer in the Coachella Valley in 1932, not 1937.

"The Happy Wanderers" was a weekly syndicated series originated by KCOP-TV in Los Angeles during the 1950s and 60s. It featured Slim and Henrietta Barnard as motorists searching the back roads of the Southwest for curiosities and scenery. The sponsor was Ford Motor Company, and maps highlighting each week's subject could be picked up at Ford dealerships. The *Press Enterprise* obituary also mentions an interview with Cabot that had appeared in the New York *Times* Travel Section the previous year (May 10, 1964). The *Times* article begins with a description of the Pueblo: "[S]tanding in the desert like a genie's creation, is a 35-room structure that has been described as 'the most fantastic building in Southern California.'"

This outline of Cabot's life follows the pattern he seems to have perfected through many retellings. It appears that a journalist composed the biographical summary from memory; it might have taken a different coloration if written by Cabot's wife or his son.

In a side box, the *Sentinel* reported that on the day of the funeral, flags flew at half mast and Desert Hot Springs city offices closed at 10 a.m.

Index

Description	Location
Acade'mie Julian	Articles: 264, Explanatory Notes #197
Addington's Cafe	Articles: 141, 249
Alaska	Articles: 2, 93, 118, 170, 193, 267; Forward, Chronology, Yerxa Survived Lawless Alaska, Introduction, Three days at Pueblo, Obituary
Alfred, the druggist	Articles: 164, 165, 166, 167
Anderson, Bill	Articles: 2, 110, 116, 117, 141, 142, 189, 248, 250, 280, Introduction
Angel of the Mountain (San Jacinto)	Article: 68, Three days at the Pueblo, Explanatory Notes #68
Angel View	Explanatory Notes #68, Three Days at the Pueblo
Ayres, Lew	Articles: 194, Explanatory Notes # 194
Bakersfield, CA	Articles: 6, 29, Cabot's Chronology
Banning, CA	Articles: 2, 33, 34, 36, 41, 110, 111, 120, 127, 158, 172, 183, 261, 269, 279, 280, Explanatory Notes #61
Banning, General Phineas	Articles: 279
Barrymore, John	Articles: 193, 194, 195, 269
Baxter, Warner	Articles: 193, 201, 202, 203, 204, Explanatory Notes #201
B-bar-H Ranch	Articles: 36, 49, 59, 93, 96, 110, 158, 191, 192, 193, 195, 199, 204, Forward, Introduction, Three Days at the Pueblo, Explanatory Notes #93, 193
Beebe, Ford	Articles: 2, 15, 16, 50, 51, 109, 111, 123, 141, 280, Explanatory Notes 15
Belt, Bob	Articles: 116, 280
Bender, Charles	Articles: 193, Explanatory Notes #191

Berkeley, CA	Articles: Cabot's Chronology
Blind Canyon	Articles: 177, 186
Blythe, CA	Articles: 137, 163, 165, 269, Introduction, Explanatory Notes #139, Obituary
Box Canyon	Articles: 165
Bradshaw, William D.	Articles: 279
Cabot, John	Articles: 196, 267, Cabot's Chronology, Yerxa Survived Lawless Alaska, Obituary
Cabot's Old Indian Pueblo	Articles: 89, 127, 142, 200, 216, 229, 230, 231, 239, 251, 255, 263, 264, 265, 267, 269, 278, Forward, Introduction, Explanatory Notes #180,193,197, 254, 265, Three days at the Pueblo, Obituary
Cahuilla Indians	Articles: 247, 279
Carr, Robert (Bob)	Articles: 2, 3, 4, 11, 13, 14, 15, 16, 17, 23, 25, 26, 27, 31, 32, 33, 43, 50, 59, 78, 79, 88, 89, 90, 123, 140, 151, 280; On the Desert Since 1913 Explanatory Notes #2
Carr, Stella	Articles: 2, 16, 17, 31, 59, Explanatory notes #2,7
Carstensen, Mamie	Articles: 7, 20; Cabot Chronology, Explanatory Notes #7
Chapultepec Palace	Articles: 1, 95, 265, Explanatory Notes #266
Charlie, the cook	Articles: 171, 172
Chino Canyon	Articles: 247
Chino, Pedro	Articles: 246, 247, Introduction
Coffee Foundation Bath House	Articles: 116, 142, 189, 248
Coffee, L.W.	Articles: 20, 186, 280; Introduction, Explanatory Notes #20, 16, Obituary
Coleman, Bonita Hume	Articles: 193, 201,
Coleman, Ronald	Articles: 193 201, 204.
Coolidge, Old Man	Articles: 33, 45, 114, 150, 151, 152, 154,Explanatory Notes#154
Cooper, Gary	Articles: 96
Cuba	Articles: 2, 94, 95, 143, 193, 257,Forward,Cabot's Chronology, Explanatory Notes #94, Obituary
Dakotas	Articles: 2, 32, 94, 264, 266, 267, Cabot's Chronology
Decker, John	Articles: 194, 195, 269, Explanatory Notes #195
DeLong, Frank	Articles: 20, 49, 106, 110, 142, 172

Desert Hot Springs (DHS), CA	Articles: 4, 7, 16, 22, 28, 45, 50, 87, 95, 141, 146, 155, 156, 163, 174, 186, 190, 191, 195, 205, 210, 215, 238, 246, 249, 264, 265, 266, 269, 278, 279, 280, Forward, Cabots Chronology, Yerxa Survived Lawless Alaska, Introduction, Explanatory Notes #20, 24, 42, 68. 259, Three Days at the Pueblo, Obituary
Desert Sentinel, The	Articles: 51, 132, 136, 159, 263, Forward, Yerxa Survived Lawless Alaska, Introduction, Explanatory Notes, Obituary
Diaz, Porfiro	Articles: 1, 95, 266; On the Desert Since 1913 Explanatory Notes #1
Dutch Frank	Articles: 33, 34, 60, 62, 63, 115, 149, 150, 151, 152, 153, 154, Introduction
Eagle's Nest Cabin	Articles: 11, 97, 128, 154
Earp, Wyatt	Articles: 279
Eisenhower, Lt. Col. Dwight D.	Articles: 73, 137, Explanatory Notes #73
England	Articles: 128, 143, 144, 146, 193, Cabot's Chronology, Explanatory Notes #61, 143
Eskimo	Articles: 2, 95, 118, 119, 193, 197, 267, Yerxa Survived Lawless Alaska, Obituary
Eytel, Carl	Articles: 9, 60, 61, 62, 63, 64, 269, Introduction, Explanatory Notes #9, 269
Fertilla	Articles: 269. Introduction, Explanatory Notes #137
France	Articles: 128, 144, 145, 193, Forward, Cabot's Chronology
Garnet Train Station	Articles: 8, 42, 93, 109, 111, 114, 124, 128, 142, 151, 156, 158, 163, 215, 216, 242, 249, 250, 266, 278, 280
Garnet, CA	Articles: 128, 227
Gray, Hilda	Articles: 2, 3, 8, 18, 35, 58, 112, 113, 114, 140, 174, 211, 212, 214, 215, 216, 217, Introduction, Explanatory Notes #7
Green, Frank	Articles: 41, 42
Harris, Phil	Articles: 193
Houghton, Frank	Articles: 141, 248, 249
Hubbard, Lucienne	Articles: 123, 191, 192, 193, 199, 204, Introduction, Explanatory Notes #191
Hunt, John	Articles: Yerxa Survived Lawless Alaska, Introduction, Explanatory Notes #20

Huntington, Henry E.	Articles: 67, 68, Explanatory Notes #67
Indio Mud Hills	Articles: 63
Indio, CA	Articles: 20, 41, 42, 64, 111, 121, 164, 167, 172, 183, 280, Introduction, Explanatory Notes #121
Inuit	Articles: Yerxa Survived Lawless Alaska
Jersey Island	Articles: 146, Yerxa Survived Lawless Alaska, Obituary
Jones, Mr./Mrs. Stanley	Articles:161, 162
Joppo the Devil	Articles: 152
Kasler, Jay	Articles: Explanatory Notes #191
Krindler, Jack	Articles: 193, 204, 205, Introduction
Lawton, Harry	Articles: 263
Lodge, Henry Cabot	Cabot's Chronology
Lolayook	Yerxa Survived Lawless Alaska
London, England	Articles: 138, 139, 143, 145
Long Canyon	Articles: 46, 47, 109, 187, 199
Los Angeles	Articles: 4, 5, 13, 20, 31, 32, 35, 36, 41, 67, 72, 73, 143, 158, 163, 183, 210, 217, 263, 279, Cabot's Chronology, Introduction, Explanatory Notes #7, 13, Three Days at the Pueblo, Obituary
Malty the Burro	Articles: 182, 183, 184, Introduction
McCarger, Wilber & family	Articles: 59, 69, 70, 101, 142, 156, 157, 158, 174
Merry Xmas	Articles: 11, 17, 19, 20, 22, 23, 24, 31, 52, 60, 62, 89, 97, 128, 129, 151, 174, 175, 177, 178, 182, 215, Introduction, Explanatory Notes #11, 24, 68, 97, 129
Mexico	Articles: 1, 48, 76, 95, 132, 193, 219, 245, 254, 265, 266, 279, Introduction, Explanatory Notes #1, 266
Minneapolis, MN	Articles: Cabot's Chronology, Explanatory Notes #267
Minnesota	Articles: 2, 95. Forward, Cabot's Chronology, Yerxa Survived Lawless Alaska, Obituary
Miracle Hill	Articles: 4, 9, 10, 20, 24, 58, 93, 97, 112, 137, 138, 139, 146, 187, 188, 191, 193, 195, 196, 216, 248, 249, 269, Forward, Introduction, Explanatory Notes #52, 191, 193, Three Days at the Pueblo
Mission Canyon	Articles: 1, 21, 22, 49, 88, 106, 110, 142, 450, 156, 172, 199
Morongo Canyon	Articles: 12, 20

Mussen	Articles: 2, 116, 117
New England	Articles: 94, 196. Cabot's Chronology, Yerxa Survived Lawless Alaska
New York Cavalcade/Journal Americans	Articles: 93, 96, 97, 98, 99, 100, 107, 122, 128, 129, 147, 159, 169, 206, 207, 226, 228, 232, 252
New York City	Articles: 2, 15, 93, 129, 192, 193, 194, 199, 204, 205, 209, Introduction, Explanatory Notes #267, Three Days at the Pueblo, Obituary
New York Times	Obituary
Nick the Spider	Articles: 195, 197, 198
Nome, Alaska	Articles: 170, 197, 267, Yerxa Survived Lawless Alaska, Obituary
North Dakota	Articles: 94, Cabot's Chronology, Obituary
O'Donnell, Hughie	Articles: 266
Oliver, Drew	Articles: 261, 262, Introduction, Explanatory Notes #261, 262
Oliver, Harry	Articles: 259, 260, Introduction, Explanatory Notes #259
Palm Springs Villager	Articles: 60, 85, 163, 182, Introduction, Obituary
Panama	Articles: 143, 145
Panama Canal	Articles: 138, 143
Paris	Articles: 93, 138, 143, 144, 145, 197, 264, Explanatory Notes #143, 197, Obituary
Pasadena, CA	Articles: 2, 279, Cabot's Chronology, Explanatory Notes #73
Patton, George S., Jr.	Articles: 67, Explanatory Notes #67, 73
Patton, George S., Sr.	Articles: 67, Explanatory Notes #67
Pembina, North Dakota	Articles: 94, 266
Pickford, Mary	Articles: 193
Procter, Bert	Articles: 264, Explanatory Notes #264
Raskob, John J.	Articles: 204, Explanatory Notes #204
Rehse, George	Articles: 267, 268, Explanatory Notes #267
Riley, Bill	Articles: 2, 141, 250
Riley, Jack	Articles: 2, 18, 49, 58, 75, 101, 110, 114, 141, 157, 174, 213, 220

Riverside Press-Enterprise	Articles: 263, Yerxa Survived Lawless Alaska, Introduction, Explanatory Notes #24, Three Days at the Pueblo, Obituary
Riverside, CA	Articles: 2, 69, 220, 250, 268, 279, Explanatory Notes #261, 262 268
Roosevelt, Theodore	Articles: 2,
Rouse, Ethel	Articles: 156, 158
San Gabriel Mission	Articles: 279
San Gorgonio	Articles: 1, 54, 99, 147, 279, Explanatory Notes #261, 262
San Jacinto Mountain & Peak	Articles: 1, 12, 16, 68, 99, 147, 177, 193, 246, 251, Explanatory Notes #68, 246
Sang, Orr	Articles: 36, 69, 142, 214, Introduction
Schuster, Max	Articles: 193, 204
Seadler, Si	Articles: 199, 193, Introduction
Semu Hante	Articles: Three Days at the Pueblo
Sennett, Mack	Articles: 13, 14, 15, 123. Introduction, Explanatory Notes #13
Seven Palms Oasis	Articles: 4, 7, 8, 9, 36, 57, 60, 65, 116, 149, 193, 247, 278, 280, Introduction
Seven Palms Rancho	Articles: 161
Sierra Madre, CA	Articles: 2, 17, Cabot's Chronology, Explanatory Notes #2, Obituary
Sioux	Articles: 2, 32, 94, 266, 268, Cabot's Chronology
Smith, Dr. Isaac	Articles: 279
Sobol, Louis	Articles: 93, 96, 97, 98, 99, 100, 107, 122, 128, 129, 147, 159, 169, 193, 206, 207, 227, 228, 232, 251, 252, Introduction, Explanatory Notes #93, 97
South Dakota	Articles: 32, Cabot's Chronology, Obituary
Spanish-American War	Articles: 2, 17, 32, 94, Cabot's Chronology
St. Louis	Articles: 2, 8, 151, Introduction, Explanatory Notes
St. Paul, MN	Articles: 1, 32, Forward, Cabot's Chronology, Introduction
Talmage Brothers & Ranch	Articles: 8, 142, 172
Tarbutton, Bill	Articles: 142
T-cross-K Ranch	Articles: 33, 52, 88, 106, 142, 150
Thousand Palms Canyon	Articles: 62
Tipton, Charlie	Articles: 2, 123, 142

Wardman, Aubrey	Articles: 186, 280, Introduction, Explanatory Notes #20
Washington, Henry	Articles: 210
Weaver, Paulino	Articles: 279
Wells Fargo	Articles: 5
Whitewater Bridge	Articles: 261
Whitewater Canyon	Articles: 154
Whitewater River	Articles: 41, 45
Whitewater Wash	Articles: 7, 24, 163, 278, 279, Explanatory Notes #24
Wide Canyon	Articles: 186, 199
Wilhelm, Paul	Articles: 259, 260, Introduction
Willow Hole	Articles: 8, 31, 65, 149, 163, 193
Woods, Lucy	Articles: 109, 111
Woods, Walter	Articles: 2, 15, 16, 49, 123, 141, 182, 184, 280, Introduction, Explanatory Notes #15, 16
Yerxa, Frederick	Articles: 92, 94, 266, 268, Cabot's Chronology, Explanatory Notes #95, 268
Yerxa, Harry	Articles: 92, 94, 266, Cabot's Chronology, Introduction, Explanatory Notes #259
Yerxa, Helen (Nellie)	Articles: 92, 93, 94, 95, 96, 187, 199, 266, Cabot's Chronology, Explanatory Notes #7, 93
Yerxa, Mamie Carstensen	Articles: 7, 20, Explanatory Notes #7
Yerxa, Portia Fearis Graham	Articles: 265, 269, Forward, Cabot's Chronology, Introduction, Explanatory Notes #236, 265, Three Days at the Pueblo, Obituary
Yerxa, Rodney	Articles: 7, 52, 88, Introduction, Explanatory Notes #7, Three Days at the Pueblo, Obituary

ABOUT THE EDITORS

Richard E. Brown retired to the Coachella Valley in 2005. Previously he was a professor of English at the University of Nevada, Reno for 32 years.

Judy Gigante is the official Historian of Cabot's Museum Foundation. She has served has a docent at the museum for seven years and is a dual resident of Michigan and Southern California.